ULTIMATE

HAPPINESS

The Best Proven Western &

Eastern Insights About

How to Be Happier Today

Version 1.3

A Thoughtful & Helpful Book By

RICHARD HAASNOOT

Dedication

I am deeply grateful to the help provided

by Sogyal Rinpoche, Paramahansa

Yogananda, and Patricia Haasnoot as I

traveled along my path.

GRATITUDE

This work has not been a solo effort by any means. It would not have happened without the help of some key people. These people include:

- Great teachers who have taught and inspired me, including Paramahansa Yogananda, his Holiness the Dalai Lama, Sogyal Rinpoche, Ken Wilber, Dr. Martin Seligman, and Daniel Goleman. A special nod goes to Sanaya Roman whose book *Living With Joy* started my journey.

- Venerable ZaChoeje Rinpoche for his help reviewing the chapter on the middle way.

- Brother Satyananda of the Self Realization Fellowship for his help reviewing the chapter on Paramahansa Yogananda's teachings

- The great support from my family: Patricia, Holland, Van, Sam and Simba here and Tricia from afar.

Table of Contents

Chapter One.

"There must be a better way!"

On a Sunday morning a little more than fifteen years ago I muttered, "There must be a better way." This was followed by another muttering, "It must be possible to be happier than I am now."

These mutterings marked the transition between decades of pursuing success and happiness as prescribed by parents, teachers, and culture and the balance of my life spent rewriting the rules of happiness and traveling that proverbial path less traveled. I was not depressed or down. I was frustrated.

I reached the point of these frustrated mutterings after decades of hard work and sacrifice following the advice of well meaning people that I respected. As the oldest son of immigrant parents, I received a quality education, served my country in a time of war, married a wonderful woman, have two beautiful daughters, worked for two highly rated companies as a senior executive, and experienced financial success. We had it all or so it seemed by the standards of success and happiness I grew up with. There was the top of line Mercedes, a large home in the mountains, a happy marriage, loving children, buying homes for parents and kids, and more. I achieved success as our culture defines it, but not the happiness I expected.

Achieving this success included sacrifices. My oldest daughter was in her third year of high school in her third different high school, which was in the third state we had lived in over the last three years. Prior to that we had moved coast to coast for career reasons, living about two years in a place before being promoted and moving again. Once we lived in a city for less than nine months before moving almost a thousand miles to a new opportunity with the same company. In addition, there was the sacrifice of quality personal and family time to meet career needs and opportunities.

After all this, I developed a longing at a deep level for a "better way." As I learned later, the Universe responds when we ask this critical question. Fortunately, I was alert when the answers came, because many came from unexpected sources. Many of the answers were unexpected because I was a very left brain person (logical and scientific method reasoning) up to this point in my life. While the answers came from unexpected sources with new dimensions of life and knowing, the logical, critical thinking skills that were a personal core business competency also served me well on the journey ahead. The answers I sought needed to be real, practical, and proven. I was not about to change my life based on any whims or unsubstantiated thinking. What I did not know at the time was that my standard for knowing something to be true was to expand dramatically and powerfully.

A Brief Overview of My Journey

Looking back, I realize the journey began several years before my Sunday mutterings. Based on the experience of a mutual friend, my wife decided to visit a local prominent psychic. I tried persuading her not to go since I thought it was a waste of time and money. When this effort failed, I invited myself to the appointment where I expected to unmask the fraud. Instead, I listened as the psychic named people, places, times, and events from our past that no one in that city could possibly have known. Fortunately, I recorded the session so I could listen to it later. I was dumbfounded. This was far outside my realm of anything I thought I knew. All I knew for sure was that the psychic tapped into some field of knowledge that I had no understanding of. The effect of this was like a sharp poke in the ribs followed by a, "So, you think you know it all Richard?" Clearly, I did not.

Back to that Sunday. Deep inside me when I muttered that there must be a better way I quickly became committed to finding that better way. I was more than curious. I was hungry to find that better way, even though I felt clueless about where to look. I know now that my deep commitment and openness to answers from about any source were key to the success I later experienced. The first life changing answer about how to achieve ultimate happiness came in the form of a meditation and healing workshop at Esalen, an alternative teaching and human potential center in Big Sur. Sogyal Rinpoche, who led the workshop, completely redefined for me the human capacity to be happy and was the first ultimately happy person I met. At first, I could not even pronounce his name. I learned he was a Tibetan Buddhist but I had little understanding of Tibet and even less of Buddhism. I quickly learned more about both. "Rinpoche" is a title given to highly accomplished masters (masters of themselves) in Tibetan Buddhism and is a level just below that of the Dalai Lama.

In this first seminar, he spoke without notes for hours on topics of great importance and, at times, complexity. Everything about him was different than anything I had experienced before. Most impressive was his demeanor. There was spontaneous laughter and happiness that seemed to come from a very deep, authentic place. I had never been with someone so consistently and deeply happy. He was also very humble and dressed simply. By studying annually with him over the next three years, I became inspired to commit my life to learning more about the path of being ultimately happy and actually walking day by day along that path. For almost 15 years, he has served as a daily inspiration for how happy and wise humans can be. Chapter 5 provides more detail on the contribution of Buddhist philosophy and psychology to achieve ultimate happiness.

At the conclusion of these four years, I was deeply committed to a regular meditation practice. By itself, this led to ever-increasing levels of consistent happiness. While the changes were gradual from my perspective, friends who saw me infrequently experienced profound changes. While I appreciate how the path he outlined contributed to more consistent happiness, I also know from Sogyal Rinpoche's example that I still have almost unfathomable progress to make along the path. On a clear day, I can see Sogyal Rinpoche a million or more steps ahead of me on the path to being ultimately happy. The next giant step for me occurred when I studied the teachings of Paramahansa Yogananda. He is the founder of the Self-Realization Fellowship, an acknowledged Avatar (enlightened being), and author of the perennial top-selling book, *An Autobiography of a Yogi.*

More than any other single teacher he contributed to my journey towards being ultimately happy. Yogananda, who passed in 1952,left an incredible breadth of teachings through his lessons, including three years of weekly lessons. His teachings are an inspired combination of three major spiritual sources—Jesus, Krishna, and his personal, enlightened teachers in India where he grew up.

He based his spiritual teachings on scientific energy principles known to the most advanced teachers. The exceptionally clear and practical teachings cover everything from proper diet to the major scientific spiritual laws governing our world. Kriya Yoga, his most powerful teaching, is one of the most advanced scientific spiritual practices that significantly accelerates overall progress and leads to much great happiness in a shorter time than any other known practice. The hundreds of thousands of worldwide Kriya Yoga practitioners over more than fifty years speak to its proven effectiveness. Another major contribution to my life has been Yogananda's expressions of love for the Divine which are overwhelming in their power and beauty. Whether expressed through poetry or teachings, it is very clear to me that he knew the Supreme Being. His love is an inspiration to me. It led to recognition of the power love can have in our lives, a power well beyond close, personal relationships.

The combination of three years of inspired weekly lessons, advanced meditation techniques, and his inspiring love of our Supreme Being contributed to my major strides along the path to being ultimately happy. The comprehensiveness of his proven, practical program was exactly what I needed. Chapter 6 provides a comprehensive overview of the most powerful elements of his teachings that contribute to becoming ultimately happy.

During this period of connecting with Yogananda, I also read many books by Western teachers and philosophers. Of these, the works of Ken Wilber, the greatest living philosopher of our time, have made significant contributions to helping me understand the world we live in. His powerful thinking produced an integral map that removed much of the mystery of life. I could now see where I was on the evolutionary path of life and the next steps that lay ahead. The clarity of his powerful thinking created a map that has helped me better navigate my way to the goal of being ultimately happy.

In addition to Ken Wilber's work, the emerging science of positive psychology, although only about a decade old, has helped me to understand some practices proven to contribute to greater happiness. Maybe their greatest contribution to date is their research revealing that most of the things that Americans think will make them happier actually have little or no ability to do so. These myths are discussed in detail in Chapter 3.

The other major contribution by Western science is emotional intelligence. While most people view the emotional intelligence as a set of workplace competencies, effective emotional understanding and management does contribute to our ability to become ultimately happy. Chapter 14 focuses the specific elements of emotional intelligence that make the greatest contribution to becoming ultimately happy.

In my quest to find a better way I have studied and been influenced by the works of many wonderful writers and teachers. Deepak Chopra, Margaret Wheatley, and Sanaya Roman are just a few of the people I am deeply grateful to for sharing their insights and practical advice. What led me to write this book was an observation that there was no one single source that did two things. First, there was no book that combined the best of Eastern and Western understandings about how to become ultimately happy. If you search Amazon.com you will find that there are over 80,000 books with the word "happiness" in the title. While I have not read all of them, clearly the most popular books on the subject provide a very limited perspective, either Eastern or Western and typically only a specific subject from that perspective.

Second, there are many books that provide recommendations about "what" you can do to be happier, but very few that then help you with "how" to use the "what" to actually become happier. Sure, there are many personal growth books but they also tend to focus on only one or two very specific practices. Achieving the important goal of becoming ultimately happy requires numerous practices integrated into a proven program of five sequential steps, which are detailed in Chapter 15.

To help you understand the progress I have made along my path, I will share with you two descriptive introductions. I used the first one about fifteen years ago and the second one is from the last six months.

Here is the first one I prepared as a part of a seminar I participated in about 15 years ago.

> I grew up in New England as the oldest son of immigrant parents. As a kid I wanted to be a meteorologist and had my own weather station. I

did well in high school which helped me get into the six colleges and universities that I applied to. I went to Penn State where I graduated with a degree in pre-law. I was deeply involved in extracurricular activities, including being president of a campus wide student government organization and a national student government organization as a junior.

My first year of law school was interrupted by a change in my draft deferment during the Vietnam conflict. After going through Navy OCS, I served my active duty in San Diego.

I then joined Procter & Gamble in sales where I was promoted quickly over the next nine years to a senior position. At my request I then moved into advertising or brand management where I was also promoted quickly to senior positions over the next seven years. After 16 years at Procter & Gamble, I left to join the Gallo Winery as vice president of marketing. There I had the pleasure of producing more than a one hundred of the Bartles and Jaymes "Frank and Ed" humorous commercials.

I am married and have two daughters.

Here is the second introduction that I used recently as a part of my participation in Dr. Martin Seligman's authentic happiness coaching program.

Yosemite after a snow storm is a national treasure transformed. It is almost like the whiteness celebrates the pure beauty that is so uniquely Yosemite.

Sedona is famous for being a red rock cathedral, but sprinkle snow here and there and it is also transformed. The contrast of red and white accentuates both. There is a sense that grace has visited this center of vortex energies.

Backpack into the desolation wilderness with a camera on board. Photograph rock fissures split apart by centuries of freezing and thawing. People view the close up photo and imagine it is a satellite photograph taken from several miles up when it is only several inches away.

These pictures of beauty live on paper and in my mind. As mind pictures they remind me of the perfection our Supreme Being created for us. As mind pictures they inspire the creation of new ideas that meet the needs of a small business or corporate giant. As mind pictures they arouse gratitude and kindness towards all who cross my path.

As pictures they bring me home, home to discover inner beauty. The outer journey shows the way for the inner one where we discover the beauty and wisdom that resides behind the veil of who we think we are but are not. Closing my eyes to the outer world I discover a beauty and grace unimaginable just a short time ago. The answers without words reside there. From this place I first encounter happiness and know from my teachers that joy lies further ahead, many miles ahead for me, but there as a star to guide me.

Inevitably, I return to the outer world with a glow to guide me. From this point, I embark on a life of service, hoping to share the light unconditionally with all who care to gander or touch.

The dramatic differences between the two introductions reflect some of the changes in my life over the fifteen years. The first introduction describes what I have done in my life while the second reflects more of who I am. The first introduction describes the major events in my outer world while the second describes more of my inner experiences.

As such, these differences reflect the major change in life focus that happened over these fifteen years. I realized that becoming happier was an inner experience requiring inner work. As a result, I increasingly focused on managing and disciplining my thoughts and emotions so that I would make choices with happier and happier consequences.

What I have learned through almost two decades of intensive study is reflected in this book. I deeply believe in the substance that makes up *Ultimate Happiness*. It represents the best of the proven and practical wisdom about happiness. There is nothing in this effort that I have personally invented. Instead, I have drawn from the best

Eastern and Western teachings and research to integrate for the first time the best of the known. The focus of this book is on the best proven and practical understandings that contribute to helping us achieve ultimate happiness. Enjoy!

Chapter Two

Ultimate Happiness

There is a known and proven path to ultimate happiness, and we know the description of the destination. It is a place where we are 100% happy, 100% of the time.

Happiness—A Definition

I could ask one hundred people to define happiness and how to achieve it. I would receive diverse responses. Out of these one hundred, maybe one, but probably no person would correctly define ultimate happiness or accurately define how to achieve ultimate happiness. This is at the core of our challenge today. As we will see in the next chapter, the vast majority of what westerners think makes them happy actually contributes to unhappiness and even depression. We do a little better when it comes to describing happiness, but we are so far from understanding ultimate happiness today and most people have no appreciation of how happy they can be.

The level of happiness is so low today that we have come to accept very low expectations.

Thus, my first job is to attempt to define what it means to achieve ultimate happiness. Some readers will find the definition a fantasy while others will question its desirability. For the first group, I suggest that you translate the fantasy into inspiration to learn and experience more. For the second group that questions the desirability of ultimate happiness, please consider the more modest goal of becoming happier than you are now. Open your mind to the possibility of becoming happier and for now do not struggle with the desirability of ultimate happiness. As you become happier, the vision of ultimate happiness may become clearer and more desirable.

Western Definitions

Dictionaries use words like enjoyment, pleasure, satisfaction, cheerfulness, and fortunate to define happy and happiness. These words begin to define the challenge since they suggest so little of what ultimate happiness is. Dr. Paul Ekman, a professor of psychology at the University of California in San Francisco, identifies seven dimensions of happiness--amusement, the delight of meeting a challenge, relief, excitement/novelty, awe/wonder, sensory pleasures, and calm peacefulness.[i] As we will see later, these are more helpful than the dictionary definitions, but still misleading in some ways.

Eastern Definitions

Eastern wisdom traditions are especially helpful in understanding happiness primarily because they have extensively studied happiness for thousands of years, which is in sharp contrast to positive psychology's ten-year history and the overall psychological history of about one hundred fifty years (most of which was spent studying unhappiness).

Of these traditions, Buddhism may be the most helpful and accessible for westerners, but other traditions are also very helpful. Other eastern religions (Hinduism and Islam, for example) and philosophies (Lao Tzu and Patanjali, for example) also offer wonderful insights and assistance.

Western definitions of happiness suggest pleasure is a component. Buddhists dispute that pleasure is a part of happiness. His Holiness the Dalai Lama offers a wonderful contrast between happiness and pleasure.

> We should distinguish pleasure from happiness. Happiness is understood here to refer to a deep sense of fulfillment, accompanied by a sense of peace and a host of positive qualities such as altruism. Pleasure depends upon the place, the circumstances, and the object of its enjoyment. One can get pleasure at certain times and not at others. It is bound to change. Something that is pleasurable at one moment might soon give rise to indifference, then to displeasure and suffering. Pleasure exhausts itself in the enjoying, just like a candle burns down and disappears.
> By contrast, a deep sense of fulfillment does not depend upon time, location, or objects. It is a state of mind that grows the more one experiences it. It is different from pleasure in almost every way.
> What we seek by disentangling ourselves from the influence of destructive emotions is the kind of inner stability, clarity, and fulfillment that we are referring to here as happiness. [ii]

Happiness is an inner experience. *Today most people rely on external stimulus for happiness. This misplaced focus is the cause of so much unhappiness.* When we turn the spotlight of our attention inward, we achieve our greatest progress. All the skills we need to achieve ultimate happiness are the skills of mastering our mind.

It is a profound insight when we realize that happiness is an inner condition influenced almost entirely by the mind's condition. When the mind focuses 100% on positive thoughts and emotions, 100% of the time, we achieve ultimate happiness. Ultimate happiness is that simple. But mastering the mind to achieve the contentment and clarity the Dalai Lama refers to is more difficult than any task we have ever undertaken. When we first focus on our thoughts, we quickly realize there is a never-ending torrent that is highly resistant to control and discipline. As soon as one thought ends another takes its place. As we examine the thoughts individually, we wonder why they popped into our attention since they appear have little relationship to anything. When we examine a sequence of thoughts and emotions, we discover another apparently random flow. Some thoughts and emotions storm into our mind and dominate our attention. And since most thoughts and emotions are negative, this often creates a mood that settles in for an hour and even days. At the end of even a cursory examination of our thoughts and emotions, we sense the enormity of the task of mastering the mind so that we only have positive thoughts and emotions.

Mastering the mind is not artificial, short term stifling of thoughts and emotions. Rather, through a long-term process, we transform the beliefs that trigger our negative thoughts and emotions. The transformation occurs as we gradually realize the essence of who we really are. By focusing inwardly, we discover this essence and how it is in such sharp contrast to our current belief structure. Ultimately, the new, deeply held, and heart-felt beliefs support an inner experience of ultimate happiness.

Happy, Joy, and Bliss

Sometimes we use these three words as synonyms for each other. This is understandable when we do not know the important differences between them. Of course, knowing these differences is difficult when happiness is the only one of the three we have limited experience with and we have almost no experience with joy and bliss.

The wisdom traditions make important differentiations between the three words. While dictionary definitions of joy suggest it is "intense and especially ecstatic or exultant happiness," the wisdom traditions teach us that joy is not the high level of happiness that many believe today. The traditions further indicate that bliss is something we rarely if ever experience today.

The traditions define happiness as the positive feelings we experience from an egocentric perspective. From this perspective, we define our reality by beliefs built through experience with our five senses. There is a strong belief that we are individuals and we focus primarily on our individual needs. Research indicates that 98-99% of people today live life from an egocentric perspective. The egocentric life orientation creates both positive and negative results. It creates its best results when its focus expands beyond just the self.

Ultimate happiness is the highest positive experience we can have from an egocentric perspective. Put another way, ultimate happiness is the most satisfying, rewarding, and inspiring life that we can achieve before having the opportunity to experience joy.

Joy is the next level of positive experience and we gain access to it when we loosen our attachment to the egocentric perspective. We experience joy when we have disciplined the mind enough to connect with our soul. A clear, consistent intuition emerges with this connection, and we realize that intuition is the voice of our soul. Our soul is the spark of divinity in all of us. Ignorance (maya) obscures our ability to connect with our soul as long as we live from an egocentric perspective. Joy is a positive experience beyond ultimate happiness. Importantly, to fully experience joy we first need to experience ultimate happiness. By removing negative thoughts and emotions, we open the door to the emergence of soul contact and influence. Living life from an egocentric perspective is a barrier to joy. The closer we come to achieving ultimate happiness, the more we experience joy in our life.

The wisdom traditions indicate bliss is the next level of positive experience beyond joy. The experience of bliss is incapable of description and the Ageless Wisdom indicates bliss is something "...about which speculation is fruitless." The earlier statement that the highest level of positive experience virtually everyone can have is ultimate happiness needs some slight modification. We can have brief peak experiences of joy triggered by special circumstances, like meditation and some drugs. But these brief and rare experiences typically do not have an immediate effect on our baseline happiness that is fairly stable. It requires long term, proactive interventions to create a happier life. These peak experiences can inspire us to undertake the interventions necessary to become happier.

Ultimate Happiness: The Inner Experience

When we achieve ultimate happiness, there is an absence of negative emotions and thoughts and the pure presence of several major positive thoughts and emotions. The four major ones are peace, love, compassion and a hunger to learn.

When we achieve ultimate happiness, we are very peaceful. My primary life teacher advises people to be "actively calm and calmly active." When we are inwardly calm, we can venture into optimally rewarding and productive activity. The person living ultimate happiness is calm, free of distracting negative emotions and thoughts. All of our attention focuses on the present and none on the past or future. Through a calm, peaceful focus, we experience objective reality clearly. We fully absorb events as they unfold. Objective reality is free of judging, fear, anger, and all other negative emotions and thoughts.

When we live ultimate happiness, thoughts and feelings of love dominate our experience. We experience a deep sense of gratitude and appreciation for all of life. There is a sense of awe and wonder for all of creation. We feel connected to everyone and everything. Love expands beyond emotional, romantic, and sometimes lustful love to an ever-expanding circle of love. The experience of love expands from a single individual to family and friends to our community, nation, and planet. There is a kinship with the world around us.

When we live ultimate happiness, we experience a deep compassion for all of life. Compassion goes beyond empathy to a desire to relieve the suffering of others. That desire inspires actions to actually help reduce the pain others feel. The objects of compassion range from other humans to other living entities, like animals, plants and our planet.

When we live ultimate happiness, we have a hunger to learn. We understand that ignorance is the primary barrier to living ultimate happiness and that continued learning is a requirement for further progress. We know that the more we learn, the more we understand how much we do not know. Increasingly learning shifts from acquiring knowledge from external sources to expanding wisdom, which comes from inner knowing. We view everyone and everything as a teacher. We know that every event presents the opportunity to learn, especially the painful events we do not want repeated in our life. We stop the cycle of painful repetition through learning. When we live ultimate happiness, we have the greatest use of our knowledge and intelligence. A key reason is that fear, which limits the use our intelligence and creativity, no longer affects us. We achieve excellence even on complex tasks that in the past caused us to struggle. We are equally adept with details and the big picture. We are highly creative because of our ability to integrate diverse inputs. Life is much easier and more fun. When we live ultimate happiness, we purposely do no harm. We have a clear understanding of universal moral and ethical principles and the vast majority of the time we live in accordance with these principles. We have a deep desire to do what is right and we let go of the need to be right.

Ultimate Happiness: The Outer Appearance

While ultimate happiness is an inner experience, others easily notice ultimate happiness in a person. We immediately see someone who is unlike all or certainly most other people we know. Seven characteristics sharply contrast a person experiencing ultimate happiness from people who have not reached this level.

Calm and Curious

The person living ultimate happiness is markedly calm. They can be very active but there is no frenzied activity or expressions of stress. They act with purpose. Their use of skillful means produces the right results the first time. They exhibit the characteristics of someone in flow or in the zone since the activities are fun and enable them to use their key strengths. Conversations reveal a deep curiosity about other people and situations. They love learning. When they encounter difficulties, they view it as an opportunity to learn. Their reaction to difficulties is positive and even enthusiastic which is in sharp contrast to the frustration and anger that most people exhibit.

Remarkably Insightful and Creative

The insights from an ultimate happiness person are remarkably helpful. In a minimum of words, they provide feedback that solves the most complex and bewildering problems that other people face. They quickly grasp the key facts. While apparently conflicting facts confound other people, they see the interconnections between facts and perceive the big picture that eludes other people. When they communicate insights, they present it as a suggestion, which enables others to consider the insights in a non-threatening manner. Their suggestions often include highly creative ideas that provide unique solutions to long-standing challenges.

The person living ultimate happiness is capable of this because fear, anxiety, and a preoccupation with either the past or future does not limit their thinking ability. This enables them to utilize 100% of their thinking capacity, whereas others may experience 50% or greater diminishing of their abilities because of negative thoughts and emotions.

Humility and Simplicity

Humility is a defining quality of the person living ultimate happiness because they keenly recognize how much they do not know. There is no arrogance or egocentric posturing. In no way do they view themselves as better than any other person. While they are typically more skilled and successful than most people, they recognize that arrogance only creates barriers between themselves and others. They also know that the greatest success comes from tapping into the collective intelligence of many people instead of relying on whatever abilities an individual possesses. Since they know their happiness is an inner condition, they live very simple material lives. They live comfortably, but not austerely. They minimally satisfy basic needs with high value solutions. Styles and fashions do not dictate their exterior appearance.

Friendly and Welcoming

The first image of the person living ultimate happiness is a smile—warm and inviting. They are friendly even to people who have previously been rude to them. Consistent with their calm demeanor, their friendliness is like greeting an old, trusted friend. They radiate their cheer to everyone who crosses their path. In many ways, they are the mental sunshine that attracts others. They maintain a friendly and welcoming attitude even when others challenge or attack them. They quickly understand divergent views and break down initially negative barriers because of their curiosity and desire to understand alternative views.

Caring and Helpful

The person living ultimate happiness is available to help as needed. They do not force help onto others. They provide the care and help that others indicate they want. They inquire into the well-being of others without prying. Because they are trustworthy, people feel comfortable being open and honest with them. People quickly sense the sincerity of their caring and desire to help relieve concerns, worries, and suffering. Their advice is warmly received and their heartfelt reaching out creates quick and strong bonds with others.

Lightness and Humor

The person living ultimate happiness laughs easily, usually at themselves and never at the expense of others. They tread the path of life lightly. They calmly and lightly handle events that others classify as failures and disasters. There are no heavy negative emotions and thoughts, only a desire to learn from life's unexpected twists and turns. They see life as a drama in which their role is to help and care for others. They know that taking life seriously creates barriers to doing what is right since "taking life seriously" often involves some degree of negative thoughts and emotions (like fear and anger) that stifle the creativity needed to solve a challenge. Lightness also creates clarity of vision, especially seeing perspectives that others do not see because of their negativity.

Trusted and Respected

Because of their ethical conduct, others have a high level of trust and respect for them. They develop strong bonds with others. Others seek their advice because they know the advice will be objective and with no hidden agendas attached.

A Map of the Journey

The journey to achieving ultimate happiness starts in a mostly unhappy place and progresses through stages of increasing happiness. As we progress through the stages the basis for and source of happiness goes through dramatic change. From my studies, I have outlined my best judgment of what the journey looks like.

10 Steps to Ultimate Happiness

1. <u>Barely a Trace of Happiness</u>: I am happy once or twice a month. There is considerable fear, anger, and unhappiness in my life. I am familiar with depression and it is not fun. I work so I can earn money to pay my bills. In my relationships, I frequently experience conflict and negativity. There is not much meaningful activity or fun in my life. My exclusive focus is on my needs and I have very little time, energy or interest in helping others. Life is mostly a struggle and there is little opportunity for fun. I never experience calm and quiet moments where I feel peaceful. I am not sure if I could be happier, but if I were to be happier other people would need to stop being mean and unfair to me. Life is competitive and because life is unfair I seldom experience winning.

2. <u>Slightly Happy</u>: I am happy about once a week. There is significant anger and unhappiness in my life. I primarily focus on my needs and rarely spend time providing in-depth assistance to others and their needs. I frequently find myself in intensely negative moods. I work so I can earn money to pay my bills, but sometimes I would like something better. In my relationships, there is considerable negative tension and almost no sharing of positive thoughts and feelings towards each other. I consider myself to be a very competitive person. Fun seems to be limited to one or two times per

month, with only about two or three really fun times a year. I seldom experience calm and quiet moments where I feel peaceful. There is a possibility that I could be happier, but the important people in my life (family members, marriage partners, and bosses, for example) would need to treat me better and more fairly.

3. <u>Moderately Happy</u>: I am happy about two or three times a week. I am competitive and I enjoy winning. I feel anger towards several people in my life, people either currently in my life or in my past. Most of the time, I feel either unhappy, bored, or neutral. Most of my life I have worked to earn money so that I can pay my bills, but I plan to find a job where I can do more of what I like to do. In my relationships, there are frequent and sometimes extended periods of conflict and anger, but we seem to have the ability to resolve many of our differences. I have fun about once a week, usually on the weekends. There are not many calm and quiet moments in my life, but several times a year I feel peaceful, often while on vacation. I sense that I could be happier than I am today. I would probably feel happier if I had a better job, earned more money, and lived in a better neighborhood.

4. <u>Very Happy</u>: I am happy several times a week. While I have negative feelings and even anger toward some people currently in my life and in my past, I feel modestly positive about most people who are in my life today. While I am sometimes in a negative mood for a day or two, most of the time I feel comfortable with the routine of life. My job is pretty rewarding. I would like to continue doing

this type of work and make a career of becoming very skilled at what I do. I enjoy the recognition, raises, and occasional changes and added responsibility associated with my work. In my relationships, we certainly have our differences that occasionally flare up and cause hurt feelings. Other than these times, we enjoy each other's company. I have fun two or three times a week, mostly on weekends but occasionally during the week. I enjoy the very few times each month where I can experience some peace and quiet. I know that I could be happier if I earned more money, received a promotion to a job with greater diversity and more responsibility, and experienced more of the good life.

5. Exceptionally Happy: I am happy at least once a day. I rarely get angry with others, although I can feel occasionally annoyed and upset by others. Most of the people in my life are good folks who try hard to do what is right. While I experience negative thoughts and feelings most days, they seldom last long enough to settle in and become a bad mood. I have a good career. I have already been promoted and look forward to more promotions that will provide more money, challenge, and opportunities to use my skills. I find the opportunities to use my creativity and ingenuity to be some of the most rewarding parts of my career. I really enjoy the recognition and like my chances to experience even more of the good life. I like the opportunity to compete with others because it provides a real test and measure of my abilities. In my relationships, we really like each other and enjoy being together.

People tell me that I am fun to be with, in part because of my positive and optimistic outlook on life. I find opportunities to have fun almost every day. I feel positive about my prospects to be even happier. I occasionally seek out good books and an occasional seminar, some of which have opened my eyes and inspired me about greater possibilities. While I think most of my opportunity to become happier will come from having greater financial security and a more comfortable material life, I sense that having more quiet and peaceful time will enable me to learn more about the world around me and myself.

6. <u>Phenomenally Happy</u>: I am happy several times a day. I pride myself in being even tempered and I almost never express anger or upset to others. Even when I have the internal experience of anger, most of the time I can easily resolve my concerns and let go of the anger. I feel lucky and grateful that there are so many good people in my life. When I experience negative thoughts and emotions, I am pretty effective at letting them go and moving on. I am able to use my positive attitude towards life to occasionally cheer up others. I have a very good career that gives me a lot of freedom to use my skills. I am well recognized and compensated for my work. I really enjoy being promoted and the challenge of new assignments. Increasingly, I feel like I am on the fast track and I really savor all the perks that come with my job. While I still enjoy occasionally competing with others and winning, I do not take it as seriously as I once did. In my relationships, we

care for each other and there are frequent nonverbal expressions of love and respect. Most of the time we can easily resolve our differences, but when we have trouble doing so, we have resources and skills that enable us to break through to a resolution. I have fun multiple times each day in each of my important life roles. I increasingly enjoy expanding my understanding of life through books, seminars, and discussions with friends. While this experience is more occasional than regular, I really benefit from the moments spent learning. Increasingly, I think I can become happier more through learning more about myself and life than through more money and material stuff. I work very hard at creating quiet and peaceful times each day in my life-- reading a good book, journal writing, taking a walk with my dog, or developing my photography skills.

7. <u>Inspired Happiness</u>: I am happy most of the time. I very seldom get upset or angry with other people because of my respect for their views and rights. I understand how people with different views and outlooks each make a contribution. I see strength in diversity of thinking and beliefs. I feel fortunate to have a network of friends who respect and care for each other. Increasingly, I become aware of any negative thoughts and emotions as they occur and I can usually let go of them within a few minutes of becoming aware of them. After some trial and error, I discovered a career that I find highly rewarding. I not only have the opportunity to be creative, but I increasingly enjoy the cooperative and collaborative experience of working with

others. This experience of working closely with others is about equally important to the compensation and recognition I receive. In my relationships, there are very regular expressions and demonstrations of positive feelings. Many people know me best for my smiles and my inclination to give someone a hug. I am very good at coping with internal negative emotions and thoughts and consider myself to be a positive, optimistic person. Learning more about myself and life has become a central theme of my life. I frequently dive deeply into a topic by reading several books, attending a seminar or two, and discussing the topic with others. I frequently feel inspired and hopeful about my ability to become much happier. Increasingly, I find myself able to use what I learn to become more successful and happy. Creating quiet, peaceful, learning time is a major priority.

8. <u>Transformative Happiness</u>: I feel like I am happy all the time, although once or twice a week I experience some mildly negative thoughts and emotions. They are more like a cloud that briefly shades the sun and then moves on. I actively seek out people with different points of view and ways of thinking. Increasingly, I find that I learn something from most people in my life, even some people I might previously have not respected or even liked. I feel that my work is a means for fulfilling some sense of purpose I have about my life. It provides me the opportunity to do what I am really good at and enjoy. When I am with others, we naturally and easily cooperate with each

other, and there is never any sense of competition between us. Organizational perks and positions of power are not very important. The opportunity to do good work and learn from each other becomes more important every day. In my relationships, in addition to really liking and respecting each other, there is a deep trust of each other. In my relationships, there is great diversity of lifestyles and cognitive abilities, which makes them fun and rewarding. I do not take my relationships for granted, and look for opportunities to be appreciative of what we have. I increasingly recognize that to become happier requires more internal focus and less external focus. I eagerly seek to understand myself better, primarily by increasing my self-awareness of the beliefs that drive my thoughts and emotions. I am able to use this awareness to slowly and steadily change some of my most dysfunctional beliefs. Today I invest about equal effort in learning more about my external world and focusing on my inner world of thoughts and emotions. My learning about the external world focuses mostly on understanding life's bigger picture and my learning centers mostly on the writings and lessons of the greatest teachers of the present and past. The focus on my inner world primarily involves fairly regular meditation, journal writing, and spending time appreciating the beauty around me. From both my inner and outer work, I see a path to much greater happiness.

9. Integral Happiness: I am happy almost all of the time. Almost nothing upsets me, and when there is something, I am skilled at quickly letting go of the

negative thoughts and emotions. There is very little fear in my life because I feel I have a good understanding of life's dynamics. I understand the fundamental laws of wisdom that guide and shape the world that I live in. Most of the time, I live my life in accordance with these laws. I strive to develop my personal and interpersonal abilities so that I made better serve and help others. My life is filled with inspired meaning and purpose that centers on making this world a better place for everyone. My work is seamlessly integrated into all other aspects of my life. My entire life is dedicated to a purpose well beyond myself. In my relationships, there is frequent sharing of the gratitude and appreciation we have for each other. When another person is troubled, a deep sense of compassion leads me to want to help relieve their suffering. I celebrate the diversity of the broad network of people I regularly interact with and learn from. There is almost no sense of superiority between any of us. I am deeply committed to doing what is right and have no need to be right. I frequently express my caring and love for others. While I rarely stumble, I am deeply committed to doing no harm to others. I spend increasing time focused on my inner world. Meditation has become one of my most important daily activities. My study of the external world is almost exclusively focused on the teachings of enlightened wisdom mystics, sages, and prophets. The quantity of my study is far less important than the quality of my study. I seek a deep inner knowing and relevance from the teachings of these enlightened masters.

10. <u>Ultimate Happiness</u>: I am 100% happy, 100% of the time. Negative thoughts and emotions do not visit my awareness. I constantly experience a deep inner calm. Even when I am focused on activity, it does not disturb my inner calm. Being centered on this inner calmness enables me to access the very best of my cognitive and inner knowing abilities. I quickly and easily identify win/win directions that consistently serve more than just the higher purpose of a few. My life activity focuses on facilitating the greatness of others, not myself. This deep desire to serve others often is expressed as compassion when I actively seek to relieve the suffering of others. I consistently focus on the powerful positive qualities of others. I live life constantly in flow or in the zone because I fully utilize my unique strengths. I seek assistance from those who are best qualified, not those with the superior organizational position or longevity. In my relationships, smiles and expressions of love abound. I humbly acknowledge the greatness of others. I live life simply, focused only on the functional necessities of life. My quick sense of humor primarily focuses on poking fun at myself. Although I neither seek nor want recognition from others, I find others enjoy being with me. I continue to be inspired by and learn from enlightened wisdom teachers. My regular meditation practice becomes deeper each day. The combination of learning from enlightened wisdom

teachers and deep meditation are the most
important priority each day of my life.

In truth, most people probably have a center of gravity in
one of the steps, with lingering influence from the
previous step, and some characteristics of the next step.
The primary purpose of this ten-step outline is to
illustrate the major changes we experience on multiple
dimensions. I hope that this illustration provides a clearer
picture of the journey ahead.

The Achievability of Ultimate Happiness

At this point, ultimate happiness may feel like an attractive
possibility but not achievable or ultimate happiness may
not be attractive to you. For those who do not find the
vision of ultimate happiness an attractive goal, the
negativity most likely traces to egocentric beliefs. Maybe
you are most comfortable judging others and feeling
better than others. If this describes you, your options
include doing nothing or considering becoming happier
than you are today using the thinking and skills outlined in
later chapters. Most people can agree to become happier
without the necessity of agreeing to the vision of ultimate

happiness. As they become happier, the vision of ultimate happiness becomes more attractive.

If you find the vision of ultimate happiness attractive but question its achievability that is a good place to be. The vision of ultimate happiness is outside of the personal experience of most of us. Since we have little or no personal experience with ultimate happiness ourselves or with an ultimately happy person, it is very understandable to question the reasonability and achievability of the vision.

As next steps, please consider the following thoughts:

- It is reasonable to be intrigued and even inspired by the possibility of ultimate happiness. The thought of being 100% happy, 100% of the time is thrilling. It is also reasonable to believe the knowledge presented in this book about how to achieve it. But eventually this belief needs to be transformed into a deep inner knowing of the truth of ultimate happiness. Inner knowing develops by personally experiencing the effectiveness of the recommended practices and their results. Inner knowing also develops as we increasingly shift the focus of our consciousness from the external to the internal world.

- Consider critically engaging this book's key points to determine their applicability and relevance to you. Do not placidly accept anything. Relate it to your personal experience and inklings you have about what happiness really is. The knowledge in this book runs counter to so many of today's beliefs. These beliefs are the cause of massive levels of unhappiness. Contrast the description of a person living ultimate happiness in this chapter with your perceptions about happiness today and you will discover that "massive levels of unhappiness" is not an exaggeration. We have such a low level of happiness today that we cannot see how much happiness is possible. Just because our expectations are very low does not mean that they are true. In fact, ultimate happiness is real and possible for those who know its truth and how to navigate the journey to achieving ultimate happiness.

- I am writing this book because of the inspiring people I met who live ultimate happiness. When I first met a person living ultimate happiness, the experience completely redefined for me how happy humans could be. I studied personally with this person several times over four years and each experience deepened by understanding and conviction about the possibility of achieving ultimate happiness. This inspired me to embark on a life long journey to understand how to achieve ultimate happiness. This book reflects what I have learned and used while on this journey. Along the way, I have experienced a few other people living ultimate happiness who exhibit the characteristics outlined in this chapter and who achieve this state using the same skills and processes outlined in this book. I am walking my talk. My experiences guide and shape the suggestions in this book to ensure their practical ability to help people take bold strides forward.

I know ultimate happiness is achievable. The good news is that while it is an ultimate destination every step we take towards this destination contributes to a greater and lasting level of happiness than we now have. The journey itself is one of ever increasing happiness.

Research today indicates that we are very far away from being 100% happy, 100% of the time. The best current research indicates that far less than half of us are happy a fairly small percentage of the time. The truth is that we are unhappy more than we are happy. In fact, the level of deep unhappiness, like depression, has never been higher. Research further indicates that we are becoming less happy than we were twenty years ago. Net, not many of us are happy, the periods of happiness are brief, and we are becoming less and less happy.

I want to be very clear about how difficult the journey is to achieve ultimate happiness. The journey includes changing almost every belief we now have about how to be happier. This is exceptionally difficult work, primarily because we have so little skill and experience changing deeply held beliefs. The journey requires a major life perspective shift from focusing on our outer world of events and people to our inner world of thoughts and emotions. Again, this is exceptionally difficult work because we have almost no experience or skills today to do this.

Achieving ultimate happiness in this life requires making ultimate happiness your most important life goal for the rest of your life. It needs to be more important than work, family, and friends. All of these will directly benefit from your ultimate happiness work, so we will enrich and not neglect these life roles.

Your current happiness starting point influences the degree of difficulty. If you have serious unhappiness problems, like being bipolar or deeply depressed, the challenges are obviously more difficult.

Even if you do not achieve ultimate happiness in this life, the balance of your life will be much happier than if you did not embark on the quest for ultimate happiness. For example, if you are happy about 10% of the time today, you could very reasonably progress to being happy 20-40% of the time. While this is far short of the ultimate happiness goal of 100% happy, 100% of the time, it is two to four times happier than you are today. These measures can be determined through validated objective assessments in combination with a personal assessment, which is the ultimate determination.

This book represents the best available, most proven resources for the ultimate happiness journey. The most important resources have proven effective for thousands of years.

There is no more important life goal than living ultimate happiness. It is the purpose of life. As we progress towards this goal, we become personally more productive and helpful resource to others. We are more successful at work, as the member of a family, as a friend, and as a member of our community. The ultimate happiness life journey has great personal and interpersonal benefits. Enjoy!

Chapter Three

The Happiness Myths

We are not happy campers on this planet. Most of the unhappiness traces to investing tremendous time and energy on efforts that we now know do not make us happier. When we invest tremendous time and energy in these efforts and they predictably do not make us happy, we have cause to be depressed. This form of deep unhappiness is at near epidemic levels today and afflicts people at younger ages than ever before.

When we believe deeply that if we invest time and effort in certain activities that will make us happier and they do not, then we have a myth. Unfortunately, there are some astoundingly powerful myths about what will make us happier. These myths include some core life beliefs taught by well meaning parents, teachers, and respected experts. When western science, through the discipline of positive psychology, turned its research and analytical spotlight onto these core life beliefs, they found that the vast majority of these beliefs do not lead to happy outcomes. The research supporting these conclusions is strong and unequivocal. Despite this support, many readers will be incredulous that beliefs like "If I have more money. I will be happier" are really myths. Please attempt to have an open mind as you review these myths and relate the conclusions to your own life. For any of these myths to make a difference in your life, you ultimately need to agree strongly with the conclusions.

Myth #1: Money

Money does not make us happy.

The belief that money makes us happy is the biggest, most deeply entrenched myth in American culture. Media images of rich and famous people that show constantly smiling and happy people only perpetuate the myth. While inconveniences like divorce and the occasional murder disrupt these images, the vast majority of images and stories present a picture of happy people. The stereotypical images are of people with lots of money smiling and people without as much money frowning. People with lots of money play and have fun while people without as much money struggle. Our culture tries to get us to believe this myth and for the vast majority of people our culture is very convincing.

The strong belief about the importance of money is in place at an early age. For example, an American Council of Education annual survey of 200,000 entering college students found the following:

- In 1971 about 50% of surveyed students said that an important reason for going to college was to "To make more money." By 1990, the percent of students agreeing with this statement rose to about 75%.

- In 1970, 39% of surveyed students said that it was important or essential to become "Very well-off financially." By 1990, 74% of students thought that it was important or essential to be "Very well-off financially."

- During the same period of time the percent of students who entered college to "Develop a meaningful philosophy of life" dropped from 76% to 43%.

More money does not make us happier.

It is a very deeply held American belief that if we have more money we will be happier. The belief is something like, "With more money we can have a bigger house, flashier car, and some of the toys of the rich and famous. With more money we will have an easier, happier life." Not only is this a myth but there is some evidence that there is a negative correlation between happiness and materialism or put another way, some research suggests that the more material stuff people have, the less happy they are. This relationship has been found in research both in the United States and in other countries.[iii] There is a strong logical basis for this hypothesis which is explained later in this chapter.

There are very large industries built around this myth. Las Vegas might not exist if people knew the truth that more money does not make them happier. The state sponsored lottery the programs might not exist if people knew the truth that more money does not make us happier. Game shows probably would not exist if people knew the truth that more money does not make them happier.

Both of these myths are also supported by highly credible, influential, and well intentioned people in our life, like parents, teachers, and friends. Interestingly, these influences tend to talk more about what success is and how to achieve it. While success is not necessarily the same as happiness, they are often presented as the same by the major belief and value influences in our life. There certainly is an assumption that success will make us happy. Success is typically a good paying, even great paying job. While success can have other components in addition to money, like a high status, respected profession, earning a high level of money is probably the most consistent component of any definition of success.

The beliefs that money and more money make us happier are so wrong that it is probably the greatest fallacy of the American dream. There is no scientific evidence to support the beliefs that money or more money make us happy or happier. In fact, the overwhelming evidence demonstrates that once we have enough money to cover essential survival needs (about $10,000), that money and more money do not make us happy or happier. Psychologist Daniel Kahneman of Princeton University, who won the 2002 Nobel Prize for economics, states unequivocally that, "Life circumstances don't seem to have much effect on happiness."[iv] From an economic perspective it is pretty clear why money does not buy happiness. Simply, the primary things that we think make us happy, like love, friendship, family, and respect, are not for sale. Some believe that both money and more money actually may make us unhappy. Dr. T. Byram Karasu, a noted psychiatrist, says "...the wish to acquire possessions and power works against the achievement of happiness."[v]

There is one minor, short-lived exception to this statement. For a brief period after learning that we have more money (like getting a raise), we are happier. This brief period usually lasts a few minutes to a few hours and in some cases, it lasts about a month. After this brief happiness spike upward, there is no residual effect of the happy event (interestingly, the same principle applies to most misfortunes). We return to the baseline level of happiness we had before learning that we had more money. This also applies to using money to acquire material possessions like a car or house. There is a brief upward spike in happiness and we then gradually return to our baseline level prior to the acquisition. Psychologists refer to this process as adaptation. As long as money or more money remains the focus of efforts to become happier, this baseline level of happiness is unlikely to waver too much.

These strong, unequivocal statements may sound reckless to some and unbelievable to others who deeply believe in the myth. I do not expect anything less given the depth and pervasiveness of the myth about money and its relationship to happiness.

While some people have already discovered this myth after years of trying to achieve happiness by acquiring more money, most people want proof that money is not directly associated with happiness. The following is a summary of some of the available proof along with citations that enable you to review the research in greater depth.

- From global and international perspectives, there is no statistical correlation between self reported levels of happiness by residents of various countries and the level of income in those countries. Put another way, there is no statistical relationship concluding that countries with higher levels of income have happier people. In addition, there is no statistical relationship between a country's level of income and self reported "life satisfaction," which is roughly the equivalent to a happiness score. The following international data demonstrates that there is no relationship between purchasing power and a person's sense of life satisfaction or happiness.

Happiness and Income in Relationships[vi]

Countries	Life Satisfaction	Purchasing Power Index (US as 100)
Russia	5.37	27
Turkey	6.41	22
Japan	6.53	87
South Korea	6.69	39
India	6.70	5
Spain	7.15	57
Germany	7.22	89
China	7.29	9
Norway	7.68	78
United States	7.73	100
Canada	7.89	85
Switzerland	8.36	96

- From an even broader historical perspective, over the last half century income levels in all Western nations have risen dramatically while reported levels of happiness have remained flat or fallen. Dr. Martin Seligman reported this research in his well documented book, *Authentic Happiness*[vii].

- The New York Times reported that over the past thirty years real income for Americans has risen 16%--real income is actual income adjusted for inflation. Another way of saying this is that over the last thirty years the buying power of Americans has increased by 16%. Despite this surge in buying power, the percentage of Americans who describe themselves as a "Very happy" has fallen from 36% thirty years ago to 29% now. [viii]

- In a separate major study done for a longer time period, United States data plotted since the mid-1950s shows that there is no statistical relationship between the percentage of people reporting themselves as being "Very happy" and "Per Person After Tax Income in 1990 Dollars". Specifically, per person income in inflation adjusted dollars rose from about $9,000 in 1957 to about $20,000 in 1997. Over these same forty years, the divorce rate doubled, teen suicide tripled, juvenile crime quadrupled, and rates of depression soared. Maybe more importantly, the percentage of people reporting themselves to be "very happy" dropped from 35% in 1957 to 30% in 1997. The income data comes from US government sources— *Historical Statistics of the U. S.: Colonial Times to 1970* and *Economic Indicators* (for data after 1970). The happiness data represents self-reported happiness levels and comes from *Trends in Public Opinion: A Compendium of Survey Data* and Dr. David G. Myers work on happiness surveys. The following chart demonstrates that while buying power has doubled since the 1950s, that the level of happiness people report has remained steady. [ix]

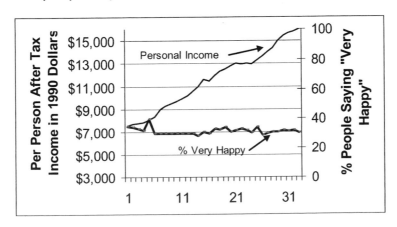

- A crucial test of the lack of relationship between money and happiness was done among people on the lower end of the income scale, including a major study among the unemployed in 42 countries. In some ways this is an acid test since money for the unemployed is presumably relatively more important than it is for the employed. Studies indicate that there is no relationship between happiness and how much various state welfare systems pay—the social support systems for people on the edge of economic viability. People are no happier when supported by generous state welfares systems than people living in societies that have less generous state welfare systems. The range of support from the least generous to most generous was about 300%--the most generous country had about three times the level of support for the unemployed than the least generous. The same conclusion held when the analysis was restricted to the 23 first world nations in the same study. [x]

- From a much narrower perspective, it does not appear that the super rich or lottery winners are much happier than the others who do not have as much money. Research among lottery winners produces mixed results. One study done among 22 major lottery winners concluded that they were no happier than a control group of average people who did not win a lottery. There was even some evidence that lottery winners had some loss of happiness. Yet, other studies suggest they may be slightly happier than the average. Net, the super rich and lottery winners are at best very modestly happier and may be no happier than the average person. [xi]

- Some researchers and writers have looked beyond just the dimension of happiness to overall subjective well-being. *The American Paradox: Spiritual Hunger in an Age of Plenty* by psychologist David Myers and *The Loss of Happiness in Market Democracies* by political scientist Robert Lane make a strong case for broad-based declines in well-being.[xii]

Why is this true? Why doesn't money or more money make us happy or happier?

It seems to me is that there are three core reasons. First, money or the things money buys is an external event and happiness is an internal experience. If we want to be happier, we need to shift from trying to find happiness in external events to finding greater happiness through internal awareness and work. Our internal beliefs guide our choice of actions and their eventual happy or unhappy consequences. As we will discover in later chapters, if we change dysfunctional beliefs then we change our actions and consequences.

Second, it seems that we can never have enough money. Gaining more money might temporarily uplift our level of happiness but then we quickly return to that happiness baseline we had before getting more money. Having experienced the temporary happiness uplift (a happiness "fix"), we become conditioned to increasing happiness, albeit temporarily, by increasing the amount of money we have. Since the higher level of happiness does not last, we set out to get even more money. This process has many of the characteristics of an addiction. Ultimately, if the cycle picks up momentum, it manifests as greed. Greed is a serious illness that frequently leads to choices that create major unhappiness. These choices include unethical conduct and sacrificing relationships for personal monetary gain.

Third, more money and the things that money buys create a series of unintended and unexpected negative consequences. When we have more money and the stuff money buys, life tends to get more complicated and worrisome. This is one reason that more money can actually create less happiness in some cases. Maybe the most frequent negative consequence is the fear of losing what we have acquired. For example, by creating a scenario of ever increasing income, we can become overextended financially which causes fear of losing all we have gained. Or when we acquire that very expensive seven series BMW, we park it in the back of a parking lot, fearful that someone will ding a door or side panel. When we were poor with the old Tercel, we never feared such damage.

Another unexpected and unintended consequence is the increased life complexity that comes with having more money and more things. For example, the addition of a second home adds the complexity of additional insurance, house maintenance and repair, and fears associated with leaving the second home uninhabited. With a second home, there are, for example, now two water heaters potentially needing replacement and two homes needing repainting at some time. With more money we enter the arena of money management and all of its associated complexities, misgivings, and opportunities for unhappy experiences. Net, more money increases complexity and fear, increases which typically offset any positives. This reason helps us understand why some studies conclude that there is a negative relationship between materialism and money and happiness—the more we have the less happy we are.

My experience parallels these three core reasons. Throughout my business career I was fortunate to achieve success that generated an ever increasing income. It ultimately led to very expensive and fast cars, multiple homes, and a complex investment plan. I was very fortunate not to personally experience the greed dimension, but I did experience no fundamental change in my level of happiness and surprising occasions of unhappiness from all the material stuff I had acquired. It ultimately led me to embrace the simplicity movement, a small social wave in the 1990's, which brought several unexpectedly positive experiences that contributed to an overall awakening to the core essence of who I really am. This awakening lead to engaging new life dimensions that did lead to increasing levels of happiness.

Along my journey I also encountered some very rich and very, very unhappy people. From my small base of personal experience, I concluded that the unhappiest people I knew were the richest people in financial terms. This not only included people who were very rich but also people who were just rich; people who made large six-figure incomes and always seemed to have a life style that was at least one step ahead of what they could truly afford and were frequently angry, grumpy, and occasionally unethical and mean.

Along my journey I also encountered people who lived simple lifestyles supported with very modest income. These were also some of the happiest people I knew. Later in my journey, I encountered a person of very simple material and financial means that became a living inspiration of ultimate happiness. This individual, who I will discuss more in a later chapter, completely redefined my view of the human potential for happiness.

This combination of academic and scientific studies combined with over fifty years of life experience pointed to a very clear personal understanding about money-- beyond the basics, money and more money did not make me happy or happier. While I expect very few readers at this point have disassociated themselves with a deep, deep belief that money and more money leads to more happiness, my hope is that I have opened a crack in your awareness to a potential new insight and belief. You should not accept anything I have said about the relationship of money and happiness without critical, personal evaluation. For this insight to be of any value you must personally know its truth. Do not accept it as truth just because someone else says it is true. For an insight to have personally transformative power capable of unlocking greater levels of happiness, the basis of the insight needs to be personal knowing.

Yogananda, the founder of the Self Realization Fellowship, summarized the myth of money and materiality, "No matter how much the worldly man acquires, he never fully enjoys his situation; for he is never satisfied, is always looking for something more, or is afraid of losing what he has."[xiii]

Myth #2: A Better Life

Many people believe that if there was less disease, crime, and pollution they would be happier. Many people also believe if they had more spacious and comfortable homes they would be happier. I have already documented that the percentage of people describing themselves as "very happy" has gradually declined since the 1940s. The incidence of people experiencing at least one bout with serious depression is ten times higher today than it was fifty years ago.

While the exact reasons for this dramatic increase are not well understood, Dr. Martin Seligman hypothesizes as to five possible causes. First, the level of self focus or individualism has steadily increased while the sense of "we" has decreased. The effect has been to limit support networks which can be readily accessed when someone feels down. Second, the self-esteem movement may have backfired in some ways with a focus on some elements that create weak or false self-esteem. Third, there appears to be a significant increase in the number of people feeling like they are victims. Victims blame others, do not take responsibility, and tend to create a learned helplessness. Fourth, with dramatic improvements in disposable income people have increasingly focused on experiencing pleasure. There is very little evidence that pleasure contributes to greater happiness but the endless pursuit followed by less than expected happiness can gradually lead to frustration and depression. Fifth, some researchers have found that children who do not have at home parenting are at significant risk of numerous negative consequences, including higher rates of depression. The trend towards two working parents may be a contributing factor.

Listening to news stories many people would think that the world is getting steadily worse off. The truth is in both short and broad historical terms, life has never been any better than it is today. In *The Progress Paradox, How Life Gets Better While People Feel Worse* Gregg Easterbrook makes a compelling case that life is far better today than it has ever been.

- First, there is one more income perspective. This is a comparison of data from the 1890 and 2000 United States census. Incomes have been adjusted for inflation. In 1890, less than 1% of American households earned the equivalent of $75,000 (in today's dollars) compared with almost 23% of households at this level in the year 2000.[xiv]

- Today's typical new home has 2,250 square feet which is double the size of the new home a generation ago.[xv] Today, 73% of homes have air-conditioning compared to almost none a generation ago.[xvi] Today, almost 70% of Americans own a home versus a century ago when less than 20% did since most Americans were tenants.[xvii]

- Today the average American works 42 hours/week compared to 53 hours in 1966 and 66 hours in 1850.[xviii]

- Easterbrook makes the following sweeping observations about how better life is today.

"Public health is improving by nearly every measure, including rising longevity and falling rates of most diseases; even forms of cancer are in decline. Environmental trends are nearly all positive, with all forms of pollution except greenhouse gases in steady decline in the United States and the European Union. Drinking, smoking, and most forms of drug use are declining. Teen pregnancy is declining. Welfare rolls are shrinking without an increase in poverty. The divorce rate has stopped increasing. Nearly all forms of death due to accident are declining. Crime has declined so rapidly that the fall has been almost eerie. Education levels keep rising, while test scores in public school performance show guarded improvement. Each year the number of nuclear warheads in the world declines."[xix]

- Since the 1990s, domestic violence against women fell 21%, rape declined 40%, robbery and burglaries declined, car thefts declined, and the number of homicides in New York City in 2002 was the same as it was in 1963, despite population increases.[xx]

- Environmentally, a quarter-century ago only 33% of our lakes and rivers were safe for fishing and swimming. Today twice that amount or 67% are safe and the number of safe lakes and rivers continues to increase. Smog is down 33% since the 1970s even though the number of cars has doubled and the number of miles driven has increased by 143%. [xxi]

- From a health perspective, the incidence of heart disease death has dropped 60% in the last 50 years and deaths from strokes dropped 70%. Since 1993, cancer mortality declined at about 1% per year. Since 1980, infant mortality is down 45%.[xxii]

There can be no doubt that life is better today on virtually every important measure, except, and this is a huge exception, happiness. As we will see in later chapters, happiness is in inner experience. What happens in our external world has very little effect on how happy we are. These first two myths make virtually an airtight case for this conclusion.

Myth #3: Work

Work with greater status, perks, and power does not make us happier.

People doing white collar work are no happier than people doing blue collar work. This conclusion is supported by research reported in the book, *Culture Shift in Advanced Industrial Society*, published by the Princeton University Press and named an Outstanding Academic Book in the year it was published. [xxiii] The proportion of white-collar jobs versus blue-collar jobs has steadily increased and today there are more white-collar jobs than blue-collar jobs.[xxiv] Despite this major shift, levels of happiness have not improved.

People with high status work are no happier than people doing manual labor. This conclusion was reached by a group led Dr. Robert Rice, a noted scholar on job satisfaction, while at SUNY Buffalo. [xxv]

There is evidence that Americans are slowly realizing that a job or career is not the answer to their quest for greater happiness. The percentage of total Americans reporting they are "extremely satisfied" with their chosen field of work has declined from 38% in 1973 to 27% in the mid-1990s. [xxvi] It may also explain why Americans are increasingly seeing work as less important in their life. In 1975, almost 50% of Americans said work was most important compared to about 35% saying leisure was most important and about 15 % saying work and leisure were equally important. By 1995 only 37% ranked work most important with about the same number (36%) saying leisure was most important and 25% ranking them equally important. [xxvii]

A significant part of this myth is related to the first myth about money. The majority of us work to earn money and, as we saw earlier, more money does not produce greater happiness.

The majority of us believe that a better job will make us happier and this is a myth. Researchers indicate that we tend to view work in one of three ways. A large group of us view work as just a job where the focus is on the financial rewards. Another large group sees work as a career where the focus is on advancement--more power, status, and perks. The evidence suggests that these first two groups are least likely to find greater happiness from their work and careers.

A fairly small third group sees work as a calling. This last group is passionate about their work because they see meaning and a higher purpose in their activities that often involves contributing to their society or even their world. They are passionate about what they do and would do their work even if they were not paid. For these people there is less separation between their work and the rest of their lives.

As we will see in the next chapter, there is evidence that people with these views about work can become happier. Unfortunately, those who view work as a calling are a small minority of today's workers. Finding work that is a calling often requires a major career change which necessitates courage and a vision. For those interested in learning more about how to make the transition from a job or career to a calling Mark Albion's book *Making A Living, Making Life* provides some excellent case studies that may inspire a vision and courage to begin the journey. Besides the understanding that more money does not equate to greater happiness, why would a "Better" job or career position make people happier? Separate research indicates that stress exists at every level within a business. While the specific nature and source of the stress varies by the nature of the work, work related stress seems to be omnipresent since there are performance objectives, deadlines, and bosses. These conditions exist in the simplest and most complex work and in the most junior and senior positions within a business.

Research also indicates that the single greatest source of stress and job dissatisfaction comes from the boss we work for. Weak supervisor interpersonal skills and dysfunctional business cultures characterize most businesses today. Both factors contribute to a pervasive stress that follows people from job to job and from position to position both within a company and at a new company. Clearly there are situations where stress is lower in some types of work and companies but meaningfully lower differences seem to be a few and isolated examples—probably about 5% of today's companies and leaders.

Surveys confirm that job dissatisfaction is high and increasing, including a recent study by the Conference Board indicating that work dissatisfaction is up sharply in recent years. [xxviii] Surveys also indicate that almost half of Americans report they are dissatisfied with their jobs, regardless of what level or type of business. With this pervasive and worsening situation, it becomes easier to understand why work as a source of happiness is a myth for most Americans.

Myth #4: Pleasure

More pleasure does not increase our basic level of happiness. This includes pleasures like vacations, sex, and the use of alcohol and drugs. Pleasure may temporarily increase happiness, but its positive effects typically last only a few minutes or at most a few hours after the pleasurable activity. Dr. Martin Seligman, the author of *Authentic Happiness* and one of the founders of positive psychology, notes, "Not only do many pleasures fade quickly, many have a negative aftermath."

Vacations and their associated activities can be fun and make people temporarily happier. Whether it is riding one of the fantasy rides at Disneyland or the local roller-coaster, there are typically happy faces during and shortly after the activity. Due to the short-term positive affect, people are off to the next ride for another happiness fix. Despite Disneyland's claim that it is "The Happiest Place on Earth", the happiness experienced there does not last much beyond the drive home. After a full day of these activities, we are typically tired, even exhausted from having fun and the happiness afterglow gradually fades.

This same process repeats itself if it is boggy boarding on ocean waves, swimming in a favorite water hole, skiing deep powder, attending a sporting event, or going to a concert. The best outcome is lots of fun and happy faces during the activity. Shortly after the activity, the upward spike in happiness gradually returns to the baseline level it was at prior to the activity.

While we may crave vacations to escape the stress and unhappiness of work, if we were on vacation all the time we probably would not be happier despite our fantasies to the contrary. We need purpose in life and a life long vacation creates boredom and a level of happiness no different than the activities that preceded it. Changing only external circumstances does little to effect our basic happiness level.

Sex is also a pleasurable activity that at its best achieves a sharp, temporary upward spike in happiness. Even in its simplest form of physical gratification only, sex can produce peak happiness moments. In its more complex forms of lovemaking and a sense of spiritual connection, the happiness peaks can be even higher and longer lasting, but they are destined to decline back to the baseline level.

Psychologists Philip Brickman and Donald Campbell described this experience as similar to being on a *hedonic treadmill.* We can scramble after more and more pleasure, but we do not get any more happiness. Because of the psychological process of adaptation (after an upward or downward spike in happiness, returning to the baseline) we keep ending up back where we started in terms of subjective experience.[xxix]

No matter how high the peak, after the climatic moment there is a gradual decline and return to the baseline level of happiness that preceded the sexual activity. For some of us, the afterglow persists longer, especially for women, but in almost all cases within minutes or maybe a couple of hours the peak happiness moment has become a memory.

For some of us the exceptional peak happiness moments can drive compulsive and addictive behavior. These people want to find a way to get more and more of the peak happiness moments into their life in an effort to live more of their life at these peaks. It is the very temporary nature of these peaks that drives the craving for more of them.

Alcohol and drugs, mostly illegal drugs, are also frequent forms of pleasure we engage in to be happier. For many of us alcohol and drugs are a form of escape from mundane, unhappy everyday lives. Different chemicals temporarily unlock a variety of happy behaviors which often are in a social setting. These behaviors can include dancing, romancing, laughter, and high feelings of being in a better, happier place. Some of these feelings can be exceptional highs, peaks equivalent to sexual highs. Depending on the chemical, there can be in experience of transcendence from the normal life we are accustomed to, like with LSD, for example.

Regardless of how high the high there is the inevitable drop from the peak experience which can be sharp and painful. No matter how high the high from a chemical experience, it is a temporary happiness increase. Unfortunately the drop from a peak experience can be so sharp and dramatic that we bypass our baseline level of happiness on the return journey and find ourselves at a lower than baseline level of happiness and may even reach a level of depression. Typically this low experience has both physical and mental aspects. The range of physical aspects can be as common as a hangover to various forms of physical depletion and discomfort. The unhappy mental aspects can include something as modest as regret to deep, debilitating depression.

It is often this sharp contrast between the highs and lows that fuel psychological dependence on the chemicals. As we know, some chemicals can also create a physical dependence or addiction which can be excruciatingly painful to break.

With all this said, the taking of chemicals, like alcohol and drugs, does not produce lasting increases in happiness. In fact, in many cases the dependence and addiction can produce persistent declines in happiness that can be difficult to reverse.

Whatever the form of pleasure seeking, if we pursue a never ending series of short, peak experiences, it rather quickly leads to boredom. While this may lead to further pleasure seeking experimentation, all pleasure seeking roads eventually lead back to boredom at best and depression at worst. This does not mean that we should not seek occasional pleasure. If we do seek pleasure, we need to recognize it is a myth that pleasure is a means of producing long term increases in our level of happiness.

Myth #5: Appearance

Dr. Seligman, the leader of the positive psychology field, comments on the relationship of physical appearance and happiness, "Physical attractiveness does not have much effect at all on happiness." There are studies that show more attractive people get better jobs and dates. Despite this evidence, personal appearance and improved personal appearance have little impact on how happy we are and our baseline level of happiness.

The fact that physical appearance does not have much if any influence on happiness levels will come as a shock to most of us. Yet, there are well known common sense sayings that provide some understanding and lessen the shock. First, there is the saying that "looks can be deceiving." In this case a beautiful personal appearance does not mean that a person is as happy as our culture might lead us to expect. Maybe more insightful is the saying that "beauty is only skin deep." As we will see in later chapters, happiness is really an internal phenomenon and life's external conditions have little influence over our internal feelings of happiness.

Despite this reality, as a culture we spend billions on creams, surgery, clothing, make-up, workout equipment, club memberships and more in an effort to improve our physical appearance. There are television shows about physical makeovers where before and after appearances are portrayed as unhappy and happy, respectively.

Efforts to improve physical appearance have similarities to our efforts to obtain more money. Often the more attractive a person becomes the less satisfied they are. We hear fashionable and highly attractive people unfavorably compare themselves to others. We hear stories of repeated cosmetic surgeries by people generally regarded as already physically attractive. It seems like physically attractive people can never be physically attractive enough.

This includes not only personal appearance but also the improved appearance of a backyard or a house's interior look. While people who experience these transformations in television shows demonstrate high levels of happiness when they first see the changes, the evidence strongly suggests that this is just another peak happiness moment destined to subside back to the baseline level before the event.

Again, the happiness we see is the temporary upward spike in happiness based on the deeply conditioned cultural belief that people with a better physical appearance are happier or that a more stylish home/room makes us happier people. It simply is not true that physical appearance affects basic happiness levels.

I offer some antidotal evidence that many of us can relate to. Those people we know who are physically attractive are seldom happy with their appearance despite the admiring and even envious looks they receive from others. They always seem to think they are too heavy. If their hair is straight they wish it had more curl. They experiment with different hair colors in a search for the best color. Experimentation with botox and cosmetic surgery seems to have become a broadly based phenomenon. While most of these comments apply more to women than men, men have their own physical appearance programs. This includes a focus on hair style, "male toys" (like cars and gadgets), and clothing. This sometimes obsessive behavior is not limited to people our culture thinks are attractive. There are many average looking folks who seem to have the same set of concerns. Even if this is not definitive proof for you, it will become clearer when you understand what does make us happy why happiness levels are not different based on physical appearance. When a changed physical appearance is associated with other changes that do make a difference in our happiness level, then there may be some contribution from the physical changes to overall happiness. These changes in physical appearance will come more from the inside, like more smiles, and less from artificial attempts to improve physical appearance.

Myth #6: Geographical Location

In the depths of a Minnesota winter people grumble, "I would be happier if I lived in Arizona now." This is another happiness myth.

If you live in Minnesota (or any cold weather state), research concludes that you are as happy on average as people living in Arizona, California, Florida, New York, or any other state. Sure, during the winter people in Minnesota complain about cold, snow, and slush. But in the summer it can be wonderful in Minnesota while in Arizona temperatures hover at about 110 degrees—yes, the humidity is low, but it is still hot and people feel trapped in their home in ways that are not too different from people living in Minnesota in the winter.

Again, changing our outer circumstances does not change our level of personal happiness.

Myth #7: Education

More education does not make us happier, nor does less education mean make us less happy. Research done among people with all levels of education proves this. My experience in academia confirms this.

This is consistent with the previous point about a lack of difference in happiness between people with either white or blue collar jobs.

Myths #8, 9, and 10: Race, Gender, and Age

People of all races report equal levels of happiness. Men and women on average report the same levels of happiness. And young people are as happy as middle age people.

There is some evidence of modest declines in subjective well being among older people. These declines trace mostly to reduced physical energy and emotional reactivity. A meta-analysis of 123 studies confirms the modest differences in subjective well being which approximates a measure of happiness. ˣˣˣ

The Good Life

Not surprisingly, many of these beliefs drive our definition of what we think the "good life" is today. The following chart lists the top ten items America's associate with the "good life" and how they relate to the myths already discussed.

Top 10 "Good Life" Elements	% of Americans Saying It's Part of the "Good Life"	Relationship to Myths
1. Home you own	90%	Myth 1: Money
2. Happy marriage	77%	Chapter 2: It does help personal happiness
3. Car	77%	Myth 1: Money
4. Children	66%	No evidence
5. Interesting job	63%	Myth 2: Work
6. Yard/lawn	63%	Myth 1: Money
7. Job that pays much more than average	63%	Myth 1: Money
8. College education for kids	62%	No evidence
9. College	52%	Myth 6: Education

education for self		
10. Travel abroad	43%	Myth 3: Pleasure

xxxi

Other "good life" elements in the next ten most frequently mentioned goals include lots of money, really nice clothes, a vacation home, swimming pool, and a second car. Again, these are all elements that we know from research will not make a long term improvement in our level of happiness. There is only one item in the next ten that does contribute to greater happiness—having a job that contributes to the welfare of society.

American's definition of the "good life" is not on a solid foundation. When we achieve most of the elements, we are no happier than we were before. Most Americans focus tremendous effort and time on elements that do not bring lasting improvements in their basic happiness level.

How Depressing

So far we have seen that our basic level of happiness is not influenced by:

- How much money we make or whether we are successful in making more money.

- The type of job or career we have, including whether it is a white collar or blue collar job, a manual labor job or a senior executive's job.

- Pleasurable activities like vacations (and all the activities associated with not working), sex, and alcohol and drugs.

- Our physical appearance, whether we are one of the beautiful or one of the not so beautiful people in physical beauty.

- Where we live, whether it is a hot or cold climate, humid or dry, lush or desert landscape.

- How much education we have.

- Our race, gender, and age.

Maybe the most disturbing and disillusioning of these is the lack of relationship of money and the things money buys with happiness. There is a deeply ingrained cultural belief that success and happiness are defined by how much money we have. While there are certainly degrees to which people embrace this belief, the vast majority of people would respond positively to the question, "Would you be happier if you had more money?"

Given the deep belief that money, work, pleasure, and physical appearance have a direct and positive influence on how happy we are, it is a shock to most of us how little influence these factors has on making lasting improvements in how happy we are.

Because we believe that investing effort in these areas will make us happier, we focus much of our attention and devote strenuous long-term effort in these areas. The efforts can include long hours of work and commuting, sacrificing vacation and family time, and tolerating high stress levels. For the most part, these conditions describe decades of our life. It is not due to a lack of effort that most people do not find themselves becoming happier. Many people when they discover that their efforts so far have not produced the greater happiness they expected, decide that they must need to work harder. As a result the sacrifices increase (working two jobs, for example) and the likelihood of finding more happiness from all this effort decreases.

Since all this effort and attention produce little or no improvement in our basic level of happiness, we might expect to find people today dissatisfied, discouraged, disillusioned, and ultimately depressed since these efforts have been so futile.

The evidence strongly suggests that this is exactly how large groups of Americans feel today. Research demonstrates that compared to 1960, ten times more people report themselves as feeling depressed today.

A separate study among adults examined the incidence of depression based on when a person was born. Despite the fact that people born earlier have had more years to experience depression, these people have much lower experiences of depression than people born more recently, as seen below:

<u>Experience of an Incident of Depression in Their Life</u>

- People born before 1914: 1% incidence
- People born around 1925: 4% incidence
- People born after 1950: 12% incidence

People born in the second half of the century were ten times more likely to have experienced an incident of depression than people born in the first half of the century despite the fact that people born in the first half of the century had many more years to experience an incident of depression.

In addition, a 2005 National Institute of Health found that "More Americans are seeking treatment for mental illness than ever before…" and that 25% of American's experienced mental illness in the last 12 months. America's incidence of mental illness may rank number one on the world.

Separate research indicates that only about 20% of Americans think of themselves as being happy while fully one-third of Americans wake up feeling depressed everyday. Separate estimates by mental health professionals suggest that only 10% of Americans are really happy.

These results led Dr. Martin Seligman to observe, "It is shocking that Americans, on average, may be victims of unprecedented psychological misery in a nation with unprecedented prosperity, world power, and materialistic well being."[xxxii] Yogananda, from a different perspective, had the same conclusion when he said, "Relatively speaking, there is very little happiness in this world, only snatches of transient pleasure for the most part."[xxxiii]

People are experiencing depression at a much earlier age than they did in 1960 with the mean age of the first

reported incidence of depression declining from 29.5
years old to 14.5 years old today.

In a study among 1,710 adolescents, Dr. Peter Lewinsohn
of the Oregon Research Institute found the following
rates of depression:

- Born 1968-1971: 4.5% experienced depression by
  age 14

- Born 1972-1974: 7.2% experienced depression by
  age 14

As we know, this dramatic rise in the rate of depression
comes during a period when purchasing power increased
and the average number of years of education increased.
Also the proportion of American people living in better
climates increased and the options to improve physical
appearance also increased dramatically. Despite all these
increases, people are clearly no happier today then there
were a few decades ago and several measures suggest we
are less happy despite all these advances in areas we
believed would produce more happiness.

These conditions should not be surprising when we
realize that the vast majority of effort by Americans to
become happier has focused on things we now know do

not make us happier. When we spend so much of our life pursuing things like more money, a better job, improved physical appearance, and more education and none of these individually or collectively make us happier, we can very naturally expect to feel depressed.

Beyond depression statistics, it is clear that very few Americans think they have achieved the "good life" despite having acquired or accomplished many of the items defined as part of the good life. For example, home ownership is at record levels, we own more cars per household than 20 years ago, and the percent of people attending college is much higher than 20 years ago. Despite these high absolute levels and improvements versus the past, only 10% of Americans feel they have achieved the "good life"—90% do not think they have...and they are probably right. Interestingly, while only 10% of the total population feels they have achieved the "good life", it is not much higher for people with $50K+ incomes or people with executive and professional jobs—only 11% of both groups think they have achieved the "good life." [xxxiv]They are right because they are not seeking the elements that truly do contribute to a "good life" that is based elements contributing to lasting happiness.

As disturbing as these myths about what contributes to greater happiness are, we should feel positive because we also know what contributes to being happier and how to change our lives so that we follow the path of happiness instead of the current path of unhappiness. Take heart, this is the only "negative" chapter in the book. The balance of the book focuses on what we know about becoming permanently happier, which is a direction that eventually leads to ultimate happiness.

Chapter Four

Western Science and Happiness

Western science knows far more about unhappiness than it does about happiness. Of the sciences, psychology is the primary one examining the subjects of unhappiness and happiness. As a science, psychology is fairly young, starting in the late 19th century compared to a science like astronomy that has been in existence since recorded time. Within the field of psychology, the primary focus since its inception and until recently has been on curing unhappiness, often serious unhappiness like schizophrenia and depression. What little attention was paid to happiness often suggested that people have little potential for happiness. Freud noted, "One feels inclined to say that the intention that man should be happy is not included in the plan of Creation." His view was that the most one could hope for was "The transformation of hysteric misery into common unhappiness." While his views were not universal, for most of psychology's history it did not pay attention to how mentally healthy people could become happier.

It has only been within the last ten plus years that psychology focused seriously on happiness. With the recent development of the field of positive psychology, western science has begun to understand what makes us happy and what does not contribute to greater lasting happiness, as noted in the previous chapter. But even with this development for every psychology journal article on happiness there are one hundred articles on sadness. xxxv

This chapter focuses on the primary findings from the field of positive psychology about what life elements tend to increase our basic level of happiness, not just provide short-term increases that fade away. This is not a comprehensive list but it does include elements that have the greatest research support and tend to be consistent with the happiness understandings of the perennial wisdom traditions that are covered in subsequent chapters. It needs to be understood that positive psychology is a very young field of science that does not yet have a great depth and breadth of research. Despite this, some very positive and practical findings can help most of us.

Happiness Overview From Positive Psychology's Perspective

Positive psychology views happiness as having three principal components. First, there is the pleasant life where the primary purpose is building positive emotions. Part of the pleasant life includes being OK with the past and having optimism and hope about the future. There is also a focus on deriving pleasure in the present.

Second, there is the good or engaged life. The focus here is on using our signature strengths to create flow in our life, and especially our work. There is also emphasis on building virtues.

Third, there is the meaningful life with a focus on serving a purpose that is larger than our individual self. There is recognition that the definition of the meaningful life changes depending upon our life stage and age.

Within this framework, there are some specific life aspects and elements that positive psychology has determined contribute to greater happiness. The balance of this chapter details the most important of these.

Married? Probably Happier

While the previous chapter indicated that many demographic factors like income, job, race, gender, and geographical location are not statistically related to happiness, being married does contribute to greater happiness. In a National Opinion Research Center survey of 35,000 Americans over the last 30 years 40 % of married people said they were "Very happy," while only 24% of unmarried, divorced, separated, and widowed people said this. [xxxvi]

Clearly not all marriages are the same. There is a range of reported happiness in marriages, from very unhappy to very happy. Not surprisingly, the level of overall life happiness also varies. Only 3% of people who say they are in marriages that are "not too happy" say they live very happy lives. Conversely, 57% of people who say they are in "very happy" marriages say their lives are "very happy."[xxxvii]

While it is not clear from the research what the specific dynamics of marriage are that contribute to greater happiness, the presence of greater love, caring, and support compared to the alternatives appear to be key factors. We know from personal experience that when we love another person we feel happier than when we do not. When there is caring and support given to another person and received from another person, we know from personal experience that we feel happier than when this is not present.

If you are considering marriage as a way of becoming happier please consider what the research says increases your chances for a long-term marriage. When most of the following factors are present, you increase the likelihood of staying married.

- You married after age 20.
- You dated for a long while before marriage.
- You are well-educated.
- You enjoyed a stable income from a good job.
- You live in a small town or on a farm.
- You did not cohabit or become pregnant before marriage.
- You and your spouse are religiously committed.

Family Background and Genetics

If you and your parents were to take a test to evaluate how happy each of you are, about half of your score is strongly influenced by how happy your parents are. Additional research demonstrates that identical twins raised apart from each other have about the same level of happiness which leads some researchers to suggest a biological or genetic link to happiness. To be clear, science has yet to discover a "happiness gene" that predetermines how happy we can be and it is not clear there is one.

The fact that the family we grow up with has a significant influence on our level of happiness makes sense and is well documented. We know separately how influential the family environment is in the establishment of values and beliefs. Since our values and beliefs have a direct and immediate influence on the choices we make, is not surprising that the family environment is so influential on how happy we are.

While we do not choose our families, we can use this insight to recognize that our values and beliefs are not universal but rather represent a unique mix and interpretation of the values and beliefs we acquired in our most formative years. This understanding's potential power is that our unique values and beliefs were consciously or unconsciously chosen at one time and can be changed in the future. This insight helps us change those values and beliefs that lead to choices producing unhappy outcomes. As we become more self aware, we discover these choices have a direct influence on our basic level of happiness. Make better choices and we have the opportunity to create happier consequences.

The danger in this understanding is that we feel we are programmed and incapable of changing. While power and influence of family values and beliefs should not be underestimated, we should not give them so much power that we feel like prisoners. Some people blame their upbringing for their current problems and the blame has so much power that it suggests these people are powerless to change. Frankly, research suggests that this is an excuse to not change and that we can change if we want to take our power back. Blaming is giving away personal power to events or people and that does make us powerless.

As we will see later in this book, there are proven, powerful techniques for adopting new values and beliefs that lead to choices capable of making us happier long-term than we have been in the past.

Work—Doing What You Are Best At

In the previous chapter, we saw that the type of job that we have (white-collar or blue-collar, executive or entry-level) does not influence how happy we are. Thus, striving to achieve a higher paying or perk filled job does not have a high probability of making us happier. We also discussed the three different types of work orientations--job, career, and calling.

While the vast majority of people tend to view their work is either a job or career, there is some evidence that if your work is a calling (a passionate sense of purpose that allows you to do what you are best at), you will probably be happier than if your work is a job or career.

Research done by Dr. Martin Seligman suggests that if we use our "signature strengths" in our work that we will be happier. He notes, "The good life consists in deriving happiness by using your signature strengths every day in the main realms of living."[xxxviii]

What are "signature strengths"? Dr. Seligman identified twenty-four that fall into six groups—wisdom, courage, temperance, transcendence, humanity, and justice. Within wisdom, for example, are the strengths of curiosity/interest in the world, love of learning, judgment/critical thinking/open-mindedness, ingenuity/originality/practical intelligence/street smarts, social intelligence/personal intelligence/emotional intelligence, and perspective. [xxxix] If you want to know more, Dr. Seligman's book *Authentic Happiness* is a good resource and you can determine your signature strengths online at www.authentichappiness.org where you can register and take the signature strengths test at no cost. Confirming the importance of signature strengths is a Gallup poll that found that the number one contributor to adding meaning and purpose to work was "The ability to realize my potential as a person."[xl]

When we know our signature strengths and find inspiring work that enables us to regularly use them, our work becomes a calling. Work then becomes much more fun than struggle and we experience a real sense of contribution and accomplishment. As we will see in later factors, a sense of purpose and helping others also contribute to increasing our baseline of happiness.

When work is our calling, it is not unusual to experience complete absorption in the present activities. This describes a condition researchers call flow and athletes refer to as "being in the zone." It is associated with greater happiness and life satisfaction. Typically we are in flow when the activities are ones that stretch but do not exceed our skills and strengths. While performing these activities there are clear goals and feedback on how well we are progressing.

When we are in the flow of our work we experience:

- Intense focus on what needs to be done in the present moment

- No self consciousness about how we are doing; we just do it

- Action and awareness are one; we are only aware of what we are doing

- A strong sense of control that is easy

- A loss of time awareness; time seems to fly and we are surprised to find out how much time has elapsed when we do pause to become aware of time

- Fun and highly rewarding activities.

Western science believes that work is second only to our family background in its ability to influence our basic happiness level. Research concludes that 20-25% of life satisfaction is influenced by work satisfaction. Remember, that roughly 50% of life satisfaction is influenced by family and upbringing conditions.

The good news is that work can make us happier when it is a calling that enables us to use our signature strengths and to be in the flow of our work. This endpoint often requires getting out of our present work that is a career or job. Before doing this we need to determine what work is our calling and then develop a plan, which can involve additional education and reducing living costs so that the leap does not cause unnecessary pain and suffering.

Positive and Optimistic Thinking

Not surprisingly, developing more positive and optimistic thinking is a powerful way of becoming happier than we are now. Positive, optimistic people have skills that enable them to cope with life's challenges better than people who are less positive.

For example, positive and optimistic people tend to believe the causes of misfortune are temporary while pessimists tend to believe the same causes are permanent. Optimists work to accept the reality of misfortune and put situations in the best possible light. Research also suggests that optimists cope with situations better than pessimists even when the causes of the situation cannot be changed.

Looking for and finding the best in a given situation obviously contributes to a greater sense of happiness than the alternative of looking for and finding the worst in a situation. Optimists are skilled at challenging pessimistic thoughts and looking for other, more positive understandings. They look for alternative explanations and the evidence to support them. They also seek to understand the implications and usefulness of each alternative. Research demonstrates that optimists have better resistance to depression when misfortune strikes. As side benefits, optimists have better results at work, live 19% longer, and are healthier. Some broad based studies suggest optimists live an average of ten years longer than pessimists do and that the longer life is happier than the pessimists' life.

I am not suggesting a Pollyannaish, rose-colored sunglasses view of the world. Positive and optimistic thinking provides major coping skills. For some people, this thinking may need to be balanced with a dash of pessimism and skepticism to prevent complacency and gullibility. Lastly, there needs to be the ability to discriminate between things we can control and those that we cannot. There is a wonderful serenity prayer that says, "O God, give us grace to accept with serenity the things that cannot be changed, the courage to change the things which should be changed, and the wisdom to distinguish the one from the other."

Optimism can be learned. The most famous positive thinking advocate and teacher was Dr. Norman Vincent Peale, the author of *The Power of Positive Thinking* and many similar themed books. When first published in 1952 it stayed on the best seller list for two years and sold two million copies, with millions more since that time. "You can think your way to failure and unhappiness," wrote Peale, "but you can also think your way to success and happiness. The world in which you live is not primarily determined by outward conditions and circumstances but by thoughts that habitually occupy your mind. "[xli] Dr. Peale's work has been carried on by others including a former student, Robert Schuller of the Crystal Cathedral. More recently, Dr. Martin Seligman's book *Learned Optimism* provides very helpful advice on how to develop more optimistic beliefs and actions. In some ways, his studies built on the positive thinking movement to develop understandings that made optimism a more powerful contributor to greater happiness. A key skill is being able to overcome helplessness by taking a more proactive role in your life, including the skills to argue with yourself about the truth and usefulness of a negative or pessimistic interpretation of a life event.

As we will see in subsequent chapters, the focus on inner conditions and the thoughts that influence our mind are the primary determinants of how happy we are and can be. As important as positive thinking and optimism are to our happiness, Western science has only discovered a small part of the role inner conditions play in our ultimate happiness. We will see broader and deeper dimensions in the next three chapters.

Forgiveness

When we forgive, we let go of anger and resentment that make us unhappy. People who do not frequently forgive carry anger and resentment with them that can build over time into hate and thoughts of revenge. This can lead to more conflict and anger that seems to become a self perpetuating cycle. An inability to forgive ensures that a negative life event will dominate the thoughts and actions of a person far longer than for a person capable of forgiving and moving on.

People who forgive have been found to have less stress and better health than people who do not. The ability to forgive also seems to produce greater levels of optimism. Forgiveness can have two objectives. First, we can forgive others, the most frequent object of forgiveness. Second, we can forgive ourselves. Forgiving ourselves or others is helped when we have some of the skills of the optimist, especially the ability to see alternative explanations and views. This ability often enables us to see things like ambiguity, good intentions poorly executed, and assumptions we make that may not be correct. All of these can open the door to forgiveness.

While true forgiveness is not easy for most of us, its contribution to greater happiness is unquestioned.

Gratitude

When we express gratitude for a life event it is usually for a positive event, one that made us happy. Expressing gratitude for the event amplifies the value and impact of the happy event. It is a method of prolonging the temporary happiness increase we experience from pleasurable events, for example. The happy memory gains intensity through gratitude. When we frequently express gratitude for a happy event or positive life condition, it is a way of recharging the happy memory and reconnecting with it. In a sense it is a method of reliving the happy event.

When we feel gratitude after a happy event, we prolong the happy feelings. The memories become richer and deeper, often more so than we actually experienced the event. The longer and more frequently we linger on expressions of gratitude for an event or person, the more power we give the event to positively influence our happiness.

Gratitude can reinforce positive life qualities that contribute to greater happiness. Even a negative, unhappy life event can be an opportunity for gratitude. For example, we can express gratitude because we kept our cool instead of getting angry like we usually do or we learned an important lesson by taking the time to examine what happened.

Gratitude can have many expressions and relationships. For example, "I am grateful for...

- The beauty in this flower which brings a smile to my face.

- The Supreme Being who created this beautiful flower

- The opportunity to share this flower with Patricia as an expression of my love.

Part of the gratitude's power is that it can have a broad and deep focus.

Researchers who have studied people who frequently express gratitude report, "Joy, happiness, and life satisfaction shot up for the gratitude group."[xlii] This makes common sense. People who spend time being thankful for positive, happy events prolong and intensify their happy experiences. Memories become stronger and longer lasting. The residue from a positive event has more influence. Gratitude, as we will see later in the book, is also a powerful method of changing negative habits into habits that make us happier.

Life Meaning and Purpose

When life has meaning and we have a purpose that excites us, we are happier. Meaning comes from our values and the belief that we can make a difference—a sense of power instead of powerlessness. It also helps to believe that we are a good and worthy person. The breadth of purpose can vary from something very self-serving to a desire to serve humanity.

The more our purpose extends beyond ourselves the more power the purpose has to make us happier. Put another way, the more we expand our view beyond just ourselves and develop a sense of altruism, the happier we are. Dr. Howard Cutler reports, "In fact, survey after survey has shown that it is unhappy people who tend to be the most self focused…"[xliii] They are also less healthy and experience more of various forms of heart disease. The same applies to meaning in life. Clinical researchers have found that the definition of meaning needs to extend beyond the "lonely self" if it is to have a positive influence on our life. These same researchers believe that the relative lack of meaning in life for many people today is a major contributor of the increased levels of depression. Researchers ranging from Victor Frankel's observations about the power of meaning in concentration camps to a host of studies over the years have confirmed the power of purpose and meaning to positively influence happiness, life satisfaction, and success. Again, when our meaning extends beyond the self, its power increases.

For some, meaning and purpose derive from religion. One of the universal elements of all religions is the identification with a higher power like God or Allah. Various studies indicate that religiously active people are somewhat happier and significantly more charitable. For example, people who agreed with the statement "my religious faith is the most important influence in my life" are twice as likely as people having the least agreement

with this statement to by very happy. Dr. T. Byram
Karasu, an acclaimed psychiatrist, notes the importance of
spirituality to happiness when he says happiness is a
function of "…being a grown-up, soulful, and spiritual
person.".[xliv]

Two factors tend to explain the relationship between
strong religious beliefs and happiness. First, religion offers
a community of shared beliefs and a support system.
Second, religion tends to answer some of life's toughest
questions and provide an optimistic appraisal of the future.
On the other hand, we have economists who generally
believe that self-interest drives behavior. This belief may
explain why they are twice as likely as other professions
to contribute no money to charities.

The suggestion that meaning and purpose have more
power when they extend beyond ourselves is counter to
deeply held Western thinking that human behavior is
highly egotistic and that we are primarily focused on self
interests. The prevailing view of basic human nature is
that humans are inherently selfish and aggressive. Over
the last several centuries there have only been minor
deviations from this view. For example, David Hume the

Scottish historian and philosopher, who influenced the development of skepticism and empiricism, two schools of philosophy, in the mid 1700s argued for the "natural benevolence" of humans and later even Darwin detected an "instinct for sympathy" among humans.

Whatever the degree of self-focus, meaning and purpose contribute to a sense of control in our life. Meaning and purpose trigger problem solving skills and provide the energy to persevere during challenging situations. Most researchers and philosophers conclude that a realistic sense of control fosters greater happiness and well being. Control also creates a sense of freedom and self determination. Researchers like Rogers and Maslow who supported the humanistic model for human behavior found that freedom and self determination were important to bringing about positive change in life, changes in values and beliefs that eventually drove different behavior that contributes to greater happiness.

Beyond Positive Psychology

Positive psychology does not represent the full scope of what the West knows about becoming happier. Maybe the single most powerful set of understandings is included in the field of emotional intelligence. Its core set of understandings revolve around self-awareness. Emotional intelligence has proven to be a greater predictor of organizational success than intelligence (IQ). I will discuss the important topic of emotions in a later chapter, where we will discover that effective management of emotions is critical to success in both Western and Eastern perspectives. I will also outline the heart of Daniel Goleman's pioneering work on emotion intelligence. There is no shortage of additional insights on how to become happier. When I searched Amazon for the number of books with the word "happy" in the title, I discovered over 6,000 different books. Searching for titles with the word "happiness" in the title, I found an additional 2,500 books. There is a great deal of similarity in the key points of most of these books. This includes advice to let go of judging, being present, being grateful, and making being happy a priority.

My focus in this chapter has been on the practices proven (mostly proven by the field of psychology) to contribute to greater happiness. In no way do I intend to diminish the contributions of writers that share their own personal experience and understandings. As already noted, there is nearly universal agreement in the West on a set of core essential understandings and practices.

Concluding Thoughts

It is encouraging that Western science has finally turned some attention to what contributes to greater levels of happiness. They have uncovered many important myths (detailed in the previous chapter) and a few factors that are associated with happier people.

We have learned that marriage and the right kind of work can contribute to happiness. We have also learned that certain ways of thinking can also make us happier—optimism, gratitude, forgiveness, and seeking meaning in life. This last group touches on an important learning that Western science has not fully appreciated. As people who have studied happiness much longer have discovered, our internal beliefs, values, thoughts, and feelings are the most important determinants of how happy we are. And the good news is that changing these is fully within our control, and we do not have to change others or external life circumstances to be happier.

This is a profoundly disturbing insight to many people who spend most of their lives blaming the external world for their woes and trying to change their external world with the belief that when they are successful they will be happier. It is far easier to ask other people to change than to change yourself, which can be truly tough, long term work. Taking back the power previously given to others (through the blame game) and using it to take control of our happiness is ultimately good news. Most people who have tried to change their external world have had little or no success and as a result they are no happier. We need to take back responsibility and the power to be happy and realize that it is up to us to change ourselves if we want to be happier.

Chapter Five

Happiness Via The Middle Way

While western science has studied happiness for a little more than a decade, Buddhists have studied happiness for about 2,500 years. Happiness has been a major focus of Buddhist research and teachings because they see happiness as an essential part of life's purpose. As His Holiness the Dalai Lama says repeatedly, "I believe that the very purpose of our life is to seek happiness."[xlv] Buddhist understandings of what happiness is and how to achieve it are the subject of hundreds of books written over the last 2,500 years. Happiness has also been the focus of countless oral discussions and teachings. Buddhist understandings of what happiness is and how to achieve it are probably the most extensive single source available to us today.

Of all the Eastern wisdom traditions, I have chosen Buddhism's perspectives on happiness for three reasons. First, as a psychology its major focus is on becoming happier. Second, it has an exceptionally extensive array of practices and insights proven effective for over 2,000 years. Third, of all the Eastern wisdom traditions (Islam, Hinduism, Lao Tzu, Patanjali, and Confucius, for example) it has the broadest availability and accessibility in the West. There are many advanced Buddhist teachers in the West and the Dalai Lama has an extensive worldwide teaching schedule and numerous very helpful books, including the bestseller *The Art of Happiness*, which he co-authored with Dr. Cutler.

Before going further with my discussion of Buddhist understandings of happiness, a brief perspective on Buddhism may be helpful. Most westerners view Buddhism as a religion, which it technically is. Experience with various forms of Christianity shapes the understandings of what religion is for most Westerners. From my hundreds of hours with Buddhist teachers, I have formed the following contrasts between Buddhism and Christianity:

- Buddhism feels much more like a philosophy than a religion.

- Buddhism is free of suggestions that it is superior to any other religion or way of thinking about life. As a result, there have been no attempts to convert me to Buddhism.

- Experience with Buddhist teachers has been free of ceremony, pomp, and circumstance. That is not to say that there is not some of this occasionally, but it certainly appears to be far less than my experiences with other religions. From my experience with Buddhist teachers, I have noted their simplicity, humility, and happy demeanor.

Buddhists believe that the life purpose for all of humans, not just Buddhists, is the achievement of greater happiness. Importantly, all humans possess the ability to be increasingly happy. In the Dalai Lama's words, "I believe that everyone of us has the basis to be happy, to access the warm and compassionate states of mind that bring happiness. "[xlvi] This is echoed by another great Buddhist teacher, Sogyal Rinpoche, "Happiness and all the causes of happiness are within ourselves. Only the foolish look for happiness outside of themselves. "[xlvii]

The "warm and compassionate states of mind" mentioned by the Dalai Lama reflect the Buddhist view of humans as essentially gentle and compassionate beings. Very few Westerners view gentleness and compassion as essential human qualities, and their actions suggest they value the qualities of anger and even violence more. One of those who did view compassion as a powerful human quality was Albert Einstein, "Our task must be to widen our circle of compassion to embrace all living creatures and the whole of nature and its beauty."[xlviii]

Fortunately, the broader Western experience does not reflect the true essence of who we really are. Over the last thirty years, several hundred western scientific studies concluded that aggression is not an essential or innate human quality. Rather, violent behavior is the result of biological, situational, social, and environmental influences. A group of twenty top Western scientists believed so strongly in this conclusion that they signed a statement saying, "It is scientifically incorrect to say that we have an inherited tendency to make war or to act violently. That behavior is not genetically programmed into human nature."[xlix]

Buddhists believe that the state of our mind determines our level of happiness more than external conditions, events, and circumstances. Since our state of mind determines our level of happiness, the key to happiness is within our control. We can exercise that control through a systematic training of our minds with the purpose of reshaping attitudes, values, and beliefs that facilitate happiness. Recognizing that we have control of most of the factors that determine how happy we are is a cause for great hope.

Knowing that we have the power to control how happy we are can have a profound impact on life. While rigorous, long-term work is required to change long-held values and beliefs, this work produces lasting increases in personal happiness.

There are a few basic beliefs that help us begin the journey to greater, lasting happiness. We need to recognize that as humans we want to be happy and free of suffering and that other humans share this desire. This establishes a common ground and link with others. By emphasizing what we have in common with others, we begin to open our hearts to compassion and altruism.

The Dalai Lama indicates the importance caring about more than just ourselves, "I think it is important to remember that in all human activities, whether it is work or some other activity, the main purpose should be to benefit human beings. Try to maintain basic human values, even at work...Just basic human goodness. Be a good person, a kind person. Relate to others with warmth, humor and affection, with honesty and sincerity. Compassion."

Having compassion for others eventually leads to a desire to serve others. The Dalai Lama's advice is "If you can, serve others. If not, at least refrain from harming them." The concept of doing no harm is a central Buddhist concept and is something all of us can aspire to. We typically need to move from doing harm to doing no harm before we can begin to serve others.

Training and Disciplining the Mind

Disciplining, training, and shaping the mind are the keys to happiness. By doing this we determine how we perceive our world because inputs from our five senses are "filtered" through the mind's cognitive and evaluating abilities. Change the mind and we change our experience of the world.

While this is a central Buddhist concept, western science agrees. Dr. Edward Diener of the University of Illinois, Urbana-Champaign, states, "It appears that the way people perceive the world is much more important to happiness than objective circumstances." Dr. Howard Cutler supports this conclusion and adds, "There is a massive body of evidence to support that assertion."[1] Conquering, taming, and disciplining the mind is neither easy nor quick. In fact, for most of us taming the mind is the most difficult, frustrating life long task we will ever undertake. The good news is there are powerful methods for taming the mind that can become part of a more comprehensive personal program. This is the focus of later chapters.

Sogyal Rinpoche is clear about the link between training the mind and happiness, "If you conquer the mind you have the master key that opens all the doors. And what is wonderful is that you find yourself and happiness when you open that door."

Through training the mind, we then can perform two other critical actions necessary to achieve happiness. First, Buddhists advise, "permit no unwholesome action" which means we need to abandon all negative actions and clear malice from our hearts. Second, Buddhists advise us to "cultivate a wealth of virtue." This means adopting positive and wholesome actions that produce greater happiness. Buddhist philosophy goes to great length to define the specific positive and wholesome actions that lead to greater happiness.

Disciplining the mind is neither simple nor quick, but this should not discourage us because efforts to increase personal happiness are part of our life long journey. We did not get to where we are today with our assorted values and beliefs overnight so we should not expect deeply, long held values and beliefs to quickly change. The process of inner discipline is very specific and precise in Buddhist philosophy and as usual, the Dalai Lama brings clarity to a complex subject in a few words, "When I speak of this inner discipline, it can of course involve many things, many methods. But generally speaking, one begins by identifying those factors that lead to happiness and those factors that lead to suffering. Having done this, one then sets about gradually eliminating those factors that lead to suffering and cultivating those which lead to happiness. That is the way."[li]

We primarily need to discipline the six major mental afflictions—attachment or craving, anger (including hostility and hatred), pride, ignorance and delusion, and afflictive doubt. Not all doubt is bad since some leads to greater understandings, but from the Buddhist point of view, all anger is wrong. Westerners view anger as warranted in some situations.

The Happy Mind

The happy mind is a calm, peaceful, and quiet mind. A calm mind it is not an insensitive or spaced out mind. The calm, peaceful mind is alert, sensitive, and experiences compassion. The Dalai Lama provides thoughts on how powerful a calm mind can be, "…if you possess this inner quality, calmness of mind, a degree of stability within, then even if you lack various external facilities that you should normally consider necessary for happiness, it is still possible to live a happy and joyful life."[lii]

Most Westerners struggle with the concept of a calm mind because they equate it with laziness. While this is understandable, experience with a calm mind reveals it is highly alert and quick. Random thoughts and feelings that normally operate as noisy chatter and distractions in the background gradually subside. On the outside, we can be highly active, but on the inside, the mind is totally focused on now. As a result, the calm and happy mind is highly productive and effective.

Compassion is very important in Buddhist thinking about how to be happy. Compassion goes beyond empathy that is feeling what another person is feeling. Compassion includes empathy and then goes the next step of wanting to relieve the suffering of other people. Compassion focuses on helping others, including acts as simple as an encouraging word, a random act of kindness, or lending a hand to help. The almost universal result of these actions is feeling personally happier and contributing to the happiness of others.

The Nature of Our Mind

There are two dimensions to the nature of the mind. First, there is the appearance of the mind, which is our thoughts and emotions. This is the aspect of mind we are most familiar with. While it is what we are most familiar with, most of us have very limited self-awareness of our specific thoughts and emotions. We are aware that we have emotions and thoughts, but we tend to spend very little time contemplating and reflecting on them. Instead, they seem to operate beyond our control to create habitual actions that frequently contribute to persistent unhappiness and occasional happiness.

The ego misuses the mind to grasp. This grasping produces limited perspective and understanding that is more habitual than a result of objective reasoning.

The second dimension is the essence of our mind. It is clear and spacious. The essential nature of our mind is pure because the basic subtle consciousness is untouched by negative emotions.

Sogyal Rinpoche utilizes an analogy to understand the transition from the appearance to the essential nature of our mind. The appearance of our mind is like a jar of muddy water. If we leave the jar untouched, the particles of mud gradually settle to the bottom of the jar and what remains is clear water above the residual mud. In this analogy, the mud is our thoughts and emotions and if we allow them to settle, the mind becomes quiet and what remains is a sense of clarity, spaciousness, and purity. Another way of understanding the difference between the appearance and the essence of mind is to look more closely at the process of recognizing, knowing, and evaluating. For example, when we experience a flower our senses of sight and smell provide us a variety of inputs enabling us to know "It is a flower." This is the objective knowing mind. The mind then moves very quickly (in a few nanoseconds—a nanosecond is one billionth of a second) to judge and evaluate the flower. For example, it might conclude, "It is beautiful," or "I do not like that shade of red." The appearance of mind is the grasping, judging mind while the objective mind is a major aspect of the essence of our mind. To experience the essence of our mind, we need to let the judging mind gradually become quiet and reside in the objective mind.

The appearance of mind (thoughts, feelings, and emotions) is out of control for most of us today. Pausing only five minutes to observe quietly our thoughts and feelings reveals an untamed torrent of random, often chaotic, never-ending stream of thoughts and emotions. There is little apparent reason for the thoughts and emotions as they jump around from subject to subject to subject. If we try to purposefully and forcefully stop the torrent of thoughts and emotions, we are successful for seconds, not minutes. Then the torrent resumes. Untamed and uncontrolled is an appropriate description for our judging, grasping mind. Sogyal Rinpoche advises that, "Speed of life fuels aggression. Slow down and become more effective—make haste slowly. Be calm."

This description of a chaotic mind may seem strange and unfathomable to many, but it is only because we spend so little time observing our mind that its real condition is unknown to us. We see the truth of this proposition when we attempt to sit quietly and maintain our focus on a word like love for as little as five minutes. We will be fortunate to maintain the focus for about a minute of the five minutes. Most of the time the mind flits from one topic to another, often topics that appear to have little relationship to each other which makes the description "chaotic mind" a bit more understandable.

By connecting with the essential nature of our mind, we experience a calmer and more peaceful world, which is a much happier experience. This essential nature of mind sees objective reality untainted by judging thoughts and emotions. The essential nature of mind is a deeply knowing mind. Residing in the objective mind opens the door to the higher mind where we access intuition and wisdom. Today, very few of us experience this essential nature of our mind, and as a result, we do not experience the clear knowing mind that enables us to do much more by doing far less.

Meditation: The Gateway to the Essential Nature of Mind Meditation brings the mind home to a state of non-distraction. In part, meditation is a process of letting the mind settle, much like letting the mud settle to the bottom of the jar. Meditation is a state of being, not thinking. By letting the thinking mind settle, clarity and spaciousness emerge. Meditation turns the spotlight of our attention from the outside world to our inner world. Buddhist's describe two basic forms of meditation— tranquility and insight meditation.

Meditation begins the process of mindfulness. It is a sharp departure from the thinking, speaking, and acting we are accustomed to. The French philosopher Pascal once observed that all of man's troubles trace to his inability to sit in a room by himself. By spending almost all our time thinking and acting, we have lost our sense of being and connection with ourselves.

Meditation has many dimensions. The focus here is on its ability through consistent long-term practice to gradually calm the mind. It does not require strenuous effort, like trying to suppress thoughts or punishing ourselves when thoughts continually arise, to tame the mind. These kinds of efforts only contribute to further stirring up the mind. The disciplining of the mind comes from internal efforts, not from any external source. The disciplining comes from being not doing.

This is incredibly difficult for most of us who are so accustomed to doing, to activity. By doing and being active, we feel productive. Sitting and letting the mind settle according to most values and beliefs is an unproductive waste of time. For the beginner, these values and beliefs are serious barriers to meditation.

Many quit after a short trial in part because of these beliefs but also because they expect quick results. Meditation's results are profound when done consistently for months and years but they may be undetectable for most when done only for a day or week.

Within months, meditation in its most basic form has major benefits. The following is a partial list of meditation's proven medical benefits:

- Lower or reduced levels of
    - Resting heart rate,
    - Muscle tension,
    - Anxiety and stress,
    - Chronic pain,
    - Blood pressure
- Improved or increased levels of
    - Visual sensitivity, hearing musical tones better
    - Concentration
    - Energy and health
    - Memory and general intelligence
    - Reaction time and motor skills

- o Feelings of connectedness to others, pleasure and ecstasy
- Lowers stress which results in less heart disease, cancer, colds, arthritis, and a stronger, more effective immune system.

Beyond these benefits, meditation gradually opens access to our higher mind or wisdom mind. Within the wisdom mind lays our intuition. While intuition is usually misunderstood and equated with a variety of feelings like instincts and gut feeling, it is the most remarkable of human abilities. Ultimately, intuition enables us to know anything at any time with no effort. Mystics, who have well developed intuitive ability, tell us that intuition is the "voice of our soul" and that our soul is our connection to the Universal mind. With a fully developed intuition, we always make the right decision with no sensory inputs or pondering by the logical mind. The "right decision" is one that is right for everyone involved in a decision, not just ourselves. While we all have intuitive ability, it is latent in most of us. Very few of us can regularly access it or distinguish an intuitive insight from the host of other feelings we have. Intuitive decisions enhance our happiness and the happiness of others.

Meditation's ability to make us more self-aware gradually opens our ability to distinguish between the types of inner feelings. Meditation also contributes to gradually calming our minds and it is with a calm mind that we can start to access intuitive insights.

I will discuss meditation further in a later chapter detailing specific actions we can take to become happier.

The Middle Way to Happiness

Buddhist psychology is concerned with how we process and react to the inevitable flow of life's events. In particular, it addresses how we respond to life's inevitable suffering (inevitable until we have fully tamed the mind). Most of us respond to life's events with actions that not only do not resolve the suffering of the moment but also ensure future suffering. These are habitual reactions for the most part, which create cycles of reoccurring and self-reinforcing actions. A deeply engrained network of neural connections in the brain supports these habits. Every time we encounter similar forms of suffering these connections create an almost compulsive reaction. The reactions are usually self-serving. Our sense of what best serves our interests is much more on autopilot than a product of careful, reflective consideration. As a result, these reactions to suffering seldom do more than perpetuate the misery and unhappiness.

Humans, when viewed objectively, are a bit perverse when it comes to processing unhappiness. In many cases we resist letting go of our unhappiness and stay very attached to it. We often take perverse pleasure in our attachment to things like self-righteous indignation and being a victim who wants others to make them happy. It is as if we enjoy our unhappiness. This is another form of the ego's grasping which causes so much unhappiness.

In part, this traces to an important dimension of our response to unhappiness. Sometimes we focus on feelings of satisfaction from our reaction that also produces unhappy consequences. It is perverse but real. For example, reacting as the wronged one enables us to play the victim, which is a perversely good feeling for many people. The focus is on ego gratification that can be very seductive. Unfortunately, the seduction usual works and after a short period of perverse happiness, we find ourselves tossed back into a sea of continuing unhappiness.

Alternatively, we have the option of focusing on the consequences of our actions or potential actions. If we choose our actions with an increasingly insightful and wise view of our actions' consequences, we would make action choices that lead to greater happiness and less unhappiness. We would see that the consequences of ego gratification do not produce lasting happiness. If the ultimate goal is happiness then we are confronted with a need for new choices, choices that greatly increase the likelihood of a happy outcome.

The middle way in Buddhism is a path that enables us to make more of these choices.

In part, the middle way allows our emotions and thoughts to flow but without becoming attached to them in a way that produces an egocentric focus and attachment.

Through the middle way, we increasingly become more detached from our thoughts and emotions. Put another way, our relationship with our thoughts and emotions shifts from a very subjective one to an increasingly objective one. Increasingly we do not let our thoughts and emotions sweep us away in directions that perpetuate unhappy consequences and that virtually guarantee more unhappiness in the future.

The middle way to greater happiness also means gradually diminishing the highs and lows of life so that life becomes more even and tranquil. Life becomes calmer and more peaceful. As we become calmer life changes. We notice more because the judgmental mind distracts us less and less. We use what we notice to make choices that reflect an awareness of the consequences from the available choices. When we are calmer, we listen and learn more. We use what we learn to make more informed choices, often choices that are different from our habitual ones that cause persistent unhappiness.

Another way of viewing the middle way is to see it as letting go of our attachment to pairs of opposites—good and bad, right and wrong, highs and lows, etc. The philosopher Ken Wilber notes the liberating effect of being able to let go of our attachment to and identification with various pairs of opposites.

> ...in all the mystical traditions, the world over, one who sees through the illusion of the opposites is called "liberated." Because he is "freed from the

pairs" of opposites, he is freed in this life from the fundamentally nonsensical problems and conflicts involved in the war of opposites. He no longer manipulates the opposites one against another in his search for peace, but instead transcends them both.[liii]

From this calmer place, we gradually become more aware of the consequences of our actions, especially how it makes us feel. As we pay more attention to our emotions, we notice that when we express feelings of love and compassion that it feels natural and happy. We notice it is good for our well being and health. We notice that loving and compassionate choices in the current moment tend to lead to more of these choices in the future. Gradually new neural networks develop in our brains that support happy choices. With this appreciation, we can better see how feelings of anger, frustration, anxiety, and fear are destructive to our well being and health. The contrast provides additional encouragement to make more of the happy choices.

As we travel the middle way we increasingly discover our essential nature. Again, the Dalai Lama's words are helpful, "It is still my firm conviction that human nature is essentially compassionate, gentle. This is the predominant feature of human nature. Anger, violence, and aggression may certainly arise, but I think it is on a secondary or more superficial level, in a sense, they arise when we are frustrated in our efforts to achieve love and affection. They are not part of our basic, underlying nature."[liv]

We get on the middle way by calming down which only happens when we discipline the mind. The mysteries of life gradually clear up. We start seeing life's challenges from different perspectives and this leads us to new choices with a greater awareness of their consequences. Ignorance gradually dissipates and clarity of mind emerges. This sounds very simple and in a way, it really is if we can only find a way for it to be simple. But the mind likes to doubt and question. The mind might conclude that the middle way sounds too good, too easy. As a result, the mind/ego judges and resists. A persistent and strong ego is a formidable foe in our efforts to travel the middle way. We got this way during the course of our entire life until now. While changing directions and getting onto the middle way is neither an easy nor a quick trip, it is entirely doable.

The basis for this is Buddhism's 2,500 years of experience with success. It is a proven path to greater happiness. Part of the Buddhist psychological approach to happiness differs sharply from Western psychology. Western psychology often attempts to understand the root of a dysfunctional behavior or negative feelings. For example, efforts often focus on determining how the dysfunctional beliefs formed, like tracing a belief back to an early life trauma. Buddhist psychology does not focus on understanding the root of the problem, but does focus on understanding the root of the mind through efforts like mindfulness.

Buddhist psychology's focus on the present, not the past, also is a remedy to unhappy conditions. Buddhist psychology has 84,000 antidotes to negative emotions, not unlike mental medicine. For example, the antidote to hate is love. If we want to stop hating something or someone then find someone or something to love. Focus energy on love, intensify the focus, and then maintain the focus. By starving energy or focus from the hate, we gradually weaken it. We replace it with an even more powerful energy, the energy of love. Our single-minded focus on love nurtures and strengthens this very positive energy. This remedy is faster and far more effective than trying to understand the root of a problem somewhere in our history. When we use an antidote, the change is often immediate. While the unhappy feeling may return, the better we become at recognizing the unhappy feeling and applying the antidote the sooner, we can eradicate the feeling from our life. Later chapters will further address antidotes since they are critical to reaching ultimate happiness.

My Experience Along the Middle Way

For me the most telling proof the middle way as a path to ultimate happiness has been personal experience, most notable with a product of Buddhist philosophy, Sogyal Rinpoche. A "Rinpoche" in Buddhism is highly revered and a level below the Dalai Lama. Many of the Dalai Lama's most respected teachers have the "Rinpoche" title. A Rinpoche is also referred to as a "Master." In the Western culture this word has generally negative connotations, like a slave master. In Eastern traditions it has a very different meaning. Yogananda says that well.

Master means one who is the master, not of others, but of himself. He has complete wisdom control of his senses. He is not a master who dominates the actions of others by the power of his commanding voice and will, but he who is the owner and wise ruler of his own actions.[lv]

Knowing him completely redefined for me the human potential for happiness. My experience with him proved to me that ultimate happiness is real and achievable. I first met him during a weekend "Meditation and Healing" workshop at Esalen, a renowned Big Sur training and retreat center. In an intimate and informal setting with about twenty people, I marveled at his pure happiness. His easy laughter, often directed at himself, and spontaneous smile were at a level I had never experienced with another person. His message of hope and practical, sage advice was inspiring.

I returned for the next three years to this workshop in what became a pilgrimage of sorts to recharge my batteries and recalibrate my definition of human potential. I remember only a few key points from his presentations, like the muddy water meditation analogy, but his humble, happy presence is highly memorable and inspiring.

Coupled with an obvious wisdom and compassion, he is the most impressive and happy person I have ever met. For almost twenty years, he has served as an inspiration for how happy and wise humans can be. He continues today to be one of my principle daily inspirations.

As I reread these words, I see how inadequate words are at describing my experience. Had I read these words without having known him I would relate to them within the narrow confines of people I had known. For me, Sogyal Rinpoche is happiness personified.

That inspiration led to regular meditation and an ever-expanding self-awareness. Along with additional study, I gradually gained an appreciation of the middle way to happiness. I saw my highs and lows as products of attachment to the events of the moment that seemed so real and important at the time, only to quickly fade in importance. This roller coaster of feelings did little to contribute to lasting happiness.

Further contributing to progress along the middle way was the ability to see life from the perspective of an observer. Increasingly I saw myself performing actions and from this perspective could see how actions did or did not contribute to my happiness. Observing gradually became more objective and less subjective. This ability helped me return to a center or middle perspective that evened out the highs and lows of life.

Most people can understand the value of evening out life's lows but why the highs? For me the lesson is that the highs were associated with events that did not create lasting happiness increases, like getting a raise or a new car. I gradually came to see the temporary and somewhat insignificant role these really played in contributing to long-term happiness. The evening out of highs and lows creates for me a more centered, balanced, and calm life that is clearly happier than where I was before this part of the journey. From this calmer life emerges the space to connect with inner wisdom, the center from which lasting happiness comes to light.

For me this has led to ever-increasing levels of consistent happiness. While the change is gradual from my perspective, friends who I see infrequently experience the change as bordering on profound. While I appreciate how the middle way has contributed to more consistent happiness, I also know from Sogyal Rinpoche's example that I still have tremendous, almost unfathomable progress to make along the middle way. On a clear day, I can see Sogyal Rinpoche a million or more steps ahead of me on the middle way.

Chapter Six

The Self Realization of Happiness

A major focus of all wisdom and spiritual traditions is happiness. Their message is one filled with hope that happiness is within our control, not our external world. Paramahansa Yogananda very concisely said, "If it is happiness you want, have it! There's nothing that can stop it."[lvi] He adds this strong warning, "It is a sin against the divine nature of the Self to think that there is no chance of being happy, to abandon all hope of attaining peace—these must be exposed as psychological errors...Infinite happiness and peace are always at hand, just behind the screen of man's ignorance "[lvii]

The message from all the traditions contains the essence of Buddhism—being happy is natural, it represents the essence of whom we really are, and that inner conditions that we control primarily determine how happy we are.

Since this message is so important, I want to present it from an additional perspective. Often different words enable more people to connect with and get a message. The additional perspective in this chapter primarily comes from Paramahansa Yogananda, the founder of the Self Realization Fellowship. An acknowledged Avatar or enlightened being, through the early 1900s until his passing in 1952, Yogananda gave us a wealth of practical, scientific lessons about how to progress along the path to self-realization of who we really are. These lessons provide specific practices and understandings proven to make us increasingly happy. The practices help us detach from the unhappy and negative aspects of our life and connect with the happy and positive dimensions.

Unlike some Western psychological practices, these are exquisitely easy to understand. For example, Western psychology often tries to understand the root of unhappy, dysfunctional behavior. This can involve extensive work to discover the life event that led to the behavior that makes us unhappy, like childhood trauma. Even after all of this work, psychology's success rate is much less than 50%. Eastern practices, like Yogananda's, are simpler and far more direct. They often can bring immediate relief from an unhappy situation. We can not only disconnect from the unhappy situation and feelings, but also quickly connect with positive and happy energy.

Despite their simplicity and directness, using these practices to become fundamentally happier requires diligent, hard work to raise permanently our baseline happiness level. In most cases, it is not easy to change deeply ingrained habits supported with firmly held beliefs. There are well-established neural networks in the brain supporting these habits and developing a new network requires starving the old network and nourishing the new network.

Before going further let me introduce Paramahansa Yogananda since he is probably unknown to most readers. He was born in India and educated by several of India's greatest yogis or wise men. In addition, strong spiritual influences included the teachings of Krishna, the founder of Hinduism, and Jesus. If you attend a Self Realization Fellowship temple, you will see the pictures of these two well-known teachers plus his three primary enlightened teachers from India. Yogananda came to the West in

1920 and over the next three decades built a world wide following through his powerful, practical, and scientific approach to wisdom and spirituality. The most powerful of his scientific practices is Kriya Yoga. He is one of the first to merge spirituality and science by suggesting practices based on scientific understandings of various levels and kinds of energy. In some ways he addressed a need articulated by Albert Einstein who said, "Science without religion is lame, religion without science is blind."[lviii]

His teachings are also very contemporary, with the original teachings in English, a language he has a great command of. Many of his writings are also very inspirational, especially those that express his love of God. Most people first learn about him through *The Autobiography of a Yogi*, a perennial top selling book even fifty years after his passing.

The balance of this chapter looks at inner conditions from Yogananda's perspective and briefly discusses specific actions we can take to become happier.

One of the reasons I find his teachings so helpful is that they are in their original English-language version. English is not the original language for most of the other great wisdom traditions' teachings. With Yogananda's teachings nothing is lost in the translation. In addition, his teachings are the most contemporary (written less than one hundred years ago, compared to thousands of years ago for most other traditions) of any of the great wisdom traditions.

The organization's name (Self-Realization Fellowship) captures one of the most attractive aspects of his teachings. My path has been more of a personal journey than one following a fixed path, which makes the Fellowship a good fit for me. The Fellowship empowers people to pursue a path of self-study along their journey to self-realization and ultimate happiness.

After more than a decade of extensive searching and studying, I chose Yogananda to be my primary life teacher. I concluded that all the great teachers taught the same lessons. The differences came in the expression and accessibility of their teachings. Yogananda's teachings best met all my needs so I embraced him as my guru for life. Today, the study of his lessons and the practice of his methods for spiritual growth are my highest daily priorities.

The Inner Path to Happiness

At our current level of consciousness, the mind creates our experience of reality. We quickly filter objective inputs from our five senses through our beliefs to form subjective conclusions. In Stephen Covey's terms, we use the moment of choice after objective awareness (created by the senses) to choose a reaction or response depending on the guidance from our values and beliefs. The vast majority of the time our responses are very quick because our beliefs have seen similar situations (or at least we think so) and know how to respond. Our responses are mostly habitual ones and usually we are unaware that we are making choices. We are aware of the stimulus and a subsequent action but most of the time we are unaware of the decision making process between stimulus and action. This lack of awareness produces a sense that we have no choice, "When she insulted me, I had to insult her back."

It also puts misplaced power in the external world, "He made me mad so I got revenge." Blaming others gives our power away; our power to make conscious choices that makes us happy. Blaming supposedly enables us to escape responsibility for our actions which we find desirable when our actions are negative—rudeness, anger, or attacks, for example. It is a myth that someone else is responsible for our actions. Blaming is really just an excuse for our negative and often irresponsible actions. Blaming fails to recognize that we are responsible for all of our choices. It seems so much easier to make someone else responsible for unhappy choices rather than owning up to the reality that all our choices are our responsibility. Unfortunately, blaming others is a choice we frequently make. It always involves giving our power to others, and this is crucial power we need to make choices that produce happiness instead of unhappiness.

Yogananda speaks to these seemingly never ending choices that appear to have control over us and lead us to repetitive bouts with unhappiness, "These patterns make you behave a certain way, often against your wishes. Your life follows those grooves that you yourself have created in the brain. Depending on how set those patterns are, to that degree you are a puppet." We often feel that we have no control, but that is because we have so little self-awareness, especially of our choice of actions.

There is a big price to pay from this lack of awareness. We continue to make choices that we feel we have little control over and many frequently lead to unhappiness. These reoccurring events follow us even when we change jobs, friends, and places that we live. When we can see this pattern by becoming self aware, we may then see that we are responsible for our continuing unhappiness, not the external world.

Yogananda reminds us of the power choice has to make us happy or unhappy, "If you do not choose to be happy no one can make you happy. And if you choose to be happy, no one can make you unhappy."[lix] And he recognizes how difficult it is to not blame others and to make conscious choices we are responsible for, "Persons of strong character are usually the happiest. They do not blame others for troubles because they see the troubles are a result of their own actions and lack of understanding. They know that no one has any power to add to their happiness or detract from them unless they themselves are so weak that they allow the adverse thoughts and wicked actions of others to affect them."[lx] Western and Eastern writers, scientists, and philosophers are clear that if we want to be happy a crucial step is to take responsibility for all our actions by recognizing that every action is the result of personal choices over which we have control. When we understand the science of how the mind works, there is no doubt that we have this control, but few of us fully exercise this control. It can be painful at first to take responsibility and easier to blame. We often succumb to being victims and give our power away. As a result, we can feel like we have no control over our personal happiness. These are all misguided perceptions when we understand how the mind really works. These choices invariably lead to unhappiness and often-serious unhappiness we call depression.

We incorrectly focus on the physical actions when the true focus of our awareness should be on the mind. Yogananda says, "Every action has a mental counterpart. We perform acts with our physical power, but that activity has its origin in the mind, and is guided by the mental captain. To steal is evil; but the greater evil is the mental act of stealing that initiates the physical theft, because mind is the real perpetrator. Whatever wrong action you want to avoid, first throw it out of the mind. If you concentrate only on the physical action, it is very hard to gain control. Concentrate on the mind: correct thoughts, and automatically the actions will be taken care of."[lxi]

This requires turning the spotlight of our awareness from our external world to our internal world. We are now back to the Buddhist counsel that the path to greater happiness comes through taming the mind. Becoming more self-aware involves self-analysis through introspection and contemplation. We seek to understand which choices lead to greater happiness. We start seeing the consequences of our actions, both for others and ourselves. We take responsibility for our consequences and use that responsibility to make ethical and right choices. When we turn the spotlight inwardly, we recognize that we are what we think we are. If we see ourselves as unhappy, we only need to change our mind to become happy. Yes, this is very easy to say and so difficult to accomplish but just knowing that being happy is within our control, not the control of others or external events, is cause for great hope and excitement.

We can extinguish this hope and excitement if we do not how to use it to affect positive change in our lives. We know how to harness this hope to specific processes to achieve the desired goal of lasting and higher levels of happiness. Part three of this book addresses this.

Actively Calm, Calmly Active

As we saw with Buddhism, it emphasizes the taming of the mind as the path to happiness. Yogananda also recognizes its importance but emphasizes the desired result from taming the mind—the achievement of a calm mind. He says, "Calmness is the ideal state in which we should receive all life's experiences...One who is naturally calm does not lose his sense of reason, justice, or humor under any circumstances."[lxii] He also advises us to "Practice the art of living in this world without losing your inner peace of mind."[lxiii]

The cost of losing our peace or calmness is high. When we are not calm, we lose our ability to think clearly. When faced with choices, the disturbed or agitated mind often falls back on habitual actions instead of clearly evaluating options and consequences. These habitual actions tend to be mostly about maximizing personal good, even at the expense of others. A lack of calmness fosters emotional decisions, which tend to reflect distorted feelings and personal needs at the expense of others. A lack of calmness also leads to decisions guided solely by logic that risk being cold blooded when we need a clear vision guided by our heart and head. The result is unhappiness and in many cases profound suffering.

If we want to be happier, we need see new options and know the potential consequences of our actions before we act or we perpetuate a cycle of habitual actions that have unhappy consequences.

When our mind is calm, we are capable of intense concentration. A calm mind is undistracted by thoughts of the past or future. It is 100% focused on now. A calm mind is the state of mind Zen Buddhists suggest in their advice, "When you wash dishes, wash dishes." It is also the state of mind connected with our ability to be in the flow (scientists' term) or zone (athletes' term). When we are in this state of mind, we are capable of our best work, often by a wide margin over the capabilities of a distracted mind. When we are calm, we have some powerful abilities, as Yogananda notes, "When the mind is calm, how quickly, how smoothly, how beautifully you will perceive everything."[lxiv]

Having a calm mind is very different from having a lazy or sleepy mind. A calm mind is exceptionally alert and capable. A calm mind is what we strive for through meditation. Despite the fact that meditation is often done with eyes closed, it does not lead to a sleepy state (unless we choose that) but to a calm and exceptionally aware and knowing state of mind. Yogananda notes the need for balance, "To be calmly active and actively calm--a prince of peace sitting on the throne of poise, directing the kingdom of activity--is to be spiritually healthy. Too much activity makes one an automaton and too much calmness makes one lazy and impractical. Peace is the enjoyment of life; activity is the expression of life."[lxv]

When we are actively calm and calmly active, we connect with our wise inner knowing and are highly attractive to others. When we are free of fear and anxiety, we are peaceful and positive with others. We manifest our best interpersonal abilities and generate powerful insights capable of resolving the most complex of issues.

Yogananda adds, "A calm person reflects gracefulness in his eyes, keen intelligence in his face, and proper receptivity in his mind. He is a man of decisive and prompt action, but he is not moved by impulses and desires that suddenly occur to him."[lxvi]

Many conditions can threaten a calm mind with anger and fear being the most threatening. When in the presence of angry or fearful people avoid that energy. We need to be uninvolved and detached. The antidote to anger and fear is peace, love, and forgiveness. An angry and fearful person is in pain and needs healing.

The most powerful healing power is love that we express from a point of peace and a heart guided by forgiveness. The calmer we become the more compassionate we become. Compassion wants to relieve the suffering of others.

We can lose our calmness for many reasons in addition to anger and fear. For example, when we experience frustration, anxiety, and interpersonal tension, it challenges our ability to remain inwardly calm. In addition being in a noisy, hectic environment contributes to nervousness that is a persistent energy making calmness more difficult. Through enough of these experiences, we become emotionally, physically, and mentally bankrupt. We lose the ability to make our best choices, to be happy, and to contribute to the happiness of others. This is a very big price to pay, but one that most of us frequently pay in a life when we value activity and doing much more than being.

We gradually become calmer each day by making regular deposits in our calmness bank account. There are varieties of ways of making deposits like reading inspiring books, listening to a wise teacher, or simple quiet communing with nature. But we make the biggest and most powerful deposits through regular meditation.

Yogananda and others teach that as we become calm we gradually gain access to our intuition, which is the voice of our soul and the spark of divinity in all of us. In Yogananda's words, "Intuition is soul guidance, appearing naturally in man during those instants when his mind is calm."[lxvii] Intuition is an often misused and misunderstood ability. Intuition is our higher mind (higher than the logical mind) which is capable of instantly knowing what is right and best for all concerned. The intuitive mind processes vast and often complex situations with no sensory inputs, like evaluating data or knowledge bases. It is a quiet inner knowing is distinctly different from instinct and gut feelings. Some scientists, like Jonas Salk and Albert Einstein, keenly appreciate intuition's power. Einstein said, "The intuitive mind is a sacred gift and the rational mind is a faithful servant. We have created a society that honors the servant and has forgotten the gift."[lxviii]

Developing a calm mind is the surest method of awakening the intuitive ability that resides in all of us. Yogananda provides some practical advice about how to utilize this powerful ability, "Before embarking on important undertakings, sit quietly, calm your senses and thoughts, and meditate deeply. You will then be guided by the great power of Spirit."[lxix]

Yogananda concludes, "When wealth is lost, you will have lost little; when health is lost, you have lost something of more consequence; but when peace of mind is lost, you have lost the highest treasure."[lxx]

Happiness Actions

One of the most attractive and powerful aspects of Yogananda's work is the practical advice that really works to help make us happier. Like any such advice, it often requires hard, long-term work to change deeply ingrained habits and realize its full benefits, but the "prize" of greater long-term happiness is worth the effort for most people.

This section provides a sampling of Yogananda's advice in brief sections. Those wanting to learn more can read some of his enlightening and inspiring books detailed in the bibliography. In addition, the Self Realization Fellowship offers a subscription series of on-going lessons that last almost three years.

Weaken Bad Habits

Bad habits hold us prisoner to repeating behaviors that consistently make us unhappy. Most bad habits are so deeply ingrained that we have little awareness of them. They seem like they are an essential part of who we are. We seldom examine or think about habits because we take the justification (our beliefs) for granted. Yogananda points out how much habits can control our life, "Success is hastened or delayed by one's habits. It is not your passing inspirations or brilliant ideas so much as your everyday mental habits that control your life. Habits of thought are mental magnets that draw to you certain things, people, and conditions. Good habits of thought enable you to attract benefits and opportunities. Bad habits of thought attract you to materially minded persons and to unfavorable environments."[lxxi]

The lack of self-awareness makes bad habits powerful. They have us on automatic pilot for so much of our life. We only become truly free when we can discard bad habits. This requires considerable self-awareness and self-control over extended periods to bring about the elimination of bad habits. Yogananda adds some practical advice, "Weaken a bad habit by avoiding everything that occasioned it or stimulated it, without concentrating upon that in your zeal to avoid it."[lxxii]

Meditation

Meditation is a frequent topic in this book because it is the most effective of the proven practices and methods for achieving the abilities and conditions necessary for lasting increases in happiness. Other processes can contribute, like time in nature, journal writing, and contemplation, but meditation is the scientifically proven "power tool" of choice for achieving lasting increases in happiness. Meditation, among many contributions, develops self-awareness and regularly calms the mind to some degree. Through meditation, we gradually allow the mind to settle usually using a mantra or breathing awareness to help maintain a present moment focus. We have already seen how important a calm mind is to our happiness. Yogananda speaks to one of the reasons meditation is so helpful in achieving the calm mind, "Real unending joy lies in attuning the consciousness to its true, ever calm soul nature by meditation, and in thus preventing the mind from riding on the crests of sorrow and happiness or from sinking into depths of indifference." [lxxiii] By "preventing the mind from riding on the crests of sorrow and happiness" he refers to traveling the middle way we discussed in the previous chapter. In addition he says, "Through meditation one can experience a stable, silent inner peace that can be a permanently soothing background for all harmonious or trialsome activities demanded by life's responsibilities. Lasting happiness lies in maintaining this evenly peaceful state of mind."[lxxiv]

The Powerful Now

A mind that focuses on the past or the future thwarts efforts to tame the mind and achieve calmness. Even when we are talking with someone, the mind can be focused on a past memory of the person or on a related event or thoughts about the future consequences of the present conversation (The mind can also be focused on something that has nothing to do with the person we are talking with!). Yogananda forcefully said, "Forget the past, for it is gone from your domain! Forget the future, for is beyond your reach! Control the present! Live supremely well now! It will whitewash the dark past, and compel the future to be bright! This is the way of the wise."[lxxv]

Improve Yourself

For most of us following Yogananda's advice or the advice from any wise teacher requires changing current habits. A life long personal growth project is required to achieve more happiness in life. Covey also addresses this as one of his seven habits of highly effective people—habit #7 is "sharpen the saw." The last series of chapters address specific, proven methods for successful achieving personal growth goals.

Despite our most fervent wishes, changing bad, dysfunctional habits that contribute to persistent unhappiness only happens when there is a deep desire and commitment to personal growth. This is not easy as Yogananda points out, "The worst pests that attack your plant of happiness are lack of desire to progress, self satisfaction and skepticism. The chill of inertia, or lack of definite, constant effort to know the truth, is the greatest ill from which our happiness plant suffers."[lxxvi]

When we can break the inertia of being stuck in old, persistent unhappiness producing habits, Yogananda details the benefits of such effort, "Your highest happiness lies in your being ever ready in desiring to learn, and to behave properly. The more you improve yourself, the more you will elevate others around you. The self-improving man is the increasingly happy man. The happier you become, the happier will be the people around you."[lxxvii]

New Interpersonal Skills

To become happier requires some fundamental changes to how we interact with others. Many of our current forms of interactions only add to our unhappiness and create an agitated mind. Examples include reactions like anger, rude responses, arguing, and quiet disdain. Yogananda's advice is the opposite of these common reactions, "The spiritual man conquers wrath by calmness, stops quarrels by keeping silence, dispels inharmony by being sweet of speech, and shames discourtesy by being thoughtful of others."[lxxviii] This is reminiscent of Jesus' advice to turn the other cheek. For most of us, Yogananda has set a very high standard but we need to understand that a calm mind contributes significantly to our ability to follow his wise advice. The major challenge is the ego's desire to defend itself, but we see the path to happiness as we sacrifice self-interest for the interests of others.

He also suggests that we reverse the usual flow of conversation from talking primarily about ourselves to speaking about subjects that interest others, "When you talk, don't talk too much about yourself. Try to speak on a subject that interests the other person. And listen. That is the way to be attractive. You will see how your presence is in demand."[lxxix]

Vigilant Self-Awareness

A key to personal growth is an ever-increasing level of self-awareness. We need to first know what we are thinking and feeling when we make choices if we expect to change bad habits. We need to convert today's unconscious choices into conscious choices through self-awareness. Self-awareness can be improved in various ways including journal writing and using Covey's suggestion to expand the moment of choice, which is the time between a stimulus and a response. By consciously expanding the moment of choice between stimulus and response, we increase our ability to make new choices that make us happier than current choices.

Yogananda's suggestion of how to use the moment of choice demonstrates the kind of energy and attitude needed to be effective, "As soon as the soldiers of wrong thoughts rally to attack your inner peace, it is time to wake up the soul soldiers of light, honesty, self control and desire for good things, and to wage a furious battle."[lxxx]

Stop Being Judge and Jury of Others

Many disturbances in our mind result from judging others. Usually the judging is negative, noting aspects of a person that we do not like, for example. These inner thoughts can be particularly intense and disturbing. When we become aware of our focus on judging others, we discover that it is usually fairly frequent and can have serious negative effects on our mood and interactions with others.

Consistent with the Dali Lama's suggestion to turn our attention from our outer to inner world, Yogananda recommends turning our judging focus from others to ourselves, "Many people excuse their own faults but judge other persons harshly. We should reverse this by excusing other's shortcomings and by harshly examining our own." [lxxxi]

Yogananda on Money and Materialism

In chapter two, we saw compelling evidence that neither money, more money, or the stuff that money buys contributes to lasting happiness increases. Yogananda adds a wisdom perspective on why money and materialism do not contribute to greater happiness.

> Why covet material extravagance? It is quite usual for people who are excessively endowed to be also excessively unhappy; for their nervous system is entangled in caring for and worrying about their possessions, never feeling quite complete and satisfied, unable to enjoy what they do have.[lxxxii]...
> The covetous man wants to have more than the next person; but when he has it he is not satisfied, because inevitably he finds someone else with still more than he. People live in a bedlam of misery created by their desires. Materially, the average American has far more than the average citizen of Europe or India or any other nation; but still he is not happy! His satisfaction is seared with anxiety and worry and unending wants.[lxxxiii]...
> When people concentrate on political and business selfishness for national and personal accumulation of power and luxuries at the expense of others, the divine law of happiness and prosperity is broken, creating disorder and want in the family, the nation, the world.[lxxxiv]

Some Personal Thoughts

During ten years of extensive searching, I gradually discovered that all the great teachers over the last 3,000 years delivered the same key core messages. Huston Smith, the great student and teacher of the world's religions, reached the same conclusion. While the exoteric (external) appearance of religions and philosophies are often different, the exoteric or core teachings are the same for all religions and philosophies whose source is God-realized teachers. We often magnify the exoteric differences to make the views we like the best somehow better than another teaching. This happens because of the efforts of well-intended people who do not possess the spiritual or wisdom development to understand fully the meaning of the God-realized teachers. As a result, their interpretations often are partially correct and incorrect and tend to be much more self-serving and narrow than the original teacher intended. The other dimension I have discovered is that while the core messages are all the same, the words used to express these messages often differ significantly. This is important because words have power and words have a specific energy. For example, when we feel hate for someone we experience a very different energy than when we feel love for someone.

Each of us also has a specific energy profile. That is, as science knows our entire being is pure energy and each of us have a unique energy profile or rate of vibration composed of our thoughts and experiences. As a result, we tend to connect best with the teacher whose words feel most comfortable to us—the best energy profile fit. This is the reason I chose Yogananda as my primary life teacher or guru. His words (his energy) had an inspiring fit for me. Others may find their best fit with other teachers who use different words to express the same core thoughts, words that have a better fit.

What is important is to connect with a God realized teacher. That is not always easy, especially when we begin our journey of self-realization. Despite this difficulty, I suggest that you use only key criteria--the teachings reflect a love for all beings, not just those who share a particular belief. It is also helpful to work with the original teachings as much as possible and to work very selectively with disciples of those teachings who may or may not possess the spiritual development to understand fully the teacher's original meaning. The original teachings of some religions and teachers have gone through major editing by more mortals who did not possess the abilities of the original teacher. The result is inevitably distortion and misinterpretation that can produce understandings that are major departures from the teacher's original intent. This makes the sorting out and connecting process a daunting task unless we rely on an awakening intuitive ability to some degree. This enables us to access our higher mind ability to better assess which understandings are the best fits for us.

Chapter Seven

What Makes Us Happy

So far, there has been a mix of bad news and good news about how to be happier.

The bad news is that most of the things American's think make them happy do not make them happy. We work incredibly long and hard to achieve things like more money, the material stuff money buys, and the self-defined good life. This news is so negative as to be devastating and depressing for some people. At some point, usually after decades of striving, we may discover, if we are self-aware, that we are not very happy or as happy as we thought we would be. If we have been "successful" earning more money, buying material stuff, and garnering items from our good life list, we may discover that we are actually less happy than we were in the "good old days" when life was simpler and we had fewer worries. We then may share the feelings of others making this discovery, feelings of disillusionment and maybe despair and depression. After all the hard work, there can also be a gasp of "Is this all there is?" We thought all the hard work and the monetary results would make us much happier than we feel now.

When news gets this bad, we tend to deny the validity of the conclusions. Many readers will not agree that money, more money, a better job, a second home, a faster car, or living in a warm climate are not associated with producing greater happiness. If so, most of their memories of being happy come from when they received a raise or bought a new car. There are the few moments and hours around the event when we felt happier. Self-examination reveals that after a brief upward happiness spike, we returned to our pre-event baseline of happiness.

This news is very hard for most of us to take. And no one book written by a guy with a crazy last name with two double vowels is going to single handedly overcome years of cultural, parental, and educational conditioning. But it may cause you to pause and become more self-aware of your experiences. You will form your own conclusions that are right for your life. Most of you will draw the same conclusions that Western scientists have that most of the items commonly on good life lists do not lead to permanent happiness increases when you achieve them.

In the past, this news may have been a dead end because there was not a good answer to this very tough question, "If those things do not make me happy, what will make me happier?" The good news is that we have an answer to this important question and behind the answer is over two thousand years of research and real world results. Making this answer even more powerful is that when we are happy we are also successful. Albert Schweitzer, the German-born theologian, philosopher, musicologist, medical missionary, and Nobel laureate said, "Success is not the key to happiness. Happiness is the key to success. If you love what you are doing, you will be successful." Those of us in the West are learning so much more about how to be happy than we did even a few years ago. Increasingly we are learning from Eastern traditions that happiness is an inner condition requiring inner work. Eastern traditions like Buddhism know this because they have studied and practiced becoming happier for 2,500 years. It has received this much focus, because they believe that happiness is the very purpose of life.

In the West, happiness was identified as one of our in an alienable rights on July 4, 1776 when our forefathers proclaimed in the Declaration of Independence, "We hold these truths to be self-evident, that all men are created equal, that they are endowed by their Creator with certain unalienable Rights, that among these are Life, Liberty, and the pursuit of Happiness." Our greatest president, Abraham Lincoln, later reminded us of a core truth about happiness when he said, "Most folks are about as happy as they make up their minds to be."[lxxxv] Unfortunately, this good start with happiness appears to have been lost over the next 150 years. Science took over from wisdom and common sense with the development of the field of psychology. From its inception, psychology primarily focused on curing various forms of mental illnesses. It has not been until the last decade that psychology turned its attention to how mentally healthy people can become happier. The field of positive psychology has made some very positive contributions, especially noting those things that do not make us happier.

We are now at a point that we can integrate all we know from Eastern and Western perspectives about how to achieve ultimate happiness. When we do that, the news is exceptionally good. Buddhist psychology outlines a path to being ultimately happy that is proven and practical. Dr. Martin Seligman, the founder of positive psychology, also indicates that there are no limits on how happy we can be. Ultimate happiness is an achievable goal.

But achieving this goal, especially for those of us in the West, requires major life changes. Today's belief systems lead to actions that primarily produce unhappiness. We need to correct a mass of major myths, which is no easy task, and replace them with beliefs that support the achievement of ultimate happiness. To accomplish this requires making the achievement of being ultimately happy our top life priority. Since happiness represents the very purpose of life, it warrants this top priority status. The achievement of ultimate happiness has far ranging benefits. It leads to greater levels of success in every aspect of our lives--work, family, relationships, and community. In most cases, success is dramatically greater than we experience today. There is no more rewarding activity we can undertake than embarking on a journey to achieve ultimate happiness.

Eastern and Western Views on Ultimate Happiness Achieving ultimate happiness is such an important and challenging goal that we need every quality, proven resource for our journey. Eastern wisdom traditions provide the greatest assistance, primarily because they have been studying the subject of happiness for centuries longer than people in the West have. If we rely only on the Eastern wisdom traditions, we miss some of the beneficial insights from Western science. Western science makes some important secondary contributions that seem especially appropriate in our culture. But there is no single Western source since positive psychology largely excludes emotional intelligence learnings that is the single most helpful source of Western practices. If we rely only on what Western science tells us, we fail to understand the critical and powerful role that meditation plays in the achievement of ultimate happiness. The combination of the two provides the practical practices necessary for a long, challenging journey.

Foundational Practices and Actions

Clearly, the most important challenge we face in achieving ultimate happiness is the mastering of our mind. Eastern wisdom traditions and Western science provide us with a set of primary and secondary practices to achieve this important goal.

The primary practices involve direct efforts to eventually master and discipline the mind so that we can calm completely the storms of thoughts and emotions. The foundational practice is meditation. Meditation is intensive practice designed initially to maintain a singular focus instead of the random cascade of thoughts and emotions that typically occupy our attention. As we will see in a later chapter, through meditation the thoughts and emotions gradually slow down and settle. When this occurs, positive emotions like love and compassion emerge to dominate our awareness.

As critical as meditation is to the achievement of ultimate happiness, we need more primary practices since meditation typically occupies less than an hour each day.

Another critical foundational practice is self-awareness or mindfulness. Through self-awareness, we increasingly become aware of the thoughts and emotions that trigger the actions with unhappy consequences. We are also able to identify the beliefs behind the thoughts and emotions. As self-awareness develops, we increasingly become adept at using what we learn to make new choices with happier consequences. There comes a point in the development of self-awareness when we can pause the rush to judgment and action to select new conclusions and actions. One of the most powerful practices is the application of an antidote to a negative emotion. With antidotes, we transform a negative emotion into a positive one. This not only provides an immediate dose of greater happiness at the moment we use the antidote, but it also helps to gradually weaken strong habits with unhappy consequences and create new ones with happier outcomes.

We broadly recognize the ability of meditation and self-awareness/mindfulness to contribute to greater happiness, in part by overcoming the negative and destructive emotions that contribute so strongly to unhappiness. A third foundational practice that we sometimes overlook is the practice and expression of love and compassion. From both Western and Eastern perspectives, love and compassion are the highest and happiest of positive experiences. Love and compassion are very similar because they both have the objective of making ourselves and others happier. When we feel love, we are happier. Often when we express our love for another person, we contribute to their greater happiness. When we reach out to help someone who is in need and suffering, we are happier. Often when we reach out to relieve the suffering of another person, we contribute to their greater happiness.

We got a glimpse of the power of love to contribute to greater happiness in positive psychology's finding that people in happy marriages have happier lives. The presumption is that happy marriages have higher levels of positive experience, including love.

To understand the universal power of love and compassion we need only to look at the exceptionally high regard the world has for Mother Theresa and Princess Diana. We admire Mother Theresa for her lifetime dedication to compassionate work among the neediest people on the planet. The almost unprecedented outpouring of love for Princess Diana when she died demonstrated the ability of millions to express love. Georges Dreyfuss, Ph.D., associate professor of religion and philosophy at Williams College, notes, "Compassion and loving kindness...exist at least potentially in the mind of every human being."[lxxxvi] From an Eastern perspective, His Holiness the Dalai Lama notes, "I believe that the most fundamental level our nature is compassionate..."[lxxxvii] He goes on to indicate the link between compassion, love, and happiness, "If our most fundamental aspiration is to seek happiness, this says something very profound about our basic nature. As I see it, happiness is intimately connected with love: In desiring happiness, we also seek love. We express our quest for happiness through the language of love. Love not only allows us to access our compassionate nature, it enables others to relate to us at the most human level."[lxxxviii] Reaffirming that love is a part of our human essence, Jesus told us that "God is love."

While we may feel that there is a shortage of love and compassion both in our life and in the lives of others, this does not deny its importance and power as a part of our essential nature. Some look at this shortage is an indication that compassion and love are fragile. The Dalai Lama has a different point of view, "I do not fully agree that compassion and caring are so fragile. Perhaps we just pay less attention to compassion and caring; we reinforce it less."[lxxxix]

Love and compassion appear to go through stages of development. For example, love starts with a love of family, especially parents. In our first few years of life, we develop a sense of self and our experience of love can become more selfish. At some point, the circle of our ability to love expands to include romantic relationships and friends. At a later stage of development, we may experience love of humanity and all sentient beings. Compassion appears to go through similar stages of development. Most people in our culture do not frequently act compassionately towards others. Our culture is strongly influenced by beliefs in individualism and self reliance which diminish our interest in helping others.

As we will see later, the evolutionary trend in beliefs is leading to greater interest in helping others. Since the evolution of beliefs is slow, the change can best be seen by looking back about one hundred years ago when organizations like UNICEF, Greenpeace, ACLU, and special disaster relief efforts either did not exist or were much less effective and prominent than they are today. We can prove the power of love and compassion to contribute to our greater happiness by reflecting on our own life experiences. Most people report their intense experiences of being in love, especially in their younger years, to be some of their happiest experiences. While there is much more written in Western culture about love (books and songs especially) than compassion, reflecting on times that we have reached out to help someone also typically bring back happy memories. People living in a Western culture tend to be less understanding of and experienced with compassion, but this does not diminish its ability to contribute to lasting increases in happiness. With more experience and skill, we learn more about its ability to contribute to lasting happiness increases.

Interestingly, the power of love extends well beyond the power to contribute to greater happiness. Western science is discovering the ability of love to contribute to greater health and even our survival. Dean Ornish, M.D., in his landmark book *Love & Survival*, notes "Our survival depends on the healing power of love, intimacy, and relationships. Physically. Emotionally. Spiritually. As individuals. As communities. As a country. As a culture. Perhaps even as a species."[xc] Dr. Ornish goes on to say, "The increasing scientific evidence from my own research and from the studies of others that cause me to believe that love and intimacy are among the most powerful factors in health and illness, even though these ideas are largely ignored by the medical profession."[xci]

Meditation, self-awareness, love and compassion create greater happiness immediately and long-term. As such, they are the primary practices for achieving ultimate happiness. Eventually, these are practices we will use every day and every moment.

Secondary Practices

Supplementing these efforts is a number of very helpful secondary practices that amplify happy experiences and weaken unhappy ones. While they are secondary to meditation, love and compassion, and self-awareness, they are indispensable for any program designed to achieve ultimate happiness.

1. Releasing Negative Thoughts and Emotions: Whenever we experience a negative thought and emotion, there are three proven methods for releasing them so that we can feel immediate relief from them. First, we can apply an antidote specific to the negative thought and emotion. There are also some more universal antidotes. When we become skilled with using antidotes, they have the ability to quickly neutralize a negative emotion and thought and replace it with a positive one. Second, we can use the Sedona Method to release even the toughest of negative thoughts and emotions. Third, for many people, visualizing the release of negative thoughts and emotions is their preferred method.

2. Forgiveness and Gratitude: Through forgiveness of others and ourselves, we weaken unhappy experiences. On the other hand, gratitude amplifies the influence and memory of happy experiences. As a

part of an extensive ultimate happiness practice, they make important day-to-day contributions.

3. Passionate, Meaningful Activities: When we have the opportunity to work on something with great personal meaning life tends to be happier, especially because helping others tends to have more meaning than actions that are only self-serving. When that same work enables us to utilize what positive psychology calls "signature strengths," we significantly increase the likelihood that we will be happier than if we are working on a job to earn money or a career to gain greater power and perks.

4. Spiritual and Religious Practice: Spiritual and religious practice can loosen the grip of an egotistical, self-serving life focus. We shift from this focus to developing our relationship with the Supreme Being and serving others. Spiritual and religious practice does not necessarily need to occur as part of a formal religion. While this is not a requirement, having the assistance of a God realized teacher is essential to optimizing the powerful contributions that spiritual and religious practice can make.

5. Becoming More Positive and Optimistic: When negative events occur, they can derail progress and even reverse progress towards our goal of ultimate happiness. In some instances, these events stall progress for extended periods. To avoid and minimize the impact from negative events we need the coping skills that optimists possess. They know how to challenge overreactions to negative events, learn about alternative responses, and get back on track.

6. Emotional Intelligence: Since negative thoughts and emotions are most often associated with triggering actions with unhappy consequences, effectively managing them becomes a high priority. While the Eastern wisdom traditions (like Buddhism and Yogananda's teachings), provide us with the practice of using positive emotions as antidotes to negative ones, we can use the tools of Western science to supplement this practice. The field of emotional intelligence, pioneered by Daniel Goleman, provides both personal and social practices that contribute to the effective management and eventual elimination of negative emotions.

7. Personal Growth Objectives and Plans: Reaching
   ultimate happiness or even becoming happier than you
   are now does not happen without continuous focused
   effort. You need specific long term and daily
   objectives with plans that fit the objective and its
   difficulty. Importantly, we can track progress towards
   ultimate happiness with validated assessments.

Taking Control

Knowing how to be happy has not been the focus of most
Western psychologists, thinkers and researchers. The
primary Western focus is on political and power interests
(usually the domination of other countries), science (how
things work and how to create new possibilities), and
economics (wealth accumulation).

The primary focus of Eastern wisdom traditions has been
on happiness because they understand that happiness is
the purpose of life. For thousands of years they have
studied, taught, and practiced how to be happier. They
have benefited from enlightened teachers who have
provided extensive practical guidance. While the
teachings of Buddha and Yogananda are the focus of this

book, virtually every enlightened teacher has focused their message on how to be happier.

Their key message is one of great hope. Happiness is within our personal control, not the external world of other people, events, and things. If we take personal actions, actions well known by the wisdom traditions, then we can become happier, almost regardless of what happens in our external world. We can achieve permanent increases in happiness even if other people do not become nicer to us or we fail to get the anticipated raise. Simply, if we want to be happier it is up to us. How happy we can be is within our control, ultimately totally within our control. This is a message of great hope in a turbulent and often fear filled world. The validity of this understanding is rooted in thousands of years of wisdom teachings taught by the most enlightened people on earth. Despite this validation, the only validation that ultimately counts for us is personal validation of the understanding that we can be happier by improving our internal world.

This is a revolutionary paradigm shift for most Americans who have counted on the material world to make them happier. We have also relied on other people to change offending behavior for more personal happiness ("If he/she would stop annoying me, I would be happier."). *The news that we can be happier solely based on personal actions is stunning and intimidating to some.* Life seemed easier when we could blame others for our unhappiness and ask them to change so that we could be happier. Recognizing that increased happiness is 100% personal responsibility is a heavy burden for many people.

Yet, for others it is freeing and inspiring. It is especially uplifting to people who have been pursuing greater happiness for decades by trying to acquire the elements of their personally defined good life. They have experienced the disappointment and maybe disillusionment of not finding happiness on this path despite hard work and sacrifices. For some of the people, the news that happiness is within our personal control is like the dawning of a new day, one filled with hope and promise. I hope you can be among these folks.

Tribute to a Tamed, Calm Mind

With a tamed, calm mind we:

- Experience love, not anger or hate

- Live securely without fear

- Are highly self-aware and alert

- See broadly, not narrowly

- Seek the highest good for all

- Perceive an abundance of beauty in our life

- Discover the essence of who we really are

- Honor the greatness of others no matter how troubled

- Know that compassion and love are the defining life energies

- Love all that is

- Smile in the face of trials and tribulations

- Laugh at fear

- Awaken an all knowing intuition

- Witness the Spirit defining all life

- Notice life is about abundance

- Understand the integration of all forms of life and existence

- Comprehend the wisdom guiding all of life

- Appreciate the appropriateness of humility

- Get the purpose of life

- Live ultimate happiness

Chapter Eight

Ignorance

The Barrier to Greater Happiness

Tell someone they are ignorant and you receive an angry response, possibly including "Those are fighting words." Despite that reaction, Yogananda makes it very clear that there is a strong connection between happiness and ignorance, "Infinite happiness and peace are always at hand, just behind the screen of man's ignorance."[xcii] We do not like to think of ourselves as ignorant, because it suggests we lack education or knowledge and that we are unaware of something. Not only do we not like to think of ourselves as ignorant, we like to think we are pretty smart and knowledgeable. Pride and arrogance serve as defenses to charges of ignorance. Pride and arrogance are the faces of a defensive ego attempting to protect its integrity and image.

But this same pride and arrogance are our worst enemies when it comes to becoming happier than we are today. They lead us to believe that we know far more than we do and, as a result, we resist learning. There are two forms of ignorance—known and unknown. Sometimes we know there is information we do not know and we choose to not learn it. We judge that it is not necessary. We decide that it is not worth knowing despite not knowing what we do not know. Then there are unknown areas of ignorance or blind spots. This area of ignorance is vast compared to the first, although most of us have little idea how vast it is.

In this chapter, I make the case that we are largely ignorant about how to achieve happiness. The evidence presented in chapter three makes a compelling case. We deeply believe that money, more money, a powerful job, warm weather, and more contribute to greater happiness. They make no lasting contribution to greater happiness. When people identify the elements of the "good life," they identify mostly elements that will not make them happier if and when they are achieved. I suggest that this adds up to massive ignorance about how to become consistently happier and to realize ultimate happiness.

Before going further, it is important to understand a key characteristic of ignorance. Ignorance is a relative state, not an absolute. Ignorance exists when we do not know vast amounts of what there is to know in general or on a specific topic.

Part of our ignorance traces to a lack of awareness of how much there is to know. Even in our area of work or career expertise, we do not know a vast amount of knowledge and, if we did know it, we would be far more capable and productive than we are now. To test this assertion, go to a book web site like Amazon and search for books in your area of expertise. For example, the last time I searched how many books had the word "marketing" in the title, I found 12,887 books and there may be an equal number of books on marketing that do not have the word "marketing" in the title. In addition, there are thousands of articles and webs sites providing information on marketing. Net, there is a vast amount of knowledge in our areas of expertise that we are ignorant about.

Ignorance is relative—a comparison between how much we know and do not know. The good news about ignorance is that it does not have to be a permanent condition. There is a remedy—learning.

Happiness Ignorance

If we determine what any one of us knows (do a complete inventory) and then compare what we know to all that there is to know, we discover that we may know as much as 1% of all there is to know. Not knowing 99% of what there is to know qualifies as ignorance. While we might intellectually acknowledge this conclusion, our rebuttal is that we know the vast majority of what is critical to know and what we do not know is not critical in our life. As right as this may feel and sound when we say it, we clearly do not know what makes us happy and how to become happier. Research says very clearly that being happy is "critical" in our life.

The previous chapters provided an overview of what Western science and Eastern wisdom traditions know makes us happy. For most readers this is new information and, as such, is personally untested. As a result, most readers still do not know that taming the mind is a key to being happier than we are today. Only actual experience will confirm this intriguing thought. This is as it should be. Until we have personal experience that a calm, peaceful mind is how to become consistently happier, we will rely on our old beliefs. Unfortunately, old beliefs about what contributes to greater happiness will not die easily or quickly. Ignorance can be very stubborn. Ignorance also extends well beyond a mistaken belief about what makes us happy. There are other major beliefs and understanding gaps that stand in the way of greater happiness. The balance of this chapter addresses the most important erroneous belief and understanding gaps.

Responsibility Ignorance

The prevailing belief in our culture is that happiness comes from our external world. We see that on the "good life" list where things like money, homes, and prestige predominate the list.

The belief about happiness coming from our external world also extends to people and events. We look to other people to make us happy. We even make promises to other people to make them happy. There is a prevailing belief that the actions of others have a very strong influence on our personal happiness.

This is probably clearest when there is conflict between people. We often believe that we would be happier if another person would stop/start doing something, like nagging me about when I will get a job. We believe in blaming other people for our unhappiness and look to them to change their behavior so we can be happy. It is not unusual to say, "You make me unhappy" to someone that we believe is annoying us. We even choose to stay stuck in our unhappy condition if the other person does not change.

The belief that someone else has so much power that they can "make me unhappy" is a broad based belief in our culture.

There are three major mistakes with this belief. First, when we do this, we put considerable power over our personal happiness into the hands of other people. Those other people include strangers, marriage partners, and friends. The other person has the power to change their behavior as requested to make us happier or to not change and we remain unhappy.

As long as we believe in giving power to other people over our happiness, we will be unhappy far more than we want or need to be. When we do this, we are victims. As such, it matters little what we do about our personal happiness. We have consciously given other people tremendous power over us—the power to make us happy or unhappy. We often give this power to people we do not like, trust, or know. Happiness is one of our most precious states and goals, yet we freely give away power over how happy we will be. Whew!

The second related mistake is that when we blame others for our unhappiness, we want them to change their behavior so we can be happy. Doing this requires infinite patience because most people will not change their behavior so we can be happier. They will not change for two reasons. First, very, very few people have any interest in changing their behavior for our benefit. If we find someone annoying, instead of changing their behavior, they are likely to say something like, "Tough. Get over it" or "You annoy me. I will change when you do." Second, in the very few instances when someone is willing to change their behavior, they come face-to-face with the difficulty of changing what are usually deeply ingrained behaviors. As we will discuss later, most people are ignorant about how to achieve personal change and growth. Thus, even positive intentions are not likely to produce the desired change.

The third mistake is a scientific one. When we understand the brain science about how we make decisions, we quickly learn that we always personally make a choice in response to a stimulus. Our beliefs determine our choice of response. People experiencing the same stimulus choose different thoughts and responses because they have different beliefs. We can blame others for making us unhappy, but the truth is we choose to let them make us unhappy. We can also choose not to let other people make us unhappy and take rightful responsibility for our choices.

So instead of saying, "You make me mad" it is more accurate to say, "I choose to let you make me mad." This is a huge shift although the words appear to be very similar. Once we shift from a belief that others have somehow forced us to be mad to a belief that we have a choice to be mad or any other response, we open the opportunity for much more happiness.

We help ourselves when we believe that the true control exists not with another person but with us. We choose reactions to stimuli based on our beliefs. Our brain processes a stimulus, by filtering the stimulus through our prior experiences with similar stimuli and the beliefs we have formed about them. This typically happens as a habitual response where the choices are made so fast that we have little awareness of the making a choice.

We are responsible for every choice we make in response to a stimulus. Understanding this, we can still choose to blame other people for our unhappiness and give them the power to make us happy or unhappy. When we do this, we choose to give them precious power.

Alternatively, we can consciously take responsibility and make personal choices designed to make us happier. When we do this, we reclaim the power to become happier. And as we will see, it takes 100% of our power to achieve ultimate happiness.

Ignorance about personal responsibility for our own happiness is at very high levels. It exists to varying degrees with some people constantly blaming their external world for their unhappiness to some people who blame others for "making" them feel unhappy most of the time and taking responsibility some of the time (even this often involves shared responsibility that includes some blame).

It is much easier to blame someone else than take personal responsibility. When we blame, we usually demand that the other person change. We do not have to do any of the hard work to change. When they do not change, then we have an excuse for our unhappiness. Even when we open to the possibility that we make choices all the time, we do not feel it is helpful. When we examine our choices, we often conclude the choice we made was the right one. We see no other viable choice. For example, a student related that his boss made them mad with their micromanaging style. When I asked if that was his choice of response, he reluctantly acknowledged it was his choice. He quickly added that their only other choice was to "kiss up" to the boss, something he was strongly opposed to doing. When asked if this was his "only" alternative, he said it was.

Thus, even when we open to the idea of personal responsibility and choice, we often have a hard time seeing new alternatives that we believe are viable options. That is because beliefs that led us to our initial choice are so strong and clear that it makes it very difficult to see alternatives. If we change beliefs and remove our ignorance of other solutions, we see entirely new alternatives that remove us from our self-created trap. For example, the student had other alternatives and I will mention just two of them.

One typically helpful and effective alternative involves discussing feelings with the boss and seeking to agree on a new working relationship that empowers the employee more. This type of discussion leads the employee new insights about the boss, especially their feelings, pressures, and beliefs. These insights often create greater empathy and understanding that enable the student to revise his opinion of the boss's intentions from micromanaging to feeling pressure to perform from their boss. It can lead to new choices where we try to help them, for example. Another alternative requires no conversation with the boss. He could release the emotions. He could recognize the emotional turmoil he choose in response to their perceived micromanaging, let the emotions go (for example, visualize breathing out the emotions) and shift attention from these feelings to a pleasant topic, like the fun you have working as part of a business team.

Clearly both of these alternatives do not sound right or feasible to someone who believes that their boss is upsetting them with their micromanagement. While this is understandable, not every micromanaging boss upsets the people that work for him or her. Different people possess different beliefs that lead to different choices, often choices that make them either less unhappy or even happy.

Ignorance About Who We Really Are

Most of us have very low self-awareness of who we really are. While there are many dimensions to "who we really are," my focus is on knowing our values and beliefs that drive the actions we take and the consequences we experience from them.

We create our beliefs through life experiences. We form most of our beliefs about life by our mid-20s. Influential people like parents, friends, and clergy play a key role in shaping our beliefs. Many times we adopt the beliefs that these influential people have and sometimes we modify them if there is a mix of influences. As we become older and experience life, we may modify them further.

Most of the time, we are not aware of creating beliefs. As we create beliefs, we often do not see that we have a choice, and if there are choices, they are between doing what is right and wrong. We seldom face multiple "right" choice alternatives. It is not surprising that we are largely unaware of the beliefs that guide almost every action we take in life.

As a result, most of us go through life on automatic pilot. Whenever we face a situation, we make the same or about the same choice, we made in a similar situation before. We rely on our habits. Habitual choices guided by well established, unquestioned beliefs determine almost every action we take in life. These actions range from the simple ones (the foods we like and think are good) to the more complex (what to do to help a loved one with a drug problem). We rarely encounter a situation where our beliefs do not quickly determine our choice of action. In these rare situations, either we do our best to adapt existing beliefs to a new situation or we seek assistance from people we trust.

At the heart of this entire process are the beliefs that determine our actions and subsequent consequences. The vast majority of us are ignorant of these beliefs. Even when questioned, we often have difficulty articulating them. When we become aware of them to some degree, we are typically very accepting of them. For us they are right, almost without question. They are so right that we often believe that any thoughtful person should have the same beliefs. We believe so strongly in them that this blinds us from seeing our ignorance of alternatives. These beliefs determine how happy we are today. It is unlikely that we will be happier in the future if our beliefs stay the same. Beliefs are that fundamental to our happiness. Despite the critical role beliefs play in determining how happy we are and can be, we spend very little time (if any) reviewing, examining, and revising them. On the road to becoming happier, we need to tame the mind. Doing that inevitably requires calming the turmoil caused by our beliefs. Since our beliefs create our thoughts and emotions, if we have different beliefs, there is the possibility for less turmoil. Turmoil usually equates to some degree of unhappiness caused by struggle, confusion, and negative thoughts. A calm mind equates to greater happiness.

This lack of self-awareness of our beliefs is a major blind spot for almost all of us. The good news is that there are paths we can follow to increase self-awareness of our beliefs. Later chapters address some of these paths.

Concluding Thoughts

This chapter focuses on ignorance as our biggest barrier to greater happiness. For some, ignorance is a very strong word and one they do not want to be associated with. That is understandable from an ego perspective, but it does not diminish the fact that we do not know a vast amount about critical elements necessary to be happier. This chapter has purposefully only touched on a small part of what we do not know. Even that small part is an imposing barrier to becoming happier. There is a vast amount of potential understanding about who we really are and how we can achieve ultimate happiness. We tend to encounter this in later stages of development (very briefly developed in a later chapter) as our inner knowing develops.

There is great hope for highly positive experiences. Today, on average humanity experiences only a small percentage of potential happiness. We have the potential to experience much greater and more consistent happiness in our life. The first formidable barrier is ignorance, which we have in abundance.

This book is committed to helping you begin to lift the veil of ignorance and see the proven paths forward to higher and more consistent happiness. The paths are well known and proven with thousands of years of successful practice. As a start, we need to see them, learn about them, and then start walking down our path.

Chapter Nine

Meditation: The Foundation for Achieving Ultimate Happiness

We want to be happier and we spend billions trying to be happier. When we buy material stuff like new homes and cars, audio and video equipment, and recreational gear, we hope the purchases will make us happier. We also spend hundreds of millions on books, seminars, and professional help with the hope that personal growth will make us happier. As we saw earlier, many of these efforts produce temporary (ranging from a few minutes to several days) happiness increases but do little to make us permanently happier.

The approach to ultimate happiness varies depending on whether we think happiness comes primarily from our inner or outer world. Put another way, our approach depends on whether we think the antidote to our unhappiness comes from personal inner work or from our external world. When we believe greater happiness is self-directed, we tap into a variety of individualistic resources, often in a self-defined personal growth program. It might be Dr. Norman Vincent Peale's power of positive thinking or Yogananda's lessons designed to assist in self-realization. The key to this orientation is that we rely on ourselves to be the agent of change.

When we believe greater happiness results when the outside world changes, then our focus is on changing elements like laws, institutions, and people. It can also mean that we need outside help, like a therapist to guide us through a change process to become happier. We view the therapist as the change agent, the person who will lead us to a happier place. This path can also lead to thinking that drugs can make us happier, either prescription or illegal.

Reliance on professional help to become happier is a risky venture. The costs can be significant and professionals do not guarantee results. Certain therapeutic options focus on discovering the "why" behind actions in the hope that the answer to that question will reveal a new direction supported by a "why" that leads to happier consequences.

Unfortunately, the professional search for "why" answers is often elusive, as noted by Dr. Martin Seligman, "One of the two clearest findings of one hundred years of therapy is that satisfactory answers to the great 'why' questions are not easily found..."[xciii]

When we review the effectiveness of western approaches (mainly drugs and various forms of professional therapy), we discover that their ability to help most forms of dysfunctional behavior is modest and on some issues, it is largely ineffective. For example, ratings of western science's ability to change conditions like depression, anger, and every day anxiety are only "mild/moderate" to "moderate."[xciv]

When it comes to deeper issues like spiritual challenges and "issues of the soul" western resources are not effective. Dr. Seligman notes, "...issues of the soul can barely be changed by psychotherapy or by drugs."[xcv]

This is a critical acknowledgement because we are gradually discovering the truth of the saying that "we are spiritual beings having a human experience." Western science has little understanding of the spiritual dimensions of life. Some Western scientists and philosophers do see the spiritual dimensions of life, and they generally are people pioneering new directions. The emerging fields of transpersonal and integral psychology offer hope that greater help is coming. Ken Wilber is the leading western philosopher whose major contributions include integrating western and eastern thinking into a cohesive map. Among scientists, Albert Einstein, the founder of quantum theory, saw the spiritual and mystical in ways that few western scientists could.

> The most beautiful and most profound emotion we can experience is the sensation of the mystical. It is the sower of all true science. He to who this emotion is a stranger, who can no longer wonder and stand rapt in awe, is as good as dead. To know that what is impenetrable to us really exists, manifesting itself as the highest wisdom and the most radiant beauty which our dull facilities can comprehend only in their most primitive forms— this knowledge, this feeling, is at the center of true religiousness.[xcvi]

When it comes to understanding how to become happier, Eastern wisdom traditions, with their more than 2,000 years of practical experience, know the actions that enable us to be happier. From my review and experience, they know far more effective actions than western science knows.

The Eastern inspired path to greater happiness is a major cost savings project when compared to the path that most people walk today. Whatever we spend today (expenses ranging from hundreds of thousands for a new house to just hundreds for jewelry, for example) to become happier becomes almost zero when we follow the most effective path to greater happiness.

It costs nothing to become happier. (One of the popular happiness books is *Happiness is Free.*) The path to greater happiness is exquisitely simple, although often excruciatingly difficult.

Maybe the lowest cost happiness practice is meditation. While it is not a magic wand, regular meditation done with increasing skill and consistency virtually guarantees a higher level of happiness within months. Over the course of years, meditation produces major personal growth in multiple life areas. We achieve levels of happiness and wisdom previously thought impossible.

Meditation involves our inner world. Simply, we gradually calm the mind by settling distracting emotions and thoughts. Through greater awareness of our thoughts and emotions, we make increasingly deliberate choices intended to produce happier consequences for others and us. As the mind becomes even calmer, we tap into an inner knowing that becomes a wise guide to choices producing greater happiness. Happiness increases steadily and slowly for as long as we follow the path.

While there are some external actions we can take, they are generally not critical and play a secondary role. While some of these can cost money, the expenditures are relatively small--books, tapes, and an occasional seminar. Even these expenditures may not be necessary. Looking for happiness from primarily outside sources will not enable us to achieve ultimate happiness.

Meditation—The Foundational Practice

Meditation is a powerful positive life action affecting everything from our health to our effectiveness at work. An earlier chapter addressed the highlights of meditation's known medical benefits.

There is considerable evidence that mediation can greatly accelerate our quest to become happier when we mediate consistently and deeply according to accepted methods and traditions. From a wisdom tradition perspective, becoming happier almost requires a regular meditation practice. Yogananda states, "Unwillingness to meditate should be recognized as among the foremost enemies of man's physical, mental, and spiritual well being…"[xcvii]

The Source of Meditation's Power

When people hear about meditation's near miraculous power, they wonder how and why it is so powerful. People's skepticism grows when they understand meditation's great simplicity—sitting quietly and purposefully taming the mind. They wonder, "How could something so simple, be so powerful?"

For our purposes, I will discuss three dimensions of meditation that contribute to its power.

First, when we sit quietly with our eyes closed, we tend to slow down. Our outside world immediately slows down because there is no overt activity like telephone calls, meetings, and reading to distract us. As we quickly discover when we begin meditating, the mind does not require overt activity to be very busy. But reducing these overt distractions does contribute to a gradual slowing down which is a step in the right direction; the direction of taming the mind to achieve a calm mind.

As we saw in earlier chapters, the best Western and Eastern sources of knowledge and wisdom all point to taming the mind as key to greater happiness. Meditation is the best method for doing this and other methods like being in nature and contemplation are helpful but dramatically less effective at taming the mind.

If you do not currently meditate then you probably question if calming the mind can really make you happier. You should not believe me or anyone else on this important point. Learning for yourself is the only validation you should accept. Fortunately, this learning is very inexpensive and requires as little as twenty minutes per day or a little more than 1% of your day.

The second dimension of meditation is its ability to connect us with our inner knowing. Inner knowing emerges as the mind becomes calm. It is though a calm mind that we can hear the soft voice of our intuition, which is our higher mind. As we saw earlier, the great wisdom traditions describe intuition as a more powerful ability than our logical mind. It is the ability to know anything without processing any sensory or knowledge inputs. This ability very slowly emerges through a quieted mind and typically does not fully blossom until higher stages of development. Nonetheless, even small glimpses of this ability are very powerful because they lead to actions with happier consequences.

Third, we develop the ability to witness ourselves as the thinker. Through meditation, we observe a constant stream of thoughts. This is witnessing. When we begin to witness our thoughts, we think that we and our thoughts are part of who we are. The more we witness, the more we realize that there is a mind generating our thoughts over which we appear to have little control. Gradually we observe our mind's seeming never-ending stream of thoughts and realize that the observed and the observer are separate. Just as when we observe a flower we know that the observed and the observer are separate.

If you have not experienced this witnessing element, what I have just said makes little sense. To provide you with some encouragement and additional understanding of witnessing's power, I share with you Eckhart Tolle's helpful insights from his popular book, *The Power of Now*:

> The moment you start *watching the thinker*, a higher level of consciousness becomes activated. You then begin to realize that there is a vast realm of intelligence beyond thought, that thought is only a tiny aspect of that intelligence. You also realize that all the things that truly matter—beauty, love, creativity, joy, inner peace—arise from beyond the mind. You begin to awaken.[xcviii]

Calming the mind contributes to greater happiness. Connecting with more of our inner knowing through a calm mind also contributes to greater happiness. Individually each aspect of mediation is a major contributor to greater happiness and collectively they are powerful enough to fuel a life long unfolding of greater happiness. While these contributions may be theoretical to you today, over the last two decades, western science confirms their power and over the past two thousand years, eastern wisdom traditions are unanimous in confirming their power.

Mediation 101

Mediation is very simple. Sit straight and comfortably with your eyes closed. Focus on something—a bodily sensation, word, or body part—for 10-20 minutes when you first start. Having done this, gradually calm down, returning you attention to your focal point whenever you notice your attention has wandered. It is that simple. There is no need to read books or attend long seminars on how to meditate.

I will provide modest additional suggestions, but they only build on the description I have provided.

Most traditions suggest mediating with the eyes closed although some suggest leaving the eyes half or completely open. Beginners and even many advanced meditators find mediating with eyes closed presents fewer distractions and temptations. When we first meditate, the body may interpret closed eyes as a signal to sleep. Meditation requires us to be very alert and aware and when we focus our attention as outlined below, we reduce the inclination to sleep.

Most meditating traditions, like Buddhist and transcendental meditation, suggest a point of focus. There are three main suggestions about what to focus our attention on. First, we can focus on our breath. We can feel ourselves breathing in, breathing out. The attention can be on the lungs or feeling the air go into and out of the nose.

Second, we can focus on a word or two, often called a mantra. Transcendental meditation provides each person with a customized mantra. Other traditions have their own mantras, like Yogananda through his meditation lessons. But it can also be as simple as choosing a word that is sacred to you, like peace, love, or God.

Third, the focal point can be the spot between the eyebrows, often referred to as the sixth chakra or spiritual eye. We do this by closing our eyes and then rolling our eyes up and to the center as if we were looking at the point between the eyebrows. While doing this may require some practice, this form of meditation can be very powerful.

In choosing which focal point is best for you experiment and start with the one that feels most comfortable and natural for you. You can always try the other methods later.

Meditation is best when the spine is comfortably straight. Meditation involves subtle energies, which flow best when the spine is straight. Teachers often recommend a chair with a straight back. Other body parts can assume a comfortable position. Putting the legs into the lotus cross-legged position is not required and neither is any particular arm position.

How long you meditate is a matter of personal choice. Some people start with only 5-10 minutes, but many people find 20 minutes to be a comfortable time shortly after they begin meditating. If you have a daily practice of 20 minutes, consider meditating 45-60 minutes once a week. Also, consider gradually lengthening the period of mediation until you reach an hour per day. You can lengthen the time over months or years. How long we meditate is far less important than how deeply we meditate. Initially, we measure depth of meditation by how long we concentrate on our focal point, breath or mantra, for example.

When we focus on our point of attention (breath, mantra, spiritual eye), we eventually discover that our mind wanders to a thought. A thought lingers while either we reflect on it or until a new thought replaces it. Our purpose in meditation is to let go of the thought and return to our focal point. When we do this, we gradually observe the mind becoming calmer. Throughout the time we meditate, we concentrate, the mind wanders, and we bring our focus back. The cycle repeats as we try to increase the time spent concentrating. It is through concentrating on our focal point that we gradually experience the mind calming. Concentration is how we discipline the mind to focus and calm down. The torrents of seemingly random thoughts and emotions that storm into our attention gradually become a mere trickle of thoughts. As the mind becomes calmer, we notice gaps between our thoughts and our purpose is to expand these quiet gaps until the gaps replace all thoughts.

The traditions suggest meditating at the same time every day and in the same location. The best times according to some traditions are early in the morning and before going to bed. Yogananda says, "When you awaken in the morning, meditate. If you don't, the whole world will crowd in to claim you...At night, meditate before sleep claims you..."[xcix]

This is the "mechanical" part of meditation. The purpose of these mechanics is to facilitate the calming of the mind. Our goal is to calm the mind by letting it settle. Sogyal

Rinpoche's analogy of a muddy glass of water gradually settling is a good one. When we do not disturb the glass, the mud settles to the bottom while clear water emerges in the top part of the glass. From this clarity emerges a deep, abiding calm that nourishes greater happiness a day at a time.

Concluding Thoughts

When I first started meditating, I approached the subject as I would most any other subject that was potentially important. I began by reading several books on how to meditate. As a novice, each book seemed to present a unique approach. Fairly soon, I recognized that they were just different ways of focusing my attention. I experimented with different focusing methods and today I use a mantra taught by Yogananda and focus on the spiritual eye. This is a personal choice while others find focusing on the breath or different mantras to be their most effective method. Again, they all have the same purpose of disciplining the mind to calm the mind.

Prior to meditating, I was a person who prized activity and seldom rested or relaxed. Initially, meditating was very difficult for me. I felt like I was not doing anything, which

made me question the value of the time I spent
meditating. In addition to this challenge, I quickly
discovered how difficult it is to maintain attention on my
mantra or spiritual eye. Thoughts and emotions flowed
chaotically in a constant stream that was highly resistant
to my efforts to tame them.

Yogananda's wise advice helped me deepen my
meditation. My mind gradually became calmer and calmer.
While this experience is beyond words, elements of the
experience include great peace, clarity of understanding,
and connection with an exhilarating and very real quality
of happiness. I had the sense that I was connecting with
part of my core essence.

Today, I meditate in the morning and later in the day.
One day each week, I host others for a one-hour
meditation with the purpose of benefiting those in need.
Meditating is my single most important activity each day.
It has unquestionably brought about highly positive
changes in my life. I am much happier. I express and
receive love far better than my pre-meditating days. I
have a deep desire to serve and help others that did not

exist previously. I trust my inner knowing more than my logical knowing, which is a dramatic shift for me. Meditation continues to be the most challenging practice I have ever undertaken. Thoughts and emotions continue to clamor for center stage in my awareness. I have periods where my focus is better than at other times. I am constantly reminded of the concentration required to discipline the mind in order to calm the mind.

We can never *know* meditation's value by listening to the descriptions provided by other people. We will never know meditation's value from external sources. We can only understand its value through personal practice.

Chapter Ten

Self-Awareness of Beliefs

Happiness is dependent on internal conditions, especially achieving a calm mind by taming the internal chaotic chatter. Meditation is often how we begin to be more self-aware. Through meditation, we experience the process of observing thoughts and emotions. Self-awareness is the next important step towards greater happiness.

It is only through self-awareness that we learn how much we need to tame and how we are progressing towards a calm state of mind. Self-awareness also starts the shift from a life focused almost exclusively on the outer world to an ever-increasing focus on our inner world. How happy we are is a reflection of inner world conditions. While meditation is a helpful introduction, we need to be self-aware beyond meditation because we spend a short time each day in meditation, and we need awareness of our thoughts throughout our day. Being aware of what we think is critical to identifying potential actions, especially actions that may produce unhappy consequences.

Self-awareness helps us make better action choices with happier consequences. We go through three steps when we create thoughts, emotions, conclusions, and subsequent actions.

First, through the five senses we experience an external event as objective awareness. For example, we see a flower or dog. When the sensory inputs first arrive, they are objective inputs—"It is a flower" or "It is a dog." At this stage, the inputs are absent any subjective evaluation. The leap from the first step to the second is often so fast (nanoseconds) that we are not aware of the first step. Ultimately, through self-awareness we can extend the time spent in objective awareness. When we reside in objective awareness, we interrupt the habitual reaction process that often either has unhappy consequences or could have much happier consequences.

In the second step, our brain evaluates the objective inputs. Our brain quickly sorts through our beliefs and experiences related to the inputs to select the most appropriate response. For example, "The flower is beautiful and one of my favorites even though it is from a lowly weed" or "I do not like this breed of menacing dog." We form these beliefs through previous experiences. A lifetime of experiences forms our beliefs, like experiences with parents, teachers, friends, enemies, animals, and plants. For example, previous experience with flowers or this dog breed influenced the subjective conclusions about them.

Despite the powerful role beliefs play in determining how happy we are, we typically do not think about our beliefs unless they are challenged or do not appear to be working. When challenged, we strongly defend our beliefs. In the rare circumstances when we feel they may not be serving us well, we discover that changing them is neither easy nor fast. Part of this difficulty traces to the well-developed neural network in the brain that supports strongly held beliefs. While we can build new networks, it takes repetition over time.

If we are not aware of these thoughts and emotions, they follow a habitual sequence, a sequence similar to living on automatic pilot. By being more aware of the stimulus, the thoughts it triggers, the conclusions reached and the subsequent impulse to act, we shift from automatic pilot to conscious, active decision making. We then have the choice to follow habitual reactions or select new responses. Doing this helps us to choose responses that add more to our happiness and the happiness of others than our quick, habitual reactions.

Stephen Covey refers to this as the "moment of choice." Recognizing that we choose every action we take and using the power of choice to select actions with happier consequences is a powerful insight into a crucial life process. This is a huge shift and it is one that most of us find incredibly difficult to make because of the power of habitual reactions. It is almost as if our habitual reactions have a mind of their own, a mind over which we seem to have little control or influence.

In the third step of self-awareness, we act based on our choice of conclusions. In this step, we have another opportunity to interrupt actions that have unhappy consequences. We observe our actions and conclude they will not have a happy outcome. At this time, we can stop and redirect our actions. This sounds easy and experience tells us just how difficult this is today for most of us. It is most difficult when strong emotions are present, like anger. It is easiest when emotions are less intense, like annoyance. As challenging as it is, only by developing self-awareness can we gradually develop this critical ability to shift actions in progress from unhappy to happy consequences.

Helping us overcome these challenges are three elements. Each element includes very helpful insights that help us achieve the self-awareness that leads to greater happiness. First, self-awareness works best when we focus our entire thought process on the present, with very little, if any focus on the future or past. It is called being present or in the moment. Through meditation, we become aware of how many of our thoughts relate to past or future events. In fact, the ego often finds only the past and future interesting.

While I only briefly address the importance of being present, it is a very important subject that is worth additional exploration. Two very good books approach being present from different perspectives--Eckhart Tolle's

The Power of Now and Spencer Johnson's *The Precious Present*. Tolle says about the present:

> Realize deeply that the present moment is all you ever have. Make the Now the primary focus of your life….pay brief visits to past and future when required to deal with the practical aspects of your life situation. Always say "yes" to the present moment…Surrender to what *is*. Say "yes" to life—and see how life suddenly starts working *for* you rather than against you.[c]

Interestingly, the ability to be present is closely associated with peak performance. Scientists have studied the phenomena of flow or what athletes call "being in the zone." In both situations, studies reveal that people achieve their peak performance, which is often 50-100% greater than their normal performance levels, when they focus only on the present. Probably the leading western scientist studying this is Mihaly Csikszentmihalyi. In his book *Flow, the Psychology of Optimal Experience* he identifies the factors associated with optimal performance. Three of the eight elements of optimal performance are:

1. The merging of action and awareness
2. Concentration on the task at hand
3. The loss of self consciousness[ci]

All three elements are dimensions of being present. These elements may be the core or essential elements of optimal performance since the other elements include clear objectives, feedback systems, challenging activity, and losing a sense of time. While important, they do not reflect the critical inner conditions needed for optimal performance.

When we are present (no energy focused on the past or future), we apply 100% of our abilities to the task at hand. Understanding this simple dimension helps explain how performance is enhanced.

Second, while in the present, we work to develop objective awareness. With this awareness, we answer these questions:

- What is happening? Experience the stimulus objectively. Be more observant. Take steps to learn more to avoid premature or incomplete conclusions.

- What am I thinking? Observe your thoughts and feelings in a manner similar to meditation, but in an active state. Pause and connect with the inner flow. Observe. Listen. Be aware.

As I face negative conditions, I check to see if the cause of the conditions is me or not me? If the latter, then I am blaming others. Are the causes isolated to this one event or are they representative of something that always happens to me? If the latter, the solution lies in the coping skills of an optimist, which we will discuss later.

- Why am I thinking this way? Ascertain what beliefs are leading to the thoughts, especially the judging thoughts. In a real time situation, this can be very difficult because the mind's habitual path is to skip this assessment since it already knows the answer and is ready to act. Typically, we become aware of the "why" through later reflection and assessment. We can then bring those insights into the present and observe, "There I go again" as you note a familiar pattern. It is important to note that this is a different "why" than the "why' therapy attempts to discover. Therapy often attempts to identify how and why we established a belief, often deep in our past and buried in a traumatic life event memory. The determination of "why' suggested here is merely to identify the reasons we think a potential action is right.

- How do I want to respond/act? As we become more self-aware and see our habitual patterns, we often search for better responses. Our habitual reactions have predictable outcomes, outcomes that frequently have unhappy consequences. Through self-awareness, we see our processes and increasingly we choose to select responses that we believe have happier consequences.

As we become aware of beliefs that consistently lead us to negative thoughts and emotions, we need to recognize and focus on them. As we focus on them we want to challenge the value and truthfulness of a belief, look at it from different perspectives, and become calmer and more resilient in the face of the challenge they present. Karen Reivich, Ph.D., has done some innovative work on developing emotional resiliency. She suggests some practical methods of diminishing the hold of negative thoughts and emotions.

- When we feel sadness because we have lost something of value or lost love, we can focus on what we have learned from the experience and experience gratitude for the opportunity to have the experience.

- When we feel anxious about impending danger, examine opportunities for controlling the situation and practice courage.

- When we feel anger because we think we have been violated, look for opportunities to have empathy, patience, and express forgiveness.[cii]

Third, there two broad resources and processes that help us develop self-awareness. One of the most helpful is reflection and contemplation used with journal writing. This is another process for examining thoughts and feelings. For example, we can explore an event that produced unhappy consequences and attempt to determine why we acted as we did and how we might act differently next time.

A second set of resources involves both personal and interpersonal assistance. Seeing ourselves objectively is not easy and may require professional help. Professional help, like a therapist, coach, or psychologist, can accelerate our ability to identify core beliefs that drive our action choices and to adopt new behaviors that have happier outcomes. Professional help is not required when close personal relationships can functionally help us see ourselves better and discover new actions that produce happier outcomes. Again, this outer help is usually most helpful when focused on a very specific issue, and only when all personal efforts to solve the issue have failed.

Beliefs: The Ego's Happiness Control Center

Since beliefs shape thoughts, emotions, and actions and each of these significantly influences how happy we are, better understanding beliefs is critical to becoming happier. As we have already seen, making happier choices requires creating new beliefs. Without new beliefs, we make the same choices we always have made. Typically, we resist changing our beliefs because we understand them to be true and helpful. We need to demystify beliefs from their almost sacrosanct status as real and true if we are to become happier. Dr. Martin Seligman, author of *Learned Optimism* and *Authentic Happiness*, provides valuable perspective when he says, "It is essential to realize that your beliefs are just that—beliefs. They may of may not be facts."[ciii]

While some of our current beliefs produce actions with happy outcomes, happier outcomes are always possible with beliefs that reflect the essence of who we really are. These beliefs flow from increasing self-awareness and opening up to our inner wisdom. This inner wisdom emerges as we develop a calm mind.

Since beliefs are so crucial to the choices we make, this section of the book focuses on some of the macro belief systems and stages that influence all of us. The balance of this chapter provides an overview of the stages of belief development known by developmental psychologists, philosophers, and Eastern sages. There is remarkable agreement and alignment between all of these sources. This consensus provides comfort and validity to critical information that can help accelerate our self-awareness and ultimately help create a calm, tamed mind contributing to much higher and consistent levels of happiness.

Overview of Belief Stages of Development

Personal experience may be the most important and credible view of the stages of development, especially belief development that we go through. This experience can come from two perspectives. First, we can recall how our beliefs about right/wrong, good/bad, important/unimportant changed while growing up for our first 20-25 years. Second, as a parent we can watch a child grow from infant to young adult. We know that there is tremendous change in beliefs in this period, but we may have limited awareness as to the stages of belief change that occur.

Western developmental psychologists have studied these stages for over a century and there are many documented studies supporting their conclusions. While there are a wide variety of research perspectives, their conclusions are consistent with each other. Some researchers have more limited view of the stages while others have a broader vision that integrates various systems into a more extensive view of these stages. Some researchers look closely at one aspect of development, cognitive development, for example, while others focus on other aspects, like spiritual development. Some of the leading Western researchers include Abraham Maslow (hierarchy of needs), Carol Gilligan (female hierarchy of moral stages), Lawrence Kohlberg (moral judgment), Jean Piaget (moral stages), William Perry (self outlook), and Clare Graves (ego and belief types).

From an Eastern perspective, the researchers, mystics, and philosophers include people like Patanjali (yoga sutras), Saint Teresa (stages of interior life), Sri Aurobindo (physical to super mind), and the highest yoga tantra.

One of the most well known and accepted view of how beliefs change through a series of stages comes from psychiatrist Erik Erikson. He studied and reported in 1956 on the evolution of beliefs from infancy to young adult and found that it follows a well-accepted path. Others have since refined his stages, but the core thinking remains in tack. His eight stages of development are ones that we become keenly aware of by reflecting on our own early life or by observing children, especially from the perspective of a parent.

Erikson's First 5 Development Stages	Belief Examples: "I believe…"
1. Trust & Hope	I can trust my mother…I cannot trust my brother
2. Will & Autonomy	I can control my father if I scream loudly enough I can have fun when I can go to Jack's house to play
3. Purpose & Initiative	I can play checkers good enough to beat my sister I can earn money by offering to help Dad with the painting
4. Competence & Work	I can get A's by studying every day I can start on my baseball team if I work extra hard
5. Fidelity & Identity	I can help others by following Mother Teresa's example. I can succeed through honesty and working harder than others work.

During the young adult stages (stages six and seven) we develop beliefs about love which determine our ability to be intimate with selected others. In these stages, we develop beliefs about what we care about the most. We may believe in a specific career plus the importance and role of a work in our life. Our beliefs about what we care about extend to how much we care about others that can range from very narrow self-absorption to compassion for a very wide range of people and causes, like the environment.

We also know some important dynamics of this evolutionary process. A review of all of the evolutionary stage development research reveals important common dynamics.

First, when we are born, every person starts in stage one. Researchers have never found someone who skipped stage one.

Second, everyone evolves sequentially through the stages. We do not skip stages.

Third, having reached a particular stage we can regress to a previous stage.

Fourth, stages have significant range. There is early, middle, and late parts of a stage. While there are basic beliefs associated with each stage, there is also a mix of highly personal variations on these beliefs.

Fifth, there is the "geek and geezer" phenomenon, a description used by the great American philosopher Ken Wilber. This concludes that beliefs typically evolve through stages up until about the age of 25. Beliefs then tend to be relatively fixed from then until about age 55 when we can progress through additional stages of development. While there is variability regarding the exact age, we do tend to evolve through stages of beliefs until we become young adults, which makes sense because this is typically an intense learning period. The stage where young adults halt their evolution of beliefs varies. We then use these beliefs to navigate life through careers, marriage, family, and friends. At some point later in life, we may discover that our beliefs have not produced the expected and hoped for results. This can lead to an examination of beliefs and attempts to formulate new ones that hopefully will produce better results.

Sixth, beliefs undergo major change from stage to stage. On some dimensions, the beliefs at one stage can be the opposite of the previous stage. Since the evolution from stage to stage typically takes considerable time (years and sometimes decades), we have the opportunity to gradually adopt new views.

Seventh, just because someone is further along the evolutionary stages, it does not mean they are a better person. The stages are not about being a better or worse person. There are very evil people in relatively advanced stages and very positive, good people living at much earlier stages of development. Each stage has its dysfunctional aspects and in some ways, the potential degree of dysfunction is greater in later stages than it is in earlier stages. As noted earlier, there are many lines of development, including cognitive ability and ethical development. For example, people with advanced cognitive development and low ethical development are capable of great harm and evil.

Eighth, as we evolve from stage to stage we expand to include a new level of beliefs and associated actions. The abilities developed in the previous stage continue with us. It is as if the umbrella gets wider and bigger. Some have called this phenomenon a nested hierarchy.

The person who has done the most to make sense of all the developmental research is Ken Wilber. Ken Wilber's work is the first that fits all these views together to create a coherent picture of how we evolve on many dimensions. He has integrated a vast array of research into a coherent and sensible system that enables us to see the value contributed by different researchers over time. His extraordinary mind has done much to advance our understanding of how we evolve. For anyone interested in learning more, I highly recommend his *Integral Psychology* and *A Brief Theory of Everything*.

Clare Graves, Don Beck and Chris Cowan—Spiral Dynamics

As noted earlier, there are numerous studies detailing the evolutionary stages that we all progress through. With our focus on beliefs, the best system for our purpose is work started by Dr. Clare Graves in the 1960s while he was a professor of psychology. Dr. Don Beck and Dr. Chris Cowen developed it further and gave Graves' thinking broader exposure through their book *Spiral Dynamics*. Researchers describe their work on belief systems as one of the three major breakthroughs in our efforts to understand complexity, with the other two being systems theory (Peter Senge's work, for example) and chaos theory (French mathematician Henri Poincaré's pioneering work, for example). Ken Wilber notes that while spiral dynamics does not include states of consciousness, it is "…an elegant model of the self and its journey through…'waves of existence.'"[civ]

Their research identified two tiers of evolution with eight stages--the first six stages in tier one and the last two in tier two. As noted earlier, there are major belief changes from stage to stage and the change is even greater from tier to tier. An extensive research database of worldwide survey data (over 50,000) is behind these conclusions. The following summarizes their stage structure:

Spiral Dynamics Tiers and Stages

Evolutionary Tiers & Stages	% Pop.*	% Power*	Power Trend
Tier One 1. Beige: Archaic, Survival	.1	0	-
2. Purple: Magical & Mystical	9	1	-
3. Red: Mythical & Egocentric	18	4	- -
4. Blue: Divine Rational Order	36	28	-
5. Orange: Individualism, Achiever	27	47	+
6. Green: Sensitive self, Relative truth, Pluralism	9	14	++

Tier Two	I	5	++
7. Yellow: Holistic, Systems & Integrative			
8. Turquoise: Psychic & Global view	.I	I	++

* "% Population" refers the percent of people on our planet at a stage while "% Power" refers to the percent of leaders and managers who are at a particular stage.

Of note, there is support for a third tier composed of the causal and subtle stages. An extremely small percentage of people live at these stages today.

The next chapter details the key beliefs of today's three major stages (based on the percentage of the population at each stage), and it provides an introduction to the first of the second tier stages—the yellow stage. The chapter also details how dramatically our definition of happiness changes from stage to stage.

The following very briefly describes the first three stages, which are collectively a small percentage of the population and declining in overall size as people gradually evolve to later stages.

Beige

At this stage, humans focus on survival by providing the basic needs of food, shelter, and safety. This is characteristic of very early humans and infants—the stage we all start at.

Beliefs revolve around fulfilling these basic needs. A key belief is that "we do what we must to survive." Actions are far more instinctual than a result of deliberation. There is no differentiated self at this stage since we experience ourselves as part of the human family. People believe in banding together to help achieve their basic needs, but at this stage, there is no organizational structure.

Purple

We evolve next to the purple stage when we have been successful enough at the beige stage to venture further into the world. To deal with the additional challenges, people assemble the first families and then clans and tribes form to help regulate families. As local resources do not meet expanding needs, groups venture into the broader world where they encounter other groups. Maintaining the peace requires the development of rudimentary social skills and rules.

In this environment, people at the purple stage believe in:

- Allegiance to chiefs, shamans, elders, and our clan who we believe know the truth and what is best for us.

- Respecting mystical elements like spirits, totems, and ghosts.

- Voodoo curses, omens and spells often dispensed by chiefs and shamans also emerge. The line between fantasy and what is real is often blurred and the result is often a high level of fear

- Communal property

- Helping each other

- Strong family and clan relationships that they describe in blood terms like "blood is thicker than water" and "blood brothers."

Today purple develops as we leave infancy and enter childhood. Children develop attachment to security blankets and characters like Pooh Bear. Among adults, we see strong purple influences in Australian Aborigines, Hitler's cult of Aryan thinking, and Japan's Kamikaze culture. Adult purple artifacts include rabbits feet good luck charms, a plastic Jesus on the dash of a car, and the good that comes from knocking on wood.

Red

After the family bonds and clans of purple have addressed the major safety needs, magical elements and fear based approaches gradually lose their control over people.

There is the strong development of an "I" or ego that often can be raw, wild, and unbridled.

People at the red stage believe in/that:

- Dominating others and are not too concerned with developing consensus
- Life is a jungle
- The survival of the fittest
- Doing what you want regardless of what others think or say
- Being a hero who clearly is in charge
- Seeing a life as not worth too much
- Enjoying life to its fullest right now and feeling no remorse or regret
- Grand gestures and sense of invincibility
- The world is made up of "haves" and "have-nots" and I am going to be a "have"

Today we see red qualities when children enter the "terrible twos." When there is not development to the next blue stage, red influences create the phenomena of rebellious youth. Throughout history, we see red influences in the frontier mentality, feudal kingdoms, epic heroes, Attila the Hun, many rock stars, and soldiers of fortune.

Concluding Thoughts

Understanding our developmental stages is a great aid to becoming more self-aware. All of us have a center of gravity in one of the spiral dynamic's stages. There is usually a mix of stage influences on our center of gravity— influences from previous stages and from the next sequential stage. The subjective nature of these influences is what makes us unique.

Knowing this we can start the process of determining where we are in the stage process. With this information, we gain access to understanding a set of important beliefs that guide our actions. We also get a peek at where we are going or can go. All of this can accelerate the critical process of expanding self-awareness.

There are many other useful tools in accelerating self-awareness. Some of the most popular are the Myers-Briggs and FIRO-B assessment tools. The feedback highlights elements of our personality formed by distinctive beliefs. Besides personal feedback, assessment tools like this also introduce us to the many other belief profiles that exist and our relationship to them. For some people learning about the other belief classifications introduces them to a powerful insight—there are other belief profile options. This insight often is the first validation of the notion that we really do have choices. Self-awareness is at the heart of the inner journey. It shifts our life focus from our external to our internal world. When developed, self-awareness is an essential tool in our efforts to tame the mind to make it calm. The journey of ever-increasing self-awareness is a key tool to creating greater happiness.

Chapter Eleven

Belief Stages and Happiness

Beliefs define actions, which always have consequences, happy or unhappy. That makes beliefs worthy of close examination. As we discover the stages through which all of our beliefs develop, we learn how we can be happiest at each stage of belief development. We also discover higher stages of development where achievement of ultimate happiness becomes an evolutionary destination. Almost three out of every four people and almost nine out of every ten managers/leaders have beliefs primarily influenced by the stages spiral dynamics labels blue, orange, and green beliefs. Each person typically has a blend of two of the three belief stages and the exact blend varies for each person, as does the relative importance of each belief. Where we are on the evolutionary spiral strongly influences the blend of beliefs. For example, we can be moving from blue to orange or strongly centered in orange with little blue or green influence. This creates a certain degree of individual uniqueness, but less than most of us currently think there is. Since most of us highly value our personal uniqueness, we tend to exaggerate our differences when the truth is that we are far more alike than we are different.

We all sequentially progress through the belief stages, although some of us may not today be at the later stages, like green or yellow, for example. People with a center of gravity in a particular stage (the belief stage with the greatest influence), orange, for example, share many of the same beliefs which leads them to join formal or informal groups of others who share their beliefs, like political parties and business organizations.

In each stage, a degree of happiness is possible. Typically, this occurs when we are true to our beliefs, since we can feel happy when we are doing what we believe to be right. In the first tier stages, we experience a small portion of our happiness potential, primarily because our primary focus is on the external world and we focus primarily on personal needs. When focused on the external world, events and other people determine so much of our happiness. In effect, with an external focus, we have limited control over our happiness. As noted earlier, higher levels of happiness are achievable when we turn our focus inward and begin taming the mind to create a calm mind. We can begin this effort at any stage and a greater internal focus provides greater personal control over our happiness. Also, the sooner we become self-aware the sooner we tame a tumultuous mind. Through self-awareness, we develop the ability to review and observe our actions and the thinking (the beliefs) behind them. With this ability, we see thinking, subsequent actions, and their consequences—happy or unhappy. These critical inputs guide future efforts to tame the mind and change beliefs to ones producing happier outcomes. Unhappiness is also possible at each of the stages discussed here. Unhappiness occurs when we are out of integrity with who we think we are as defined by our beliefs. Unhappiness also is a consequence of the dysfunctional behavior that exists at every stage. It can also occur when there is conflict with people who have different beliefs. This can be stressful and create a range of negative emotions and thoughts. As long as we have an outward focus, there will be modest levels of happiness and high levels of frustration and unhappiness. This becomes much clearer when we later understand ultimate happiness. Today most of us have limited expectations for how happy we can be and, as a result, what we call happy today we will see as unhappy in the future. The difference is that great between how happy most people are today and how happy they can be when they ultimately tame the mind.

The following sections provide an overview of spiral dynamics' blue, orange, green, and yellow beliefs with some thoughts on how these contribute to happiness and unhappiness.

Tier One

Blue: Traditional, Conformist, and Divine Rational Order

The blue stage develops in direct response to the excesses and dysfunctional aspects of the red stage. Red actions can be rough and even violent. Seemingly chaotic actions often appear to have little apparent, thought out philosophy behind them. There is little long term thinking at the red stage and little concern for the consequences of personal behavior.

People at the blue stage of belief development love law
and order and living life by rules that are defined by
authority figures, including the Supreme Being who is the
ultimate authority figure. This is a sharp departure from
life at the red stage. In the end, the power of the
Supreme Being is the only force capable of putting fear
into the hearts of reds and bringing them gradually into
line with blue beliefs.

Belief: *I believe life has meaning, direction, and purpose with
predetermined outcomes defined by power authorities.*

Blue develops in part in response to the often unbridled
chaos of the red stage, where it often seems like it is
every man and woman for himself or herself. At the red
stage, life has limited meaning, but in the blue stage, life
takes on meaning defined for many people by their
religion and its authority figures. One source of happiness
is living in accordance with religious beliefs and gaining the
favor of the religion's authority figures.

Life's meaning is usually translated into specific do's and
don'ts. These come from a code of conduct, like the
Christian Ten Commandments. This becomes a strictly
enforced code of conduct where there is little room for

interpretation or subjective application. There is a very clear definition of right and wrong. Committing wrong actions or even thinking about them often has severe consequences, like the pain suffered by Hester Prynne in Hawthorne's *The Scarlet Letter*. On the other hand, there are rewards to the faithful, like entering heaven instead of hell when they die.

Leaders often are religious authority figures who wield considerable power as custodians, teachers, and enforcers of their religion's word from the Supreme Being, as delivered through prophets like Jesus, Buddha, and Mohammed. The political leaders often need to respect and adhere to religious teachings as interpreted by authority figures. The same holds true for leaders in other fields, like business and the military. Some of the excesses of religious influence on the political world ultimately led to the separation of church and state, as seen in the United States Constitution.

This belief in rules and life's meaning has a powerful influence on personal happiness. When living in sin (not adhering to the prescribed rules), unhappiness is almost a guaranteed consequence. Unhappiness comes from personal guilt and from shame heaped on a person by other blue believers. Happiness is living strictly in accordance with the proscribed don'ts and prescribed do's.

Belief: *I believe there are rigid social hierarchies defined by Divine rules as interpreted by today's keepers of the rules.*

At a fundamental level, the social hierarchies define two groups—believers and non-believers. But the hierarchies are greatly complicated by the diversity among believers. Among Christians, for example, there is tremendous diversity including various forms of Catholicism and Protestantism. Within these forms, there is further diversity (Baptists and Lutherans among Protestants, for example) and each group has its highly committed believers.

It is somewhat amazing how various Christian believer groups can view other Christian groups almost as non-believers despite their shared belief in the Bible and Jesus. The strict social hierarchies tend to revolve around shared belief in a particular branch of Christianity. Christianity is not the only religion with this diversity, as we have learned from Muslims who have their own diversity with the Sunni and Shia groups that can view their differences as so great that they go to war and kill each other, the Iraq and Iran war, for example.

Social hierarchies today are less defined in strict and narrow religious terms than they were in the past. In the past, these beliefs defined friends and foes. They defined your proper place in society and work. In its strongest terms, Divinely defined beliefs saw believers as saved and worthy people and non-believers as heathens unworthy of any of society's benefits. It relegated non-believers to roles as servants and even slaves. While blue's ability to dominate cultures and populations has weakened considerably from the times when blue was the center of gravity for Western culture, there is still clear evidence of the controlling ability blue beliefs have on people, the Quakers, for example. This weakened influence comes from the growth of subsequent belief stages, especially orange and green.

Happiness is being accepted by others who share your beliefs and unhappiness is being shunned by these same believers. Happiness can be converting a non-believer to your way of thinking, while unhappiness can be "losing" a loved one to another way of thinking, converting from being a Catholic to being a Baptist, for example.

Belief: *I believe in bringing order and stability to all things.* When we remember that blue develops from red's highly undisciplined belief systems, we begin to appreciate better blue's positive contributions. Blue believers fear anything less than strict order to life. They believe that in the absence of order the only alternative is chaos. Blues believe everything needs to be well organized, especially a sense that everything has a place. Order and regimentation are prized and seen as the characteristics of a quality person.

People with these beliefs are happiest when this order exists. They are happy when they can see purpose and meaning. Conversely, they are unhappy when ambiguity replaces clarity of meaning and purpose. Chaos or disorder creates fear. If someone challenges life's meaning, it can be very unsettling, which contributes to a high level of unhappiness.

Belief: *I believe righteous living produces stability now and guarantees future reward, both in this life and after.*

As we saw earlier, the definition of righteous living usually comes from Divine sources as interpreted by religious authorities. There is a willingness to sacrifice today's gains for future ones. Future gains can be rewards in this life (admiration from peers and authority figures, for example) and at the end of life (going to heaven, for example). Sacrifice often includes stifling impulses through guilt. Blues believe that we build moral character and fiber by following laws and sacrificing impulses that are contrary to Divine guidance. While impulses are understandable, following them only leads to unhappiness.

To people at other stages, blue life looks stoic and unhappy. Blue beliefs limit or prohibit most of the activities traditionally associated by other stages with happiness. For example, blues minimize the focus on materialism, and they channel material well being into charitable and religious outlets.

Blue Beliefs: Past and Present

Blue beliefs dominated cultures in the past, like Confucian China and the days of knights and their code of chivalry and honor. They also played a strong role in Puritan America and the reformation and counter reformation in the 16th and 17th centuries.

Today, we can see blue influences in Singapore's highly disciplined culture, the appeal of evangelists like the Reverend Billy Graham, the Boy and Girl scouts, the Salvation Army, and politically the Christian right and fundamentalism. Blue beliefs define conservative political views while green beliefs tend to define liberal beliefs.

Tier One

Orange: Individualism and Personal Achievement

Orange beliefs develop in response to the dysfunctional aspects of a blue belief dominated culture. People tire of the strict harshness dispensed by religious authority figures for what seem like personal and not Godly reasons. Emerging oranges also see that religion increasingly cannot answer important questions or religion's answers do not fit with readily observable facts. Oranges desire greater freedom and room to make decisions that are right for them. They increasingly do not respect the blue herd mentality.

Orange beliefs form the center of gravity for American culture today and are still very influential in European cultures. Orange beliefs develop in part due to the excesses and freedom limiting aspects of blue. There is a desire to break free from the strict confines of blue beliefs.

Belief: *I believe that each individual defines personal truth and meaning based on objective and scientific thinking.*

In reaction to truth and meaning defined by religious authority, there emerges a new basis for knowing because the religion based thinking increasingly could not answer crucial questions. Historians mark the beginning of this profound change as 1543 when Copernicus announced (via a paper published after his death) that the sun, not the earth was at the center of our universe. In 1633, religious authorities (blues) forced Galileo to renounce his support for Copernicus because the thinking was heretical to prevailing religious beliefs. By the 1700s, many people accepted that the earth did rotate on its own axis (every 24 hours) and around the sun (once every year). This was the beginning of replacing religion and religious authority as the ultimate definers of truth by scientists and their scientific method. Also receiving credit as early champions of the scientific method are Francis Bacon and René Descartes in the 17th century.

Increasingly authority and truth came from scientists who conducted experiments and used their logical mind. Learning flowed from tried and true actual experience. Another important shift was the belief in change and not permanence. Blues believed in unchangeable truths while oranges believed change was an inevitable part of life. Today, oranges believe in disciplined, focused problem resolution using the scientific method in almost all areas of life. Science is an obvious area, but the thinking extends to business and the science of economics. Oranges also seek to extend science to understanding themselves through the development of the science of psychology. Oranges are happy when science or strong logical thinking defines decisions. Fact based decisions provide the most comfort. Conversely, they are unhappy when people try to convince them of something for which there is little factual proof. In a similar vein, oranges are unhappy when someone else tells them what should be true for them.

They are happiest when they find truth through their efforts and they experience it for themselves.

Belief: *I believe in acting in my own self-interest and I play the game of life to win.*

Oranges love competition. They believe it brings out the best in people and produces the best results. They believe life is a series of challenges, tests, and opportunities for them to become winners. Competition is fun for them and it reinforces their sense of self-importance and individuality. They love getting competitive juices going in business, sports, and politics where they seek to win every time they "play." They have a deep sense that there are winners and losers in life and they plan to win, not lose.

For the most part, oranges are optimistic and enjoy taking risks. They do not mind working and competing on their own because it supports their self-reliant image. They use their logical mind, technology, and science to win. They also believe that change and moving ever forward are an inherent part of how life works.

Oranges are happiest when they compete and win using their personal wits and logical thinking ability. There is no sweeter victory than out-thinking your opponents. They are unhappy when forced to cooperate since it means a lost opportunity to show how good they are personally. They are also be unhappy when they see competition as unfair, especially when it is not how well you think that counts but subjective factors dominate the outcome, like the boss promoting his daughter instead of you and your superior record of achievement. There is also unhappiness when competition crosses fairness and ethical lines and takes on more red characteristics, like "all is fair in love and war."

Belief: *I believe in personal autonomy and freedom.* John Wayne is the hero of many oranges. During the 1800s, the conquering of the western frontier saw orange beliefs blossom. Oranges believe in adventure, venturing out into the unknown, and being the first to experience or discover something. Oranges glorify first ever accomplishments from people like Charles Lindberg, Allan Shepard, Jonas Salk, Babe Ruth, and Lewis and Clark. This high degree of individualism extends to a desire to experience the new and novel, like being an early adopter of new products and technology.

Oranges want as few as possible constraints on personal freedom. This spirit guided the writing of the Declaration of Independence and the limiting of federal powers in the Constitution. Today, it is the belief behind limiting constraints of all kinds. They have great faith in individuals' ability to make the right decisions.

Oranges believe in operating independently. This spirit, in conjunction with other orange values, drives entrepreneurship. In many ways, the new frontier for orange believers is the world of business. Their optimism and self-confidence makes them willing to defy great odds for success. They glorify courage and results.

Oranges are happiest when there is freedom to do what they love. In business, they love the opportunity to compete and win. While unhappy if they lose, they usually pick themselves up off the floor and charge into the next opportunity to win. They are happy being the first person ever to accomplish something. For example, in sports there are so many numbers and records that there are plenty of opportunities to get into the record books.

Oranges are unhappy when forced to play the game of life by any blue or green (the next stage) rules. They feel stifled and they rebel in an effort to regain their freedom. Belief: *I believe in cautiously developing personal relationships and relationships are best when they help me win the game of life.*

Personal relationships are not as important to oranges as they have been for previous stages. For oranges, relationships are often part of competitive plan to win. It is not unusual of oranges to manipulate others to get what they most want—to win. Oranges are very slow to trust others. Relationships tend to come and go even important relationships like marriage. As long as a relationship contributes to orange's personal needs, it continues. In their decision about who to marry oranges may consider how helpful their mate will be in winning at business and life.

Once in relationships, oranges can be cold and factual. Criticism of others is often very straightforward, cold-blooded, and insensitive. Oranges have limited concern about feelings (facts only please) and there is little concern if the relationship ends, since there is little long-term commitment to relationships. Oranges believe relationships are unpredictable although they are often quick to project their motives and beliefs onto others. Oranges may demonstrate warmth towards others, but in many situations, it is insincere as they attempt to manipulate others for their purposes, usually winning at something. Not surprisingly, oranges can lack remorse or conscience, especially when an important opportunity to win is on the line. While oranges like to be fair and scrupulous, they are not reluctant to do what it takes to win. They often justify harm done to others as one of the prices of competition, and that by teaching others a lesson, they actually help the other person. The orange relationship attitudes lead to more short term relationships than blues experience and is one of the reasons blues criticize oranges. Blues advocate families and family values while oranges tune out what they consider the preachy nature of blues.

Oranges are happy when relationships work to help them achieve their life goals. Certainly, love can be a component of relationships but love can be fleeting if the continuation of the relationship, like a marriage, threatens the achievement of other life goals. Oranges are happy when relationships do not restrict their freedom and when they are not too complicated. Oranges prefer to invest their energy more in achieving personal goals than personal relationships.

Oranges can be unhappy and run from a person who wants a very close, long-term relationship. A fear of commitment is characteristic of some oranges. Oranges can be unhappy when someone is unethical with them, especially when it happens in competition. They dislike being on the losing side and the on the receiving end of another person's painful lesson.

Belief: *I believe that the world is a rational and well-oiled machine with natural laws that can be learned, mastered and manipulated for my purposes.*

Oranges have little doubt about their abilities to master their world. This includes both people and the earth itself. Unlike previous stages that held the earth in awe or fear, oranges have no such concerns. Through science, they are confident they can learn nature's secrets and then use them for their personal and business gain. All of this gives them the confidence to achieve material abundance and the good life.

Oranges are happy when they use science for personal gain, especially the accumulation of money and material stuff. As noted earlier, they are usually in competition for this abundance and are unhappy when their best skills do not win.

Belief: *I believe living fast and stylishly.*

Oranges love living at high speeds. They work and party fast and intensely because it is required to win. They admire speed and have no respect for laziness or a slow pace of life. Intelligent, hard work is a given and they are constantly testing new ideas through experience and with their logical mind.

Oranges love style. How they look and the opinion of others is very important. They conform to prevailing images of success, fashion, and style. Flashy, fast cars, beautiful men and women, and stylish clothes are prized by oranges.

To a certain degree, oranges are happy when they have the right look, but it also seems that they can never look good enough. As a result, how an orange looks can be source of both happiness and, more often, unhappiness. Oranges are one of the biggest consumers of cosmetic surgery, stylish clothing, and expensive cars.

Orange Beliefs: Past and Present

Orange beliefs drove much of the colonialism of the British Empire. The Cold War symbolized orange competition on a global scale. The language of the Cold War was clearly orange language, for example, the description of an arms race. Orange beliefs drove the development of capitalism and today these beliefs dominate business culture. Wall Street and Chambers of Commerce today are havens for oranges. Competition is so prevalent in life that it seems that devoted orange believers are willing to compete on just about any subject. The fashion business would fall on hard times without oranges. Oranges disproportionately consume everything from cosmetics to breast implants. There might not be a Rodeo Drive if there were no oranges. Among men, hunting, especially trophy hunting, is a strong orange activity, as are most forms of sports.

Tier One

Green: Sensitive Self, Relative Truth, and Pluralism

Greens rebel against orange's excesses of individualism and material greed. They see orange personal gains coming at the expense of others and the planet. The only power that seems to count in the orange world is economic and hierarchical power. Greens dislike the harshness of competition and that competition brings out the worst in people, especially unethical behavior and damage to weaker foes for personal gain.

Belief: *I believe in reaching decisions through reconciliation and consensus.*

This is a sharp departure from oranges who believe that personal organizational and economic powers produce the best decisions. When businesses embrace this green belief, through increased use of teams, for example, it can be very disconcerting to oranges who find they need to seek the views and agreements of others that they previously ignored or simply told them what to do. Orange team members are a major source of team conflict since they see teams as a waste of time ("I do not need a team to tell me what needs to be done. I already know.") and a threat to their previously unchallenged personal power.

Greens believe in building strong, harmonious relationships through an emphasis on dialogue and human bonding. Again, oranges find this soft and unnecessary. Greens emphasize listening to a wide range of views before reaching a decision through consensus. Where there are differences they work hard to reconcile them and are willing to go to great lengths to achieve broad-based agreement. To do this they stress togetherness and understanding of the others' needs and opinions. This is a difficult task when we realize that greens also invite diversity of thinking into the decision making process. Diversity can make it difficult to achieve a sense of community.

Driving this effort is the green belief that everyone is beautiful in their own way. Greens believe there is room for everyone's views. Greens distrust and dislike organizational hierarchy because they believe we are all equal.

For greens, relationships are important, in sharp contrast to oranges who specialized in relationships of convenience and personal gain. Greens believe that being liked and accepted by your social network is far more important than winning or material gain. Again, this is the opposite of orange beliefs.

Greens are happy when people get along and arrive at consensus decisions. They really enjoy the strong relationships that often develop as part of the decision making process. Greens are unhappy when they encounter orange's attempts to impose their personal will on decisions.

Belief: *I believe in subjective, nonlinear thinking, which creates warmth, sensitivity, and caring for the earth.*

Oranges' dependence on logical thinking and economic factors almost to the exclusion of other considerations led greens to seek a better belief system. While they appreciate the contributions of logic and science, greens supplement these factors with personal feelings. Greens view orange decisions as too cold hearted and often cold blooded when it comes to valuing people and the planet. Greens feel responsibility for their community, which can be as small as the street they live on and as broad as concern for our planet. Their sense of equality often

leads to a belief in sharing society's resources among all.
Greens are happy when they feel their efforts contribute
to sharing and environmental responsibility. Conversely,
they are unhappy when they encounter orange's waste
and greed.

Belief: *I believe in the rights and equality of all people.*
Greens view the orange beliefs as responsible for the
economic, political, and social damage and injustice. In the
quest for personal success, greens believe orange beliefs
create victims that need defending.
Green beliefs led to social programs like welfare, political
programs like rights for woman and blacks, and social
programs like environmental organizations. They can be
passionate in their defense of justice for all.

Belief: *I believe the human spirit needs to be free of greed,*
dogma, and divisiveness.
Greens rebel against orange greed and its damage to
relationships. Greens think competitiveness creates
divisiveness and believe that teamwork, collaboration, and
cooperation are the remedy. They also believe that
accepted orange dogmas contribute to divisiveness and
narrow thinking. Greens open their minds to alternatives

to capitalism (more sharing models) and world problems (the 1983 Brandt Commission recommendations, for example).

  Belief: *I believe in spirituality as a means to develop greater harmony.*

While religion is very important to blues, its importance diminished for oranges. Greens embrace spirituality, both religious and increasingly non-religious experience. Greens seek inner peace as a way of enriching their lives and developing their potential. They believe in active exploration of spiritual traditions, including revisiting some purple traditions. Greens have been the primary force behind much of the loosely described New Age interest. Greens believe in a purpose beyond self-interest and actively seek answers and meaning. Their openness can lead to a wide range of quasi-spiritual and spiritual interests, ranging from channeling to Buddhism, for example. From their spirituality, they develop a greater interest in caring, harmonious relationships.

They also seek answers beyond the scope of traditional science, because increasingly science is unable to answer some fundamental questions, the nature of consciousness, for example. This leads to an interest in metaphysics and various forms of scientific spirituality. They seek to reconcile science and spirituality. For example, David Bohm, the great English quantum physicist, saw many common understandings between quantum physics and wisdom traditions. His conversations with the Indian sage Krishnamurti are striking for their broad agreements on the workings of the universe.

Belief: *I believe it is better to live plainly and simply.* Greens believe in preserving the earth's resources, which leads them away from the excesses of orange's conspicuous consumption. The simple life is increasingly equated to the good life. While simplicity was a belief of some blues, greens believe in living simply but without the sternness and sense of sacrifice common to blues.

Green Beliefs: Past and Present

The development of green beliefs is more recent than previously discussed stages. We can see green beliefs in Susan B. Anthony's efforts to gain the right to vote for women. The civil rights movement is also evidence of greens' interest in the equality of all people.

Today, we see green beliefs guiding organizations like Greenpeace, the ACLU, the World Council of Churches, animal rights, Doctors Without Borders, and deep ecology. We also see it in the development of business teams, the lyrics of John Lennon, and sensitivity training. Jimmy Carter was the first president with strong green beliefs.

Tier Two

Yellow: Holistic, Systems & Integrative

The next very big step in belief evolution is the second tier's yellow stage. For most readers this stage will be the most difficult to relate to since less than one percent of the world's population is at this stage today. Despite their few numbers today, yellow beliefs are important because many greens are poised to take the next step and yellow is a stage that will contribute to major progress on the planet.

Belief: *I believe in making life decisions by connecting with my inner-directed core being.*

Yellow is the first stage where life's spotlight shifts from the outer to the inner world. They gradually develop an inner knowing or intuitive ability that is distinctly different from green's gut feel or the emotions of other stages. The dictionary defines intuition as "The act or faculty of knowing or sensing without the use of rational processes; immediate cognition."[cv] The wisdom traditions define intuition as a higher mind ability (the logical mind is the lower mind) that can know anything without needing or processing sensory inputs.

With their emerging intuitive ability, yellows get to the core of an issue quickly. They solve complex problems that befuddle and defy solution for people at earlier stages. People at earlier stages might form study groups, seek a wider range of inputs (especially greens), or seek answers from higher authorities in an organization. When science attempts to answer complex problems, it tends to investigate the parts of a problem in an effort to understand the overall problem. Paradoxes and uncertainties are unsettling to the scientific approach. Yellows do not seek answers in understanding the parts but in understanding the whole. Paradoxes do not frustrate yellows. They see systems by examining the whole and how it connects and interacts with other wholes.

While yellows do not go out of their way to create green's harmonious relationships, they are not bulls in a china shop either. They do not spend time or energy on perfunctory niceties, interpersonal gamesmanship (a strong orange belief), or trivial subjects.

In resolving problems and making decisions, they value good content, clean information, and open channels for finding out more on their terms. They have no need for status or displays of power. They recognize that the best solution can come from anyone, anywhere in an organization or group. They seek to learn from everyone, all the time. Yellows are only interested in the best solution for everyone involved. The best solution always considers long-term interests and needs. Functionality is a key component of good decisions.

Belief: *I believe life is an up and down journey from problem to solution, so I accept both chaos and order as normal.*

Out of chaos come new solutions and learnings that make life better when we use our capacity to learn from situations. Yellows know that out of chaos comes the opportunity for profound, breakthrough win/win/win outcomes. While challenges can be complex, yellow's abilities enable them to make decisions that are remarkable simple, especially in the execution of the solution.

　　Belief: *I believe in personal integrity and standing firm for what I know to be right.*

Yellows are impervious to coercion, bribery, or intimidation. They have no desire to please or control others or allow others control of them. They reject anything artificial or unethical in relationships while seeking spontaneity and simplicity. Their internal validation makes them relatively immune to external pressure or judgment.

　　Belief: *I believe all stages are right and contribute to progress on the planet.*

Yellow is the first stage to appreciate the previous stages. All the previous stages think other stages are wrong and my stage is the right and best belief system. For example, consider what would happen if four people were in a room, one person each from the blue, orange, green, and yellow stages. Within a very short time, the blue, orange, and green participants would discover they have major differences and that they do not like each other. All three would find the yellow participant likeable and understanding.

Yellows see the legitimacy of each belief system and respect their right to exist. In fact, they see each stage as a dynamic force contributing to the well-being of all people. They see stages as aiding the development of people and providing a progressive path forward. Yellows do not necessarily agree with all the beliefs of earlier stages, but they are understanding and respectful of each belief system.

Belief: *I believe that knowledge and competency supersede rank and status.*

Yellows have little use for hierarchy and rank. They are only concerned with who has the answers, experience or knowledge to accomplish the task. The people with the greatest ability (a combination of skills, experience, and knowledge) have the most authority, regardless of tenure, status, or even feelings. As yellow influence increases, there will be fewer perks, fancy offices, and status symbols.

Belief: *I believe in personal freedom but without harming others or indulging in excessive self-interest.*

Yellows favor appropriate technology, minimal consumption, and a deliberate effort to avoid waste and clutter. They enjoy life but do not go to excess or become slaves to their human appetites. In part, this is a reaction to the excesses that can occur in the previous stages. Yellows do not go to the simplicity and restraint extremes of some blues.

Yellows celebrate the magnificence of existence, appreciate the value of being, and place less value on material possessions than any of the previous stages. Their appreciation of what they have comes from an increasing ability to be reflective.

There is great personality diversity in yellows. They can be gentle or ruthless and angry or calm. The specific circumstances of the moment and the overall interest they have in an event or topic influence their choice of behavior.

Belief: *I believe there are natural hierarchies, systems and forms.*

Yellows see life in systems and seek to integrate what other stages may see as disparate parts. They integrate apparent differences into interdependent, natural flows. Yellows see open systems that interact in a dynamic manner. They see that system control is neither desirable nor possible.

Yellow Beliefs Today

There are limited high profile examples of yellow beliefs today. One of the most notable is system theory and Peter Senge is one of its best-known proponents. He and others are also champions of learning organizations. Yellow movie stars have Paul Newman personality characteristics. Television got a peak at some yellow beliefs in the early episodes of Northern Exposure.

Concluding Thoughts

The discussion of the evolution of beliefs has been brief in an effort to provide a useful overview. I have used the spiral dynamics model for the discussion and the book with the same name provides considerable more detail on what is a fairly complex system.

Part of the complexity traces to the spiral nature of how our beliefs evolve. My discussion has focused on descriptions of pure stages, when in fact most of us are a blend of stage beliefs. Even when our center of gravity is in a particular stage, orange for example, there are influences from the previous and next stage. The more entrenched we become in our center of gravity stage, the more the beliefs of the previous stage diminish. As we mature in a particular stage, we see the emergence of influence from the next sequential stage.

For our purposes the spiral dynamics model helps us know ourselves better. It acts as a belief road map detailing where we have been, where we are now, and where we are going. For our journey, we can rely on this very accurate and validated road map. We can also supplement it by studying other evolutionary lines of development to round out our awareness of who we are and what is ahead.

By becoming self aware of the beliefs that define our choice of actions, we take a big step towards making more conscious choices and fewer habitual choices. In the language of Covey, we move from reactions to responses

by expanding the moment of choice. We use the
expanded moment of choice to understand the belief
leading to an action and determining if there is another
belief that will lead to a better action choice. That better
choice is usually a choice that will make us feel happier
than the old belief led us to feel.

The ultimate purpose of increasing self-awareness of our
beliefs is to consciously identify beliefs that are not making
us as happy as we want to be and then developing new
beliefs that drive actions with happier consequences.
Again, at the stages that most of us are at today, we can
become happier when we identify beliefs that drive
actions with unhappy consequences and then change to
them to ones with happier outcomes.

Science has discovered the only practice that can
accelerate progress through the stages is meditation.
Studies prove that four years of meditation (about an
hour per day) is capable of moving a person forward by
two stages of development. This is major growth,
especially when we consider that for many of us two
stages of growth brings us into the yellow stage of
development. Studies reveal that other practices (like

journaling) can accelerate progress by only about a half stage. Again, meditation is the only scientifically proven practice of accelerating growth through the belief stages. Certainly reaching later stages of belief development does not guarantee greater happiness. Happiness requires consistent, conscientious inner work at every stage to ensure greater happiness. We can choose to do inner work like meditation at every stage. The interest in doing this inner work increases as we progress through the stages and is especially evident when we reach the yellow stage of development. At the yellow stage, there is a dramatic reduction in fear as life becomes more understandable. The reduction in fear removes or greatly diminishes one of the most devastating negative life forces that creates high levels of unhappiness.

As we progress through the stages and reach the second tier, we significantly increase the opportunity to achieve ultimate happiness. In both second and third tier stages we become increasing attracted to doing the inner work necessary to achieve ultimate happiness. To be clear, we can achieve high levels of happiness at first tier levels if the necessary inner work is done.

Chapter Twelve

Six Happiness Beliefs

In earlier chapters, we saw how beliefs strongly influence our actions and how our actions' consequences impact our happiness, positively or negatively. Given our belief's strong influence, it is important to embrace beliefs that have happy consequences. Fortunately, the world's great teachers tell us that there are beliefs that contribute to greater happiness.

These wisdom based beliefs reflect an understanding of the fundamental laws guiding our universe. As such, they enable us to live more purposefully and in alignment with those understandings. A life aligned with the essence of who we really are is a happier life. Happiness is both our birthright and a natural consequence of living life connected to the essence of who we really are. The best method of discovering and connecting with our essence is through meditation.

Embracing these beliefs is a major part of living ultimate happiness and preparing ourselves to move onto the next level of positive experience, which is joy. From the egocentric perspective, beliefs determine our thoughts, emotions, subsequent actions, and their consequences. When beliefs are this central to our happiness, it becomes critical that we have beliefs that nurture increasing levels of happiness. The beliefs suggested for your consideration in this chapter are rooted in the deepest understandings of our universe's fundamental laws. As such, they provide the promise of ultimate happiness when they become a major part of an on-going plan to become happier.

The six happiness beliefs and understandings in this chapter are consistent with the teachings of all the enlightened teachers over more than four thousand years starting with Lao Tzu in 2,500 years BC and ending in current times with enlightened teachers like His Holiness the Dalai Lama. In between are the founders of the world's great religions and the enduring enlightened philosophers and thinkers who contributed the perennial wisdom teachings.

There certainly are more than six happiness beliefs. For example, John Marks Templeton wrote the *Worldwide Laws of Life* in which he articulates "200 eternal spiritual principles." The six beliefs and understandings presented here have the greatest ability to contribute to greater happiness when we live life guided by them. They reflect the most fundamental laws of our Universe.

Belief One

There is a Supreme Being who is the Guiding Hand for all that is. We awaken our understanding and personal knowing of the Supreme Being through spiritual practice and living. Gradually, we understand that we are spiritual beings having a human experience. The more we awaken to our divinity the happier we are. We are happiest when this divinity guides our thoughts and actions.

The wisdom and religious traditions are unanimous in their recognition of a Supreme Being. While the name given to the Supreme Being varies, God and Allah for example, the exoteric definitions from all the world's great religions and wisdom traditions are remarkably similar. The Supreme Being is an all-powerful Being for at least our planet. He is omnipresent and omniscient. As such, His presence is undeniable. Even men of science like Einstein and Dr. T. Byram Karasu, chairman of the department of psychiatry and behavioral sciences at the Albert Einstein College of Medicine acknowledge the existence of a Supreme Being. Dr. Karasu notes, "We are born with the knowledge of God. God is an imprinted knowledge that can be forbidden or denied, but it cannot be erased."[cvi] He adds, "The knowledge of God is no knowledge. It is a mystical experience."[cvii] In addition, national surveys indicate that 80% of people believe in a divine power.[cviii]

Researchers report that interest in spirituality has been steadily increasing the last twenty years. Wade Clark Roof, a professor of religious studies at the University of California at Santa Barbara, says, "What's driving the interest in spirituality is a sense among people that their lives are not properly fulfilling,"[cix] I might add that it is part of their awareness that they are not as happy as they thought they would be and they are seeking a better way. For centuries, the Supreme Being has communicated laws or rules through Their prophets and teachers that define proper thoughts and actions. While these laws or rules

take different forms from different teachers and prophets, their core meaning is the same across all religious and wisdom traditions. Huston Smith, the last century's greatest researcher and writer of religious traditions, clearly makes the case for this conclusion in his writings. From a science perspective Dr. Karasu notes, "The basic teachings of Western and Eastern religions, as civilizing forces, are indistinguishable. They all advocate honesty, kindness, faithfulness, loyalty, and the like."[cx]
The teachings tell us that as humans we have a spark of divinity in us. It has various names, including our soul and Buddha nature. While our preoccupation with the physical aspects of life clouds our awareness of this spark of divinity, when we turn our attention inward, we gradually awaken to the understanding that "We are not human beings having a spiritual experience. We are spiritual beings having a human experience."[cxi] This quote is from Pierre Teilhard de Chardin (1881-1955), a former French Roman Catholic priest, geologist, paleontologist, and philosopher-theologian, noted for his evolutionary interpretation of humanity and the universe and his insistence that such a view is compatible with Christianity.

Knowing the Supreme Being is critical to knowing whom we really are as noted by Shri Mataji Nirmala Devi, "You cannot know the meaning of your life until you are connected to the power that created you." She was an enlightened teacher in Gandhi's ashram.

The teachings are also clear that the more we live life consistent with the spiritual laws the happier we are. Yogananda notes this, "In the spiritual life one becomes just like a little child—without resentment, without attachment, full of life and joy."[cxii] A life guided by spiritual principles is essential as noted by Buddha, "Just as a candle cannot burn without fire, men cannot live without a spiritual life."[cxiii]

Many people tend to equate a spiritual life with a religious life. Public opinion research indicates that the majority of people see spirituality and religion as different. People seeing them as different tend to view spirituality positively and religion negatively.[cxiv] It is clear that a spiritual life can exist both within and without a religion, a thought echoed by His Holiness the Dalai Lama, "This is my simple religion. There is no need for temples; no need for complicated philosophy. Our own brain, our own heart is our temple; the philosophy is kindness."[cxv]

There are two bases for belief in a Supreme Being—faith and inner knowing. When our inner knowing is not strongly developed, we rely on faith. We base this faith in a Supreme Being on the words and actions of revered teachers like Jesus and Krishna. In the absence of inner knowing, we rely on external authority. This is the basis for most people who believe in a Supreme Being. Gradually through meditation and study, we go beyond faith to deep personal knowing of the Supreme Being's existence. Through inner knowing developed via meditation, we can have personal experience of the Supreme Being's existence. One of Yogananda's descriptions of meditation is "concentration to know God." With the development of our inner knowing, we no longer need just faith as the Buddha advises, "Believe nothing, no matter where you read it, or who said it, no matter if I have said it, unless it agrees with your own reason and your own common sense."[cxvi] In this case, common sense has the deeper meaning of inner knowing which is not the traditional use of the phrase.

Many people think that science and God are separate and that science cannot prove the existence of God. This adherence to a belief that only science determines what is real and not real is dangerous. Again, Dr. Karasu, who is a highly acclaimed psychiatrist by his peers and a leader in his field notes some sage perspective.

> Those who endow researchers with the sole source of truth are forfeiting that power. Scientists are limited by their scientific role. After all, they are asked to collect data on certain subjects and build hypotheses to explain them. Yet the database they are willing to explore can, at its best, represent only part of reality. Scientific research is typically not designed to examine all of the wondrous and intangible forms of human experience. It cannot explain everything. The illusive idea of God, in contrast, has the extraordinary capacity to explain everything: it encompasses not merely measurable phenomena but phenomena personally felt and subliminally sensed, which can even include revelations that can only be communicated through spiritual or mystical channels. Unlike science, the concept of God extends beyond the scientist's tangible world.[cxvii]

Well said.

Belief Two

Love and compassion are the primary energies defining and shaping our Universe. The Supreme Being is loving and compassionate. When we love and are compassionate, we connect with the essence of who we really are. We are happiest when living a life infused with love and compassion. We are happier as we expand love and compassion into wider and wider circles–loving yourself, family, community, country, and ultimately all that is.

Chapter seven identified love and compassion as fundamental actions we can take (along with meditating and being self-aware/mindful) to elevate our baseline of happiness. I also indicated that very close relationship between love and compassion. The Dalai Lama makes the link between love, compassion and happiness very clear, "We express our quest for happiness through the language of love. Love not only allows us to access our compassionate nature, it enables others to relate to us at the most human level."[cxviii] Because of the central role that love plays, I will focus on substantiating it with an understanding that it has a clear, unbreakable link to compassion.

The enlightened teachers for centuries have delivered one consistent message that love is the defining energy of the universe. Jesus was one of the first to tell us that God is love, but he certainly was not the last. More recently, Yogananda and the Dalai Lama have reminded us of love's defining power. The Dalai Lama said, "When we feel love and kindness toward others, it not only makes others feel loved and cared for, but it helps us also to develop inner happiness and peace."[cxix] And Pierre Teilhard De Chardin added that "Love is the affinity which links and draws together the elements of the world...Love, in fact, is the agent of universal synthesis."[cxx] Lastly, the American essayist and poet, Ralph Waldo Emerson (a leader of the philosophical movement of transcendentalism) said very succinctly what love is when he said, "Love is our highest word and the synonym for God."[cxxi]

One of the greatest revelation sources is the more than twenty volumes in the Ageless Wisdom series, which is the science of spirituality. It reveals that the primary energy influence in our universe is an influx of love and wisdom energy, which is one of seven potential defining energies.

Love is probably the number one musical topic with some very direct messages from some of our most popular musicians, like Bob Merrill's 1961 song *Love Makes the World Go 'Round* and the Beatles' 1967 song *All You Need is Love.* Rocker Jimi Hendrix added memorable perspective when he said, "When the power of love overcomes the love of power the world will know peace."[cxxii]

We do not need to rely on external sources to know this for ourselves. If we reflect on the happiest times of our life, they almost certainly were times where love was the predominant energy or feeling. Life is at its best when we are "in love." The object of our love is usually another person, significant other or family member, but we can also love everything and everyone, a family dog or flower, for example.

The combination of respected external authority and internal personal validation strongly suggest that love represents the essence our being. As such, the more love we have in our life, the more happiness we experience. Western science also suggests this with its finding that married people are happier than unmarried people are.

Love is a universal antidote to negativity. When feeling negative feelings like anger, fear, or hatred, we can pause and become self aware of what the energy feels like. After effectively applying the antidote of love, we can also pause and assess what the energy feels like. There may be no more dramatic and convincing proof of love's power to make us happy than this sharp before and after contrast.

Our first experiences of love tend to be very narrow and single dimensional. Love usually starts with love of our parents when we are very young and then shifts its primary focus to personal romantic love. The breadth of our love world may remain this narrow until our own family develops and it extends to children.

Our capacity for love is well beyond this rather small and tight circle of people closest to us. We have the ability through spiritual practice to expand gradually the circle of love to more people, a community, a country, our planet, and ultimately all that exists. While this may seem inconceivable today, again the enlightened teachers and prophets are unanimous on this point also. It becomes more realistic when we remember that the defining energy of our universe is love. Since the Supreme Being is love, it means that love is omnipresent. As such, there are no limits on our ability to love. As a result, there are no limits on our ability to be happy when we live a life infused with love.

An ancillary, but very important benefit of love is its healing power. There are many studies supporting love's healing power. Dr. Dean Ornish wrote a book on the scientific basis for the healing power of love. He notes that if you answer "no" to the question "Does someone love you" that "…you may have *three to five times* higher risk of premature death and disease from *all* causes"[cxxiii] than a person who answers "yes."

Acting on this belief requires us to proactively seek opportunities to experience and express love and compassion. By cultivating and nurturing love and compassion, we directly contribute to increasing our baseline level of happiness. Here are some suggestions about how to bring more love and compassion into your life.

Compassion not only involves empathy or feeling what another person is experiencing, but also wanting to relieve any suffering a person experiences. An important dimension of compassion is directly relating with the suffering and relieving it, and not engaging our judging mind to provide help that another person does not feel that they need. You can experience and act on compassionate feelings by:

- Becoming a volunteer in Red Cross Disaster Services. After being trained, you have the opportunity to actively help people who have experienced a natural disaster like a hurricane, tornado, earthquake, or flooding.

- Volunteering in organizations serving the neediest people in your community. Potential organizations include soup kitchens, the Salvation Army, and Habitat for Humanity.

- Reaching out to help people in your personal circle of compassion. You make personal sacrifices to help someone you know is suffering. The help can range from something as simple as listening to their plight to actively helping with a solution.

We often feel it is easier to be compassionate with a wide range of people than it is to love a wide range of people. When we live life from an egocentric perspective (blue, orange, and green levels within the spiral dynamics system), we often find that our circle of love barely extends beyond ourselves to include a significant other or marriage partner and family. We may also find that love is expressed only conditionally. We express love when someone reciprocates. However large our personal circle of love, we have the opportunity to proactively experience much higher levels of love in our life. As we expand our circle of love, we also can consider expressing love unconditionally. To bring more love into our life, we can:

- Discover beauty. When you experience beauty, it often becomes easy to feel love for the object of your attention. Taking your camera and going on a "beauty quest" is a wonderful method to experience the undiscovered beauty that is often very close to you right now.

- Express love. Spending quiet time reflecting on those people you already love enables you to deepen your appreciation and feelings of love for them. Taking the next step and sharing these thoughts and feelings can

be a deeply rewarding experience for you and the
other person.

- Expanding the circle of love. As you begin to
  recognize the power of love, it is natural to seek
  opportunities to expand the number of people within
  your circle of love. For example, you can expand from
  family members to friends. Often the starting point is
  recognizing specific qualities in a friend that we love.
  This seed then has the opportunity to grow into love
  for the whole person. Doing this often requires a new
  understanding of what love is. When the circle of love
  is small, we experience love in romantic and lustful
  contexts. Even when the circle expands to include
  family, there is a special "blood" connection. When
  you can expand the circle of love beyond romantic and
  family love, you open up a world of rich and happy
  opportunities.

Belief Three

Change is constant. From a narrow perspective, change
is evolutionary and from a broader one it is truly
revolutionary. The direction of change is towards
increasing levels of understanding who we really are

and capabilities to be happy. We cannot control the broad direction of change, but moment-to-moment our choices determine the pace of change and how efficiently and effectively we participate in the change process.

Change is inevitable, on going, and never ending. This strong statement may be at odds with your current understandings and even wishes, but please consider the following evidence.

Science tells us that the earth started as a mass of rocks composed of various minerals in solid, molten, and gaseous form. Among the more than 3,000 different types of minerals is significant evolutionary diversity ranging from simple, base minerals to more sophisticated crystals, diamonds, and uranium. When the mineral kingdom first existed, there were no plants, animals, or humans.

The next major change in life on the planet was the development of the plant kingdom. It probably started with green algae and evolved until the plant kingdom today includes about 260,000 known species. Plants evolved from simple algae to complex forms like flowers and trees, with degrees of complexity within them.

The animal kingdom developed after the plant kingdom and represented another major change. It initially differentiated itself by two characteristics--being multicellular and ingesting food for energy. Today there are more than 2 million animal species ranging in complexity from invertebrates like sponges and worms to vertebrates like horses and dogs.

The next evolution change led to the human kingdom which is different from the animal kingdom primarily because of the brain size and the capabilities it enabled like speech and thinking. Meaningful differentiation within the human kingdom is along lines of cognitive development, interpersonal capabilities, and our beliefs. Each evolutionary step from minerals, to plants, to animals, to humans represents revolutionary change. The record of millions of years of change is clear. To suggest that this degree of revolutionary change has ended with the human kingdom is foolish. It flies in the face of all that science knows and what the wisdom traditions tell us. Change is on going and never ending.

We do not need the perspective of millions of years to see change. It happens moment to moment—I am thirsty/drink water/no longer thirsty or I am angry/furious/venting/peaceful. We age day to day and our beliefs undergo revolutionary change from infancy through several adult stages, as we saw in earlier chapters. As noted scientists have changed their view of the brain from an earlier view that is was largely unchangeable to now seeing that the brain is highly moldable or in scientific terms that the brain exhibits a high level of plasticity. Change is everywhere and constant.

Attitudes toward change vary. Some people resist change and do not see change as inevitable. They want to preserve the "good old days" and resist change because "if it is not broken, don't fix it." Often these people see change as bad because it leads to a lower quality of life, as they define quality. They often resist change and find themselves unhappy during the struggle, which threatens their desires. When resistance fails, they can be even unhappier.

Other people embrace change and want to be active participants in the change process. They are comfortable with ambiguity and uncertainty because they trust that the basic direction of change is positive. They are comfortable destroying old structures and beliefs to build new ones. Most people are in between these two views. They want to retain some elements of their current life and change other elements.

Is change good or bad? Yes. Change is good or has happy consequences when guided by universal spiritual laws and it is bad or has unhappy consequences when these same laws do not guide both the change process and the resultant change. Even this badness can be good if we eventually learn from our mistakes to resume change in the right direction.

Regardless of our attitudes, both external and internal changes happen. From a macro perspective, we are gradually evolving through the human kingdom on our way, according to some of the wisdom traditions, to the spiritual kingdom. That is too mind boggling for most of us, so we can focus on something like the evolution of belief systems and their related cognitive abilities which was briefly outlined in chapter eleven. We can choose to actively and consciously participate in this evolutionary process.

We can become change agents and facilitators, primarily for ourselves and secondarily for others. We need an understanding of the universal laws, where we are today, and where we want to go. Using these elements, we can navigate a path of purposeful change that can be as narrow as becoming more physically fit to broader and longer efforts to change beliefs with unhappy consequences to beliefs with happier consequences. While we can be aware of the much broader direction of evolutionary change and possibilities, we inevitably need to come back to the present moment. The key decisions are determining where we are now and the next steps we can take to become happier.

The focus needs to be on the now or the present. That is the only place in time where we can effect change. We cannot change the past. We can influence, but not control, the future by the choices we make in the present. The effectiveness of these moment-to-moment choices determines our pace of change. Effectiveness is a function of making choices consistent with universal laws and utilizing proven change processes, like the ones outlined in later chapters.

We virtually assure greater happiness by heading in this direction.

Belief Four

There are inevitable consequences to every thought we have and action we take. The consequences are positive for positive thoughts and actions and negative for negative ones. Consequences can happen somewhere between immediately after a thought or action to in the deep future. Universal laws of ethical conduct taught by history's great teachers, prophets, and sages define positive and negative thoughts and actions. Consequences gradually teach us how to live in accordance with the essence of who we really are.

At some level, we do not believe there are consequences for all our actions. When we do something we know to be wrong and "get away with it," it seduces us into believing that there were not and will not be any consequences.

To avoid consequences, we may compound our original wrong action with more wrong actions like lying and intimidation. We do this to avoid consequences. Most of us learn these beliefs and skills at an early age from siblings, friends and even parents.

We may be aware of Jesus' teaching that "as we sow, so shall we reap" and may even have a vague understanding of karma. Simply, karma is the law of cause and effect and is analogous to Newton's third law of motion as it relates to physical objects.

All the world's great religions and wisdom traditions make it very clear that there are consequences to every thought and action we have. The Ageless Wisdom provides helpful understandings about karma:

- "The Law of Karma is today a great and incontrovertible fact in the consciousness of humanity everywhere....This great law—at one time a theory—is now a proven fact...."[cxxiv]

- "...the Law of Karma, rightly understood and rightly wielded, can bring that which produces happiness, good, and freedom from pain, with its chain of consequences..."[cxxv]

More recently, Deepak Chopra noted the law of karma as one of his seven spiritual laws of success. His statement of the law is: "Every action generates a force of energy that returns to us in like kind...what we sow is what we reap. And when we choose actions that bring happiness and success to others, the fruit of our karma is happiness and success."[cxxvi] Driving the point home, he says, "Whether you like it or not, everything that is happening at this moment is a result of the choices you have made in the past."[cxxvii]

Swiss-born psychiatrist Elisabeth Kübler-Ross, an expert on understanding death and bereavement (her 1969 book *On Death and Dying* is a classic), provides a similar perspective looking at the end of life, "I believe that we are solely responsible for our choices, and we have to accept the consequences of every deed, word, and thought throughout our lifetime."[cxxviii]

Karma is a complex topic, but here are some general points. First, we incur negative and positive karma from our actions and thoughts. We often think of karma as just a law of retribution but it is balanced and fair. So much of the focus is on negative karma that we may forget there is good karma. Unexpected and apparently unexplainable good life events probably have a karmic connection. Second, the determination of positive and negative karma or consequences depends on whether our thoughts and actions are in accordance with basic laws of the universe.

As mentioned earlier, all the world's great teachers taught these laws in various forms, like Christianity's Ten Commandments and Buddhism's three unwholesome actions and thoughts, which are greed or lust, hatred and resentment, delusion that creates confusion in the mind. Third, we experience karmic effects at different times ranging from immediately to later lifetimes. For example, we wonder at why bad things happen to apparently good people. The answer in many cases is that a bad event is part of paying a karmic debt incurred earlier. Fourth, karma plays an important evolutionary role in helping us to learn to differentiate between good and bad actions and increasingly live a life in accordance with our essence as defined by universal laws. Fifth, we incur karma based on both our thoughts and actions. For example, what looks like a kind and helpful action might be motivated by thoughts of manipulation with the intent to swindle. Despite the appearance of the action, the karma in this instance would be negative. Our degree of knowing and intent determines the severity of karma. For example, accidentally killing an animal has less severe consequences than premeditated killing.

It is difficult to moderate previously incurred negative karma, but the choices we make every moment going forward in life determine most of our future karma. We have the choice to have thoughts and take actions that create positive karma. Determining the thoughts and actions creating good karma is not difficult. Religious, spiritual, and wisdom teachings are a wonderful source. Also, as we consider thoughts and actions we can get in touch with our inner feelings which are a good barometer of what is right and wrong. When we feel positive, uplifted, and loving, we can be sure the thoughts and actions have positive karmic consequences.

For those readers who started reading this as skeptics, nothing I have said may have made you a believer. That is as it should be. You need to base any acceptance on inner knowing. You develop this through both meditation and study of wisdom traditions.

Belief Five

We are happiest when we give to and serve others while acting compassionately to relieve their suffering. Giving triggers receiving. Serving others is the best way to grow personally.

Compassionate giving and service connect us with our essence,
which enables us to serve others better.

The only way you can know the truth of this belief is to live it. I awakened to the truth of this belief when I served as a Red Cross volunteer. While a leader in our local chapter, our community experienced a one hundred year flood that quickly became a major disaster by national standards. I experienced giving of my time, energy and emotions to the desperate needs of people who lost their homes. I also experienced the outpouring of giving from the community and much of this giving focused on donations to the Red Cross chapter. While managing the giving was a logistical challenge, we easily overcame the challenge with a strong sense of compassion that energized our efforts. This several week experience deeply touched me. From that point forward, I increasingly dedicated my life to serving others. My desire to serve and help relieve the suffering of others by outlining a comprehensive path to happiness is the primary motivation for this book.

To make the case for giving and service, I am sharing with you the words of people far more understanding than I am about the value of giving and service to others. I do this in the hope that their inspired views touch you with the deep truth of this belief.

His Holiness the Dalai Lama

If you want others to be happy, practice compassion. If you want to be happy, practice compassion.[cxxix]

Albert Schweitzer: 1875-1965, German-born theologian, philosopher, musicologist, medical missionary, and Nobel laureate

I don't know what your destiny will be, but one thing I know; the only ones among you who will be happy are those who have sought and found how to serve.[cxxx]

Bible

As you give, so shall you receive.[cxxxi]

Deepak Chopra

The universe operates through a dynamic exchange…giving and receiving are different aspects of the flow of energy in the universe.

And in our willingness to give that which we seek, we keep the abundance of the universe circulating in our lives. (The Law of Giving from *The Seven Spiritual Laws of Success*.)[cxxxii]

Zig Zigler, Master salesman and motivator

You can get everything in life you want if you will just help enough people get what they want.[cxxxiii]

Discover how much happier you are when giving instead of hoarding, helping instead of demanding help for yourself, and sharing instead of greedily accumulating all you can for yourself.

Belief Six

We are what we think. Our beliefs define our ordinary reality. Change our beliefs, and we change our reality. Greater happiness is a belief change away.

As we saw earlier, we choose responses to every stimulus received via our five senses. Our beliefs define our choices. Our choices define our perception of reality. Buddha said it succinctly, "The mind is everything; what you think, you become."[cxxxiv] Making the same point another way, Buddha said, "All that we are is a result of what we have thought."[cxxxv]

The power of the mind plays a direct role in determining how happy we are. In the third chapter, we saw how optimistic beliefs and expressing gratitude positively influence how happy we are. I have also pointed out recent brain research concluding the brain is capable of significant change. Net, we are capable of changing our beliefs, which changes our choices and the consequences we experience. Ideally, if we change our beliefs, we develop new ones known to be conducive to greater happiness.

This all sounds easy, but it is not. For the most part, we do not know how to change beliefs and any previous experience probably produced modest, short-term success. We do not know because very few people teach both happiness supporting beliefs and how to transform existing beliefs with these new ones. I have dedicated this book to being a resource to help you achieve this happy transformation.

The benefits of knowing we can change our beliefs open up another powerful possibility. When we realize that it may only be our beliefs that hold us back from our dreams, we understand the wisdom of Henry Ford's (inventor of the Model T and founder of the Ford Motor Company) statement that "Whether you think you can or not, you are right."[cxxxvi] Knowing we do not have to be prisoners of our doubts and that we can transform doubts into hopes and dreams eventually enables us to believe that we can be virtually anything we believe we can be. Getting to this point requires opening our mind to new possibilities. Dick Sutphen, poet and metaphysical teacher notes, "Minds are like parachutes, they only function when they are open." [cxxxvii] The biggest barrier to greater openness is overcoming decades of beliefs that consistently produce unhappy consequences. Getting unstuck from such fixed, strongly held beliefs requires an open mind that can then engage in the five step growth process outlined in a later chapter.

Concluding Thoughts

For me these beliefs are very supportive of greater happiness. They flow from years of practice and study. While the teachings of many wise and enlightened teachers for several thousand years are basis for the beliefs, there is a deep personal inner knowing of their truth. This inner knowing provides hope, inspiration, and ultimately increasing levels of happiness.

Knowing that there is Guiding Hand over all that is provides comfort and direction. Instead of a chaotic, random chance world, there is a plan. Love guides that plan. Love is the defining energy of our world. When we live a life infused with love, we are our happiest. Our experience confirms this understanding. What a thrill to know that love is the defining energy and that our essence is a being of love.

Part of the plan is constant change. By being an active, aware participant in the on-going change, we increase our chances for happiness, especially when universal laws guide our moment-to-moment choices. When these laws guide our choices, we create positive consequences or karma and have our greatest influence over our future happiness. We also know that giving and serving others leads to greater happiness for others and us. Love, giving, and serving others are powerful antidotes to whatever negative energy inflicts us.

Lastly, since our beliefs define our reality and we have great influence over which beliefs we embrace, there is this final element of hope that there is a path towards greater happiness and we know the direction and processes for moving ever forward. For me this is exciting and inspiring. We are not stuck. We can change. We know what kinds of change produce greater happiness. We also know the change process we need to engage to accelerate progress along the path.

All we need is a few more understandings and tools and we are fully equipped for a life long journey of increasing happiness. The next chapters provide these.

Chapter Thirteen

Seven Secondary Greater Happiness Practices

In addition to the primary practices of meditation, love and compassion, and self-awareness (mindfulness), seven secondary practices can make significant day-to-day contributions to greater happiness. While they are secondary, their power and ability to help us should not be underestimated. Used individually or in groups, they can make direct and measurable improvements in our level of happiness, both short-term and longer-term. This chapter discusses five of the seven practices. The next two chapters address the remaining practices. As an overview the seven practices are:

1. Releasing negative emotions and thoughts

2. Forgiveness and gratitude

3. Passionate and meaningful activity

4. Spiritual and religious practice

5. Becoming more positive and optimistic

6. Emotional intelligence

7. Personal growth objectives and plans

Practice #1: Releasing negative emotions and thoughts

There are three proven methods for quickly and effectively releasing negative thoughts and emotions. While these methods provide immediate short-term benefit, they also play an important role in the longer-term effort of becoming ultimately happy. Of the three proven methods, applying an antidote comes from the Eastern wisdom traditions while the Sedona Method and visualization have a more Western origin.

Antidotes

Applying an antidote to negative, unhappy emotions and thoughts is a highly effective and proven method of becoming happier. When we become skilled at this practice, it produces almost instantly happier feelings. The practice is simply stated. When we feel negative and unhappy, we shift our focus from these feelings to the appropriate positive and happy antidote. For example, patience and tolerance act as specific antidotes to anger and hatred. When through self-awareness, we become aware that we feel anger, we consciously refocus on feelings of patience. Initially, this is a very challenging practice since we are unaccustomed to and unskilled at this practice.

Developing the ability to apply consistently an antidote to unhappy thoughts and feelings typically goes through four stages (anger is my example):

1. Impossible: We think it is impossible to interrupt an angry moment. We remember angry moments and the momentum and intensity of those moments. These memories are a formidable barrier to exercising patience. If our level of commitment to applying the patience antidote to an angry situation is not at the "I will" level then we stall at this stage. Becoming skilled at applying the right antidote in a variety of unhappy situations takes time, practice, courage, and persistence.

2. Could Have: By reflecting on a previous angry moment, we see how we could have been more patient. Maybe we can see ourselves pausing and taking a few deep breaths. For the first time we get a glimpse of a possibility.

3. Tried and Learned: We apply the patience antidote in an actual situation with mixed results. Maybe we

pause a little, but then the anger resumes. We see how pausing and patience would have helped. We see how we could be more effective. We commit to a better effort next time.

4. Getting Good: We develop diverse antidote application skills. We proactively anticipate possible angry situations and mentally prepare to be patient. We get better at visualizing being patient and our self-awareness helps us detect anger's early warning signs. We constantly learn and explore additional skill development.

Eastern wisdom traditions know about the effectiveness of applying antidotes to unhappy conditions. From a Buddhist perspective, the Dalai Lama observes:

> …we…claim that our negative emotions can be rooted out and eliminated. This premise is based on the fact that our positive states of mind can act as antidotes to our negative tendencies and delusory states of mind. So, the second premise is that as you enhance the capacity of these antidotal factors, the greater their force, the more you will be able to reduce the force of the mental and emotional afflictions, the more you will be able to reduce the influence and effects of these things.[cxxxviii]

Of note, Yogananda's lessons, which in part reflect Hindu and Christian influences, also strongly support the application of antidotes to unhappy conditions. I find particularly helpful his advice to look for beauty or something or someone to love when we feel unhappy. Buddhist texts identify 84,000 negative thoughts and emotions and their corresponding antidotes. This reflects the depth of their study and understanding of negative thoughts, emotions, and antidotes, an understanding that surpasses anything in the West.

Applying antidotes to unhappy conditions has short and long-term benefits. Short term, we can shift quickly from feeling unhappy to feeling happy. The happy condition may last for a few moments or maybe an hour or so. Then another event occurs and we feel unhappy again. We can apply an antidote to feel happy again. The benefit of this approach is shortening periods of unhappiness and increasing periods of happiness.

Longer term, each time we apply antidotes in response to habitual unhappy feelings, we contribute to the reduction and eventual replacement of the unhappy habitual reaction. As noted earlier, a well-developed neural network or "wiring" in the brain supports habitual reactions. When we apply an antidote to an unhappy condition, we starve the unhappy neural network of energy and nourish the development of a new neural network in the brain. Since weakening well developed neural networks and building new neural networks takes time, we need to be persistent and consistent in applying an antidote to an unhappy condition. Applying antidotes to unhappy conditions is a very effective method of gradually converting unhappy feelings into happy feelings. Yogananda is very clear on the power of good and bad habits.

> Good habits are your best helpers; preserve their force by stimulating them with good actions. Bad habits are your worst enemies; against your will they make you do the things that hurt you most. They are detrimental to your physical, social, mental, moral, and spiritual happiness. Starve bad habits by refusing to give them any further food of bad actions.[cxxxix]...to form a new and good habit, just concentrate in the opposite direction.[cxl]

While progressing along the paths of meditation, love and compassion, self-awareness, and secondary practices like antidotes, we eventually reach a point of dispelling the blinding ignorance about the essence of who we really are.

The Dalai Lama notes this ignorance is resolved by applying the ultimate antidote:

> Applying antidotes such as love and compassion can significantly reduce the degree or influence of the mental and emotional attachments, but since they seek to eliminate certain specific or individual afflictive emotions, in some sense they can be seen as only partial measures. These afflictive emotions, such as attachment and hatred, are ultimately rooted in ignorance—misconception of the true nature of reality. Therefore, there seems to be a consensus among all Buddhist traditions that to fully overcome all of these negative tendencies, one must apply the antidote to ignorance—the "Wisdom factor."...The "Wisdom factor" involves generating insight into the true nature of reality.[cxli]

We gradually access this "true nature of reality" through meditation and self-awareness. Both of these fundamental practices contribute to a calmer mind from which these crucial insights emerge.

Western science is beginning to discover what eastern wisdom traditions have known for thousands of years. Dr. Howard Cutler observes:

> Interestingly, the consensus among modern anger researchers such as Dr. Zillman and Dr. Williams is that methods similar to the Dalai Lama's appeared the most effective. Since general stress lowers the

threshold for what may trigger anger, the first step is a preventative: cultivating an inner contentment and a calmer state of mind, as recommended by the Dalai Lama, can definitely help. And when anger does occur, research shows that actively challenging, logically analyzing, and reappraising the thoughts that triggered the anger can help dissipate it.[cxlii]

While Western science does not fully appreciate the power of applying antidotes to unhappy conditions, it is getting closer to appreciating what the Eastern wisdom traditions have known for over 2,000 years.

Sedona Method

An alternative to using an antidote to free ourselves from negative feelings and thoughts is the Sedona Method. Lester Levenson developed this process for releasing negative thoughts and emotions and today Hale Dwoskin continues the work. The Sedona Method includes techniques for releasing unwanted negative thoughts and emotions.

The Sedona method can be learned in a few minutes and be highly effective for a lifetime. The Sedona Method does not require changing any beliefs or believing in something new. After releasing negative thoughts and emotions people often feel a sense of lightness and relaxation. Typically, this sense deepens over time as we become more skilled.

Their most popular method requires four simple steps.

1. Sit quietly and focus on an issue in your life. Allow yourself to feel whatever you are feeling in this moment.

2. Ask yourself one of the following three questions, "Could I let go of this feeling?", "Could I allow this feeling to be here?", "Could I welcome this feeling?" Answer the question honestly. A "yes" or "no" are equally OK. Proceed to the next step regardless of your answer.

3. Ask yourself "Would I?" By asking this question, you are seeking to determine your willingness. If your answer is "no", then ask yourself "Would I rather have this feeling, or would I rather be free?" Even if your answer is still negative, go on to the next step.

4. Ask yourself "When?" You may be surprised to find yourself easily letting go.

5. You can repeat these four steps as frequently as you need to do to feel free of the feeling. In the beginning

and with deeply entrenched negative thoughts and
feelings, it may require a few repetitions. In most
cases, there is a noticeable lighter and freer feeling
after completing the first four steps.

When I first started using the Sedona Method, I found
immediate benefits. The transformation from a negative
and heavy feeling to a light and peaceful one was almost
miraculous. Increasingly, I found myself using the Sedona
Method in a variety of situations, including driving, where I
wanted to release a negative thought and emotion.

If you are interested in gaining freedom from negative
thoughts and emotions, please learn more about the
Sedona Method either by reading the book with the same
name or visiting their web site at www.sedona.com.

Visualization.

Visualizing a desired outcome is a proven and effective
technique used by a wide range of people, including
athletes, people in healing practices, and the releasing of
negative thoughts and emotions. Athletes will often use
visualization to rehearse in their minds a successful
outcome. Probably the most familiar is the ski racer
standing at the top of the hill with his or her eyes closed

visualizing the twist, turns, and bumps on the course they are about to race down. In the healing practices, Jeanne Achterberg's breakthrough book *Imagery in Healing* demonstrated the powerful role visualization can play in the curing of serious diseases.

The power of visualization is also very effective at releasing negative thoughts and emotions. In its simplest and often most effective form, we only need to sit quietly, connect with a negative thought and emotion, and visualize releasing it. The exact form of visualization varies by person. For example, I find it very effective to see my negative thoughts and emotions floating away in a balloon. I also find it effective to visualize myself releasing negative thoughts and emotions when I breathe out.

Of the seven secondary practices outlined in this chapter, these releasing techniques provide the fastest transformation from negative thoughts and emotions to positive ones. When we use our self-awareness in combination with these techniques, we can become noticeably happier in a very short period.

Practice #2: Forgiveness and gratitude

Forgiveness is a practice to reduce or eliminate negative thoughts and emotions, and gratitude is a practice to retain and amplify positive thoughts and emotions. Both contribute to being happier and have the ability to produce an instantly happier state.

Regarding forgiveness, research suggests there are some expected benefits from having a forgiving attitude. For example, these people tend to make better friends and be better coworkers. The research also suggests there are personal benefits for the person with a forgiving attitude. They tend to be happier, healthier, live longer, have fewer incidents of clinical depression, and experience more success in life.[cxliii]

On the other hand, people were not very forgiving experience several negative life aspects. Everett Worthington, a professor of psychology at Virginia Commonwealth University and a pioneer in forgiveness research, found these people experienced more stress related disorders, lower immune system function, and higher rates of divorce.[cxliv]

The practice of forgiveness is universal to all religious and spiritual traditions. Through forgiveness, we loosen the grip of negative thoughts and emotions. As with antidotes, it is easiest when we can quickly forgive perceived transgressions and injustices against us. Dr. Seligman notes that people who are good at forgiving also are happier people.

There are various methods of forgiving and factors to consider when we forgive others. First, we can forgive quickly, with no need for thinking or reasoning as to why we are forgiving. This type of forgiving tends to be used by people who are experienced with forgiving and have concluded earlier that it is always the appropriate remedy to negative feelings like revenge and anger. Typically, they have learned from experience that harboring grudges and urges to gain revenge only makes them unhappy, especially when they act on these thoughts and feelings.

Second, many people require reasoning and reflection before they can forgive. In this situation, they would like to forgive but first they need a reason to do so. The reasoning can include questioning if they have their facts correct and empathizing with the other person or group.

At the conclusion of the reasoning process they decide that further engagement, attacks, or revenge are just not worth it based on either moral principles or consideration of the happiness consequences.

Everett Worthington in his book *Forgiving and Reconciling* suggests four steps to forgiving. First, he suggests recalling the hurt of a situation. It is important that we have a clear picture and understanding of what it is we want to forgive. Second, we develop empathy for our perceived transgressor or transgressors. We want to see the event from their perspective, especially trying to understand the facts and feelings from their perspective. Third, he suggests an altruistic gift. This does not need to be a material gift, but a gift of ourselves like compassion and caring. Fourth, he suggests that we make a commitment to forgive publicly. This often requires the courage of our convictions and, as a result, when we do forgive, it is a purposeful, powerful act for us. Lastly, he suggests that we hold on to the forgiveness experience so that the good deed is not lost. It is a proven method for amplifying the positive experience of forgiving in our memory.

While I have discussed forgiveness primarily as a method of letting go of negative thoughts and emotions, it has far greater potential benefits. As mentioned earlier, forgiveness is a fundamental teaching of all the world's great religions. They make it clear that forgiveness has far-reaching life effects. Jesus articulates this clearly when he said, "For if ye forgive man their trespasses, your heavenly Father will also forgive you: But if ye forgive not men their trespasses, neither will your Father forgive your trespasses."[cxlv]

While Worthington suggests publicly forgiving, there are situations where that is not appropriate. The only benefit of forgiving that we can count on is a personal one. We hope that forgiving will benefit people when we do it publicly, but we cannot and are not responsible for their reactions. Publicly forgiving may not be appropriate when the person we forgive disputes their need for forgiveness. In their heart they may believe the person doing the forgiving is the transgressor and that any actions they took were defensive and justified. In this situation, publicly forgiving may provoke additional negativity-- arguing, anger, and accusations, for example.

In all cases privately forgiving is appropriate. It is a practice where we let go of current unhappiness and probably prevent additional unhappiness. Simply, forgiving is letting go of unhappiness for empathetic reasons or because it is the right, virtuous thing to do.

Forgiving is proactive action to resolve negative, unhappy consequences.

A different but related method is being able to say "sorry" to another person. Expressing regret for negative, harmful actions is another proactive way of resolving negative relationship issues. Often by saying "sorry", we can repair and rebuild a temporary rupture in a relationship. When the conditions are right, it can convert unhappy conditions into neutral or happy ones.

Gratitude and appreciation practice magnifies and extends positive thoughts and emotions. We can focus our gratitude and appreciation outwardly or inwardly. Since happiness is an inner experience and becoming happier requires inner work, gratitude and appreciation focused inwardly tend to be the more valuable form.

Research indicates that those people who are good at expressing gratitude receive many significant life benefits.

For example, they have better physical health and energy, experience less stress and clinical depression, and are more spiritually appreciative of the oneness of all life.[cxlvi] We can express gratitude for something as simple and basic as our breath. Breath is basic to life. Imagine being trapped underwater. We know how grateful we would feel for a gasp of fresh air. Deep appreciation and gratitude for the simple, basic parts of life that we typically take for granted can be a powerful, positive experience. Since love is such an important part of life, expressing gratitude for the ability to give and receive love is also a powerful practice. An analogy is that gratitude is like carefully tending the soil with nourishing food and water so that a plant will grow. When we express gratitude for our ability to give and receive love, we nurture both of these abilities and increase the likelihood that we will do more of both. We know that when we do express and receive love, we are happy and when we do it more often, we are happier.

We can also express gratitude outwardly to other people. For example, we can express gratitude to people who have been kind and helpful. The act of gratitude can strengthen a bond and connection with another person. Strengthening a bond with a kind and helpful environment contributes to greater happiness. While we can verbally express and share gratitude, its most powerful form may be a written expression of gratitude. This tends to deepen the experience and make it more meaningful to both the person expressing and receiving the gratitude.

Practice #3: Passionate and meaningful activity

Most of us have had the experience of performing activity where we had fun, an exceptional level of productivity, and time seemed to pass very quickly. If this was work, the experience was so positive that we would be willing to do it even if we were not paid. Researchers call this type of experience being in flow while athletes refer to it as being in the zone.

For most of us, these times are preciously few. We know we are very happy performing activity in this environment. The good news is that we know the conditions that contribute to passionate and meaningful activity. While this brief section provides a glimpse at one important aspect of this experience, you can very easily learn more about being in the zone or flow.

Signature strengths are the one aspect examined here.
Dr. Seligman uses the term "signature strengths", as we
saw earlier, to describe a set of six major universal virtues
or moral traits. After a review of 200 philosophers and
philosophies, including the Old Testament, the Talmud,
Confucius, and Benjamin Franklin, the researchers
concluded, "To our surprise, almost every single one of
these traditions flung across 3,000 years and the entire
face of years endorsed six virtues: wisdom and knowledge,
courage, love and humanity, justice, temperance, plus
spirituality and transcendence."[cxlvii] A very positive aspect
of signature strengths is that they create a win/win
outcome. We benefit from using our signature strengths
and others associated with us may be inspired or uplifted
from the experience.

While there are six major signature strengths, subsets of
these six bring the total to twenty-four.

8. Wisdom and knowledge: curiosity and interest in the
   world, love of learning, judgment/critical thinking/open-
   mindedness, ingenuity/originality/practical
   intelligence/street smarts, social intelligence/personal
   intelligence/emotional intelligence, and perspective

9. Courage: valor and bravery, perseverance/industry/diligence, integrity/genuineness, honesty

10. Humanity and love: kindness/generosity, loving and allowing oneself to be loved

11. Justice citizenship/duty/teamwork/loyalty, fairness and equity, leadership

12. Temperance: self-control, prudence/discretion/caution, humility and modesty

13. Transcendence: appreciation of beauty and excellence, gratitude, hope/optimism/future mindedness, spirituality/sense of purpose/faith/religiousness, forgiveness/mercy, playfulness and humor, zest/passion/enthusiasm

You can determine your personal signature strengths by participating in a free online assessment at www.authentichappiness.org.

Armed with this information, we then seek activities, including work that enable us to use our signature strengths the majority of the time. When combined with an environment of freedom and flexibility and activities with a higher purpose (where the benefits extend beyond

ourselves), we have some of the main ingredients
necessary to create high levels of happiness from our
activities, including work. Both freedom and purpose are
necessary to unlock the full potential from using our
signature strengths. When this exists, we transform
activities from mundane and drudgery to a happy and
inspiring experience.

Practice #4: Spiritual and religious practice
Spiritual and religious practice is personal, and it connects
us with some universal principles and truths that are
bigger than ourselves. It helps loosen the grip of an
egotistical, self-serving life focus. As noted in the previous
practice, when the purpose of an activity and even our life
extends beyond just personal benefit to benefiting and
serving others, life becomes happier.
Spiritual and religious practice is as basic as studying the
works of enlightened teachers. We are fortunate that we
have writings from enlightened teachers dating back more
than 3,000 years. Many of these enlightened teachers are
associated with formal religions. Today, enlightened
teachers like Krishna, Buddha, Yogananda, and Jesus have
a massive network of places of worship, teachers, and

writings. The greatest value from associating with religions comes when we forgo limited, surface engagement and political correctness to establish a personal connection to relate to and integrate the teachings into our life.

Engaging religious teachings from an expanded universal perspective optimizes the benefits we receive. When religious teachings become exclusive and separative (my religion is better than your religion), the teachings can actually contribute to conflict and unhappiness. Great religious scholars like Huston Smith recognize the universal truths taught by all the great religious traditions. It is an unfortunate and unhappy situation when religious believers attack and criticize people who believe differently than they do. Yogananda notes:

> How necessary it is that "my way is the only way" religionists concentrate on acquiring Self-realization, that by the incontrovertible perception of God and truth the walls of divisiveness and intolerance are thrown down to accommodate the all-inclusive One Truth, which seeks a home in shrines of every faith.[cxlviii]

We do not need formal religious association to expand our spiritual awareness. Today, many people create personalized approaches to spirituality that includes studying the teachings of multiple religions supplemented with the works of great philosophers like Patanjali, Lao Tzu, and more recently Ken Wilber. I find this more expansive approach personally beneficial, and it is one of the reasons I became associated with the Yogananda's Self Realization Fellowship. This provides a framework for personal study and development.

Whether we practice a formal religion or follow a personalized path, reading inspired works is another powerful spiritual and religious practice. Yogananda suggests reading to assimilate which means reading a short passage, like one or two pages, and then thinking about its substance and relating it to our life. This increases the benefit we receive from our reading.

Whether we follow a formal or informal program, meditation is the single best practice for developing a relationship and understanding of the Supreme Being. Meditation is a universal practice used by all religions and individualized spiritual practices.

The purpose of either a formal or an informal approach is to open up access to our inner wisdom where we gradually discover and develop a relationship with the Supreme Being. This critical relationship connects us to a broader life purpose defined by universal truths, like those in chapter twelve. What typically emerges as we develop a relationship with the Supreme Being is greater love, compassion, and a desire to serve others. All of these create major, lasting increases in personal happiness. As we develop this relationship, we discover that our greatest happiness comes when we shift from self-serving activity to selfless activity dedicated to helping others. Recall that happiness and joy are different positive feelings. Happiness is the positive experiences we have when we live from an egocentric perspective. Joy is an even greater set of positive experiences that we access when we have let go of the egocentric perspective and embrace a soul-felt perspective. Reaching ultimate happiness and moving on to joy requires developing awareness that we are not just a limited physical being. We are part of something far greater. Our soul is the personal connection with this greater presence that is the Supreme Being.

Practice #5: Loving and caring relationships

In chapter twelve, we saw that love is one of the universal laws. Therefore, it is not surprising to find loving relationships contribute to significantly higher levels of happiness than relationships where love is not as present. We saw the research supporting this in chapter four. Research also indicates that people who are married experience some significant benefits. For example, they have a lower risk of dying from cancer (the risk of someone 10 years younger) and typically are better off financially.[cxlix]

When we are part of a loving marriage or relationship, there is likely to be more love present than in an unhappy marriage or an unmarried relationship. Consistent with the universal law regarding love, higher levels of love make a direct contribution to higher levels of happiness. Regardless of how happy a marriage is today, overall life becomes happier when the people improve their ability to express and receive love. There are many couples's resources that teach methods for improving both the overall relationship quality and the giving and receiving of love specifically. Since there are only a limited number of known practices that contribute to greater happiness, developing a more loving relationship is one of the best long-term investments we can make to create a happier life. Furthermore, it is difficult to imagine achieving ultimate happiness without one or more loving relationships.

Practice #6: Becoming more positive and optimistic

We do not have to be at the whim of negative emotions that storm into and out of our life on a regular basis. We have already discussed some long-term solutions (meditation) and short-term ones like antidotes.

As we develop the foundation skill of self-awareness, we have the proactive opportunity to counter negative emotions that intrude into our life. In addition to the skills already discussed, we can learn from optimists. In psychological research, people with good coping skills are optimists, while people with poor coping skills are pessimists.

When challenging and apparently negative life events occur for the pessimist, they tend to exaggerate the negative thoughts and emotions and conclude an event has a broad and far-reaching scope and meaning. This choice of reactions can derail and even reverse progress towards their goal to be ultimately happy. The perceived negative life event's effects can linger for an extended period, even contributing to a more negative, unhappy temperament.

Optimists, on the other hand, have skills to engage the apparently negative life event by disputing and questioning their initial thoughts and emotions. Optimists have skills that enable them to rebound faster than people who are neutral or pessimists. Their key skill is the ability to dispute and challenge the validity of negative emotional responses. As optimists become aware of a negative emotion, they argue with themselves over the presence and substance of the emotion. Dr. Martin Seligman in his landmark book *Learned Optimism*, provides advice on what to do when we become aware of a negative emotion:

> Give them an argument. Go on the attack. By effectively disputing the beliefs that follow adversity, you can change your customary reaction from dejection and giving up to activity and good cheer.[cl]

When we become aware of a negative emotion, we usually can determine its cause since events or thoughts trigger emotions. Since negative emotions tend to build momentum, it is important to put this movement on pause before it builds such intensity that it overwhelms our ability to be self-aware and effectively intervene. Once we interrupt the momentum, it becomes important to determine if the emotional conclusion is warranted based on the facts. Emotions are very quick to judge and in their rush to judgment, they may overlook critical facts and perspectives. Their intensity also clouds our vision so we do not see objective facts and can quickly lock us into a firm, fixed assessment. When we can effectively interrupt the negative emotion, it is crucial to view it objectively. This process starts by asking questions like, "Did I overlook any facts? What are the facts? What questions can I ask to learn more?"

This process inevitably produces insights that were not initially present. These insights may enable us to derail the negative emotion at this step when we realize that all the facts warrant a different conclusion. Insights can defuse building anger, for example, and lead to a quick softening of our emotional response.

If this step does not terminate the negative emotion, then in the next step we look for alternative responses with the goal of determining a more positive emotional direction. We identify potential alternatives by learning more from others involved in an event, especially their intent behind an action or statement. Misreading another person's intent is a major cause of negative emotions, especially the strong negative emotions involving anger and hate. Since most of us are not very good mind readers (despite what many people apparently believe), asking questions to gain understanding and clarity about intent often quickly produces alternative reactions. In considering alternatives, we also want to identify what is changeable and fixed about a situation and to focus attention on non-personal causes, like facts, that can shift the mind's activity to more rational thought and less negative emotion.

Consideration of alternatives also involves a determination of the consequences of various options. In most instances, we have a history with a particular negative emotion that enables us to predict accurately the potential consequences of letting the current negative emotion continue on its habitual path. Negative emotions usually have unhappy consequences for others and ourselves. They create the classic lose/lose consequences. In considering alternatives to a current negative emotion, we will always have more than one option to consider. From the previous step, we may identify new facts that support a different emotional assessment and alternatives that flow from this assessment. Even in the absence of new facts, there always are alternatives to any negative emotion, although our commitment to the initial negative emotion makes it difficult to see them. We have already reviewed methods to release negative emotions that we want to consider for every negative emotion. While a releasing method is an alternative in every situation, we may identify other alternatives such as a milder negative emotion (being annoyed instead of angry, for example) or neutral emotions (choosing to walk away and ignore the stimulus, for example). These do not convert a negative into a positive (an antidote's effect) but they may be the best we are capable of at the moment and they may make us less unhappy than the initial negative emotion.

As a part of our consequence assessment, we want to determine the medium and longer-term usefulness of the current emotional response. Negative emotions tend to have a strong perceived initial usefulness, but questionable medium and long-term usefulness. Determining usefulness often focuses on moving forward in a way that has a longer-term utility, not just the immediate ego-satisfying outburst, for example.

Here is an example to illustrate briefly these steps. Imagine a situation where you are driving home after a long, hard day at work and someone cuts dangerously in front of your car triggering in you the immediate negative emotion of rage. You are self-aware so you know you feel rage. When you have experienced similar stimuli, rage has been the usual or habitual reaction. The negative emotion typically leads to immediate aggressive driving actions designed to retaliate and punish the offending driver.

Step One: You ask yourself why they might have cut you off. Your response may be the thought that either the offending driver is late for an appointment or there is a family emergency. These are both situations that have prompted you in the past to drive unsafely, even recklessly, as this driver is doing. This observation may trigger empathy, which defuses your rage, or the negative emotion overpowers the observation and you charge on with your habitual reaction.

Step Two: You know where this negative emotion of rage goes when left unchecked (risky driving of your own, for example), so you seek to determine if there are any alternatives in this situation since previous unchecked reactions have left you feeling very unhappy. You may consider alternatives like letting the offending driver go and just turning the rage over internally without acting on it, which is an alternative that produces less unhappy consequences. Alternatively, you may try a deep breathing exercise to calm down and let go of the rage, visualizing releasing the rage with each out breath. When this is effective, you return to a neutral state. On the other hand, you may apply an antidote by finding a thought or object to love. It requires a strong will and focus to fix your attention on love when you are in the grasp of rage. When this is successfully accomplished, you transform a negative into a positive.

Step Three: With alternatives defined, you pause to examine the consequence of each and your willingness and ability to act on them. You also examine the usefulness of each. In almost all cases, choosing an alternative is challenging. Momentum is with the initial rage impulse and it often has considerable power. Harnessing more logical thinking and lessening the emotional consideration is necessary to throttle back the rage. The longer the time spent evaluating alternatives, the better the chances are that we choose an alternative. When you develop these skills and apply them to the myriad of negative emotions encountered daily, you create steady progress by choosing actions with happier consequences. These coping skills also facilitate the formation of new beliefs so that you permanently eliminate the rage reaction, which is a very big step forward with long-term happy consequences.

Everything I have said may sound logical and right as you sit calmly reading this, but you know that in the real world this is tough to accomplish. As tough as it is, what is at stake is your happiness, and in this instance your safety and the safety of others. If you can create any level of pause in a reaction like rage, you have a powerful window of opportunity to redirect your impulse to act.

Using these skills at the time of an actual event that triggers a negative emotion is often very difficult. If your first attempt to use these skills in a live event fails, you may be quick to discard them. Consider starting your use of these skills after an event that triggered a negative emotion and subsequent actions. For example, in the evening record in a journal the event and develop alternative scenarios using the coping skills. Examine questions you could have asked to gather more facts, alternatives, usefulness, and consequences with a strong focus on assessing the happiness consequences. Alternatively, you can discuss the event with a respected and trusted friend who effectively uses coping skills or has the ability to remain calm in provocative situations. Either approach provides the opportunity to develop new skills in a low-pressure environment. As you become skilled in this environment, you will gradually become more effective using these skills in live situations.

Typically, we do not make this level of effort unless the rewards are valuable. I suggest that in this instance the reward is greater happiness—one of the most important needs we have.

With some especially powerful negative life events, pessimists often see them as a far-reaching catastrophe. An optimist's objective evaluation of the facts and alternatives often dissipates the cloud of catastrophe that tends to envelop pessimists. Optimists are also good at evaluating the consequences of potential action paths. These crucial skills distinguish optimist from pessimists. Pessimists may view optimists as Pollyannaish and artificially positive. What they fail to see is that the optimist's disputing, challenging, and analytical skills enable them to arrive at more positive interpretations with a solid basis. Optimists do not allow negative events to paralyze their thinking skills and lock them into thinking and emotional prisons.

Concluding Thoughts

If we are unhappy and want to be happy, we have no more excuses. Between the three basic practices of meditation, love and compassion, and self-awareness (mindfulness) and these seven powerful secondary practices, anyone who wants to be happier can be happier. The basic practices primarily contribute to steady, long-term happiness increases. It is difficult to imagine achievement of ultimate happiness without some significant use of these practices.

The seven secondary practices contribute to both short and long-term happiness increases. Practices like antidotes, gratitude, and forgiveness have the ability to immediately convert an unhappy experience into a happy or neutral one. Practices like creating passionate and meaningful activity, loving and caring relationships, and becoming more positive and optimistic contribute to medium and long-term happiness increases.

It requires purpose and a plan to fully leverage the potential of both the basic and secondary practices. Later chapters address both of these.

Overall, we are so far away from the goal of ultimate happiness that we need all of the basic and secondary practices to achieve ultimate happiness. We have so limited an understanding of how positive ultimate happiness is. I hope that readers recognize how difficult the task ahead is and that they have powerful resources to aid their efforts.

Chapter Fourteen

Emotional Intelligence and Beyond

Emotions roll in and out like clouds on a windy day. We can feel sunny one moment and like a dark cloud is following us around the next moment. The New England weather saying, "If you don't like the weather, wait a minute" seems to apply to emotions. Fortunately, we have more potential control over our emotions than the weather.

In the day-to-day quest for greater happiness, nothing is more vexing than the negative emotional storms that blow into and out of our life. They appear in a flash and can firmly attach themselves to us despite our protests. While they can drop in for a short stay, they often test our patience and go from being a brief feeling to a mood that hangs around like a bad cold. When emotions settle in, they take on mood status, and we often feel trapped and bewildered about why we feel so negative.

We have known about the need and importance of controlling emotions since the early Greek philosophers. They believed that reason must conquer the emotions, moods, and temperament, which are the cause of all trouble.

While we have already learned about some long term processes to become happier (meditation is the most effective), we also need a specific understanding of emotions and the processes we can use to manage them moment to moment. Fortunately, we know much more about emotions and how to manage them effectively than we did even ten and twenty years ago. This greater understanding flows from two sources—research by Western science and increasing accessibility in the West of Eastern philosophy and wisdom traditions. We have already benefited from various releasing methods including Buddhist and Yogananda's antidote practice as immediate relief from negative, unhappy thoughts and emotions. Western science also provides assistance through such positive psychology practices as forgiving, gratitude, and meaningful work.

Before we go further, it will be helpful to define emotions. The Oxford Dictionary defines emotion as "a strong feeling, such as joy or anger"[cli] and further adds emotion is "an agitation or disturbance of mind, feeling, passion, any vehement or excited mental state."[clii] The Latin root for emotion means, "that which sets in motion," which adds a valuable dimension to our understanding, as we will see later.

In the West, we tend to differentiate between rational thoughts and feeling emotions. For example, thought's definition is "an idea or opinion produced by thinking or occurring suddenly in the mind."[cliii] Rational thoughts involve reflection, pondering, and logic while emotions involve impulses, which may be illogical. While the West typically sees rational thought and emotions as distinct from each other, they also acknowledge that they work in "tight harmony." The major emotions are anger, sadness, fear, enjoyment, love, surprise, disgust, and shame. Buddhism sees greater similarity between emotions and rational thoughts. For example, in the Tibetan language there is no word for emotion. One word describes thought and its affective (emotional) aspects. Daniel

Goleman, the author of several books on emotional

intelligence, notes:

> In the Buddhist view, thoughts are considered to be
> normally laden with the emotions, and emotions
> are invariably laden with thoughts, so the Tibetan
> term for thought includes its affective tone. The
> Tibetan system does not hold a sharp distinction
> between thought and emotion made in the West,
> but rather understands them to be intertwined--a
> view closer to the reality modern neuroscience is
> discovering in the brain.[cliv]

Goleman comments further on emotions and thoughts

from a neuroscience perspective:

> Indeed, the Dalai Lama's challenge to the less
> separation of emotion and cognition has support in
> current findings from neuroscience. The brain, it
> seems, does not make any clean distinction
> between thought and emotion, as every region in
> the brain that has been found to play some role in
> emotion has also been connected with aspects of
> cognition. The circuitry for emotion and for
> cognition are intertwined--just as Buddhism posits
> that these two elements are inseparable.[clv]

For the purposes of this chapter, I address emotions and

thoughts from this broader view.

Emotional Intelligence (EI)

Daniel Goleman published his landmark book *Emotional Intelligence* about ten years ago. Today, there is an entire industry of teachers, seminars, and books focused on these insights. The primary focus of EI has been in the workplace where it has become the leading interpersonal development program. As such, the focus is on how organizations and individuals in the organizations can become more successful. There has not been a major focus on the EI teachings helping people to become happier. Dr. Seligman in *Authentic Happiness* provides minor mention, but it does not receive the major attention I believe it deserves.

Being emotionally intelligent can make us happier and more successful. From the perspective of success, emotional intelligence is far more predictive of success than intellectual intelligence as measured by IQ. Research indicates that IQ predicts only about 10% of success (studies indicate a predictive range of 4% to 25%). On the other hand, EI levels are the primary predictor of business success as measured by income and position.

Aside from success, emotional intelligence provides a process for effective management of negative emotions. The cost of negative emotions is high and their level is very predictive of our chances for depression, a very unhappy condition. Through the very valuable work of Daniel Goleman and others, we have proven processes and skills that enable us to effectively address negative emotions and create conditions where positive emotions can thrive.

Emotional Intelligence Overview

There is considerable reason to believe that emotional intelligence may be the most valuable contribution by Western science to the goal of becoming happier. As a stand-alone practice, it cannot lead us to ultimate happiness, which requires at least the two basic practices of meditation and self-awareness (importantly, self awareness is the most critical EI competency). As a secondary practice, along with the releasing methods it may be one of the most effective fields of study and practice capable of building and sustaining higher levels of happiness.

EI has personal and group skills that contribute to greater happiness. My primary source for this summary is Goleman's work published in *Emotional Intelligence* and *Emotional Intelligence at Work*. I recommend you read both if you want to expand your EI.

Self-Awareness

The core critical skill of EI is self-awareness. Goleman notes, "In the emotional intelligence model, self awareness--including the ability to monitor our emotions-- represents the fundamentals skill needed to be intelligent about our emotional life. Ideally, this would include detecting destructive emotions while they were beginning to build--as the Dalai Lama said meditative practice allowed--rather than only after they have captured our minds,...If we can become aware of destructive emotions as they are first starting, we have maximal choice about how we will respond to them." [clvi]

As a personal skill, it includes awareness of our emotions, strengths and weaknesses, and self-confidence. Of these, being aware of specific emotions, why we are feeling them, and how they influence our life are all essential to emotional well-being.

When we are emotionally intelligent, we recognize a specific emotion, its probable cause, and effects. Instead of general emotional awareness ("I feel unsettled."), we are aware of a very specific emotion ("I feel very angry."). We also link an emotion to a specific cause. For example, we recognize the emotion is a reaction directly linked to something just said to us. But being emotionally aware goes beyond just these factual perceptions. It also includes the ability to see an emotional state's current and future effects, including the happiness consequences. When we have this emotional awareness and an understanding of emotional management tools like antidotes, we can interrupt a negative emotion's momentum and regain our balance and perspective. This is an exceptionally valuable ability in the workplace, life, and the achievement of greater happiness.

While our discussion of self-awareness has primarily focused on thoughts and emotions, self-awareness extends to an accurate self-assessment and self-confidence. An accurate self-assessment includes the ability to understand objectively our strengths and weaknesses. Typically, this is challenging to do only from a personal perspective, and as a result, there are self-assessment tools like Myers-Briggs and the significant strengths assessment to help form an accurate picture. We need to supplement these efforts by reflecting on actual events and the strengths and weaknesses we demonstrated in them. Strengths and weaknesses constantly change since many of us learn from experiences and incorporate lessons learned interpersonal growth efforts. We also benefit from the open and candid feedback from others whose opinions we trust. In the course of this process, it helps if we can have a sense of humor about ourselves.

If we have an accurate self-assessment, we can then have a reality-based self-confidence. By accurately understanding our capabilities, we can confidently undertake challenging, complex tasks. Instead of being tentative, we can be decisive. Instead of needing to be politically correct, we can have the courage of our convictions even if those convictions are unpopular and unconventional. When we couple self-confidence with an environment where we can use our signature strengths, we can readily see how this environment contributes to greater happiness.

We also use self-awareness to self regulate ourselves, especially managing negative emotions. The most valuable aspect of self-regulation may be impulse control. At the moment of emotional impulse, we need to intercept and derail an emotion's momentum before it effectively enslaves us in its feeling grasp. Some western scientists refer to this as the refractory period where it is difficult for information to enter our awareness and emotions bias our interpretation of events. Awareness is often limited to inputs that support the original emotional impulse. When we have self-control, we do not allow negative thoughts and emotions to overwhelm us and cloud our ability to take actions with happy consequences. We retain our inner calm that enables us to think clearly and stay focused under pressure, attacks, and apparent chaos. With self-control, we prevent impulsive acts motivated by negative thoughts and emotions; which almost invariably have unhappy consequences. When instead of impulsive acts we take carefully considered action, we dramatically increase the likelihood of creating happy consequences. When we have self-control, it enables us to be more trustworthy because we are less erratic, and we adapt better to complex demands and changing priorities. Self-awareness and self-regulation also contribute to greater creativity and innovation.

Change and Happiness

People who have high EI are adept at handling change. Change is a constant in our lives and how we choose to relate to change can have happy or unhappy consequences. People who find change a threat live in fear and see life as a series of threatening challenges. People who easily adapt to change can handle many demands, shifting priorities, and multiple changes. They thrive on the change process. Instead of change making them unhappy, change is a happy activity for them. Personal flexibility and openness to the views of others is a crucial quality these people have that enables them to flow with change instead of fighting and resisting change. Another EI personal talent is being highly motivated and committed to a plan and vision. EI people demonstrate a desire to achieve through learning and risk management. As we saw previously, people participating in meaningful activity that enables them to use their signature strengths also exhibit high levels of motivation and commitment to this purpose.

Interpersonal EI Skills

Beyond the personal realm, EI also includes skills to have happier interpersonal relationships. The core skill is the ability to empathize with others. This includes being sensitive to what others experience and using this to reach out and help them in either a personal or work environment. People who can empathize with others tend to focus on a person's strengths in their efforts to help others. In an organization, empathy manifests also as political awareness of formal (organizational hierarchy) and informal (social networks) organizational power relationships.

People who are sensitive to and understand others are also great listeners. They subscribe to Stephen Covey's advice to "seek first understand, then to be understood." Good listeners gather facts and calmly assess them before making their own contributions. Their communication is straightforward and seeks mutual understanding. They share openly and bad news does not threaten them. They see failure or bad news as an opportunity to learn and do better. Because they speak with understanding, interpersonal relationships tend to be happier and more productive.

The last EI skill is effectiveness in social situations. We see this in effective communication used to influence results, the ability to resolve conflicts, and leadership that inspires others to achieve goals, especially where change is involved. People with effective social skills use cooperation and collaboration to connect with others to form lasting bonds. In business, these are particularly important team building skills.

While I have focused on separate EI competencies, they also interact with each other. For example, self-awareness can increase our empathy. As we become more aware of our own emotions, we become better at reading the emotional experiences of others. Reading the emotions of others is mostly (up to 90% in some studies) done by observing and assessing non-verbal communication.

Buddhism: Beyond Emotions

Buddhism distinguishes between constructive and destructive emotions. When a destructive emotion is present, it prevents the mind from seeing reality. Destructive emotions cloud our ability to understand, and they create a gap between appearances and reality. They create distortion and the results are less freedom, well-being, and happiness.

The Dalai Lama articulates a clear distinction between constructive and destructive emotions when he says, "...when a destructive emotion arises--the calmness, the tranquility, the balance of mind are immediately disrupted. Other emotions do not destroy equilibrium or the sense of well-being as soon as they arise, but in fact enhance it -- so they would be called constructive."[clvii]

Personal experience confirms this observation. We feel unbalanced when a negative or destructive emotion is present and balanced and centered when a positive or constructive emotion is present.

Constructive emotions bring us closer to a spiritual self-realization and the ability to see reality while destructive ones block the path to self-realization. As such, emotions play a pivotal role in our spiritual life, which is the most important aspect of life. Destructive emotions make it difficult to connect with our intuition and the essence of whom we really are. This is a very powerful negative consequence.

In addition to their consequences, destructive and constructive emotions also differ by the motivation associated with them. The motivation for destructive emotions is egocentric. These emotions relate to defending or serving personal needs. On the other hand, constructive emotions are altruistic or selfless.

Two of the most powerful constructive emotions are compassion and love. Ricard Matthieu, a Buddhist monk and interpreter for the Dalai Lama, notes their differences, "The technical definition of compassion is the wish that others may the free from suffering and the causes of suffering, while love is defined as the wish that others be happy and find the causes for happiness."[clviii] Buddhism suggests our ultimate goal is to rid the mind of all emotions. The critical moment is eliminating emotions by stopping them at the moment they surge into our mind. The initial surge quickly leads to triggering a chain of thoughts and feelings that eventually take over the mind. If a negative emotion appears, we apply the antidote as quickly as possible. As a part of disciplining the mind, we also want to eliminate positive emotions. While positive emotions play a constructive role, there is great benefit to eventually eliminating them also. The Dalai Lama notes, "It might be thought that if one gets rid of all emotions, one will become as torpid and unresponsive as a log. But this is completely false. When the mind is free, it is lucid and clear. The sage who is completely at peace and free from disturbing emotions has a much greater sensitivity and concern towards others' happiness and suffering."[clix]

Buddhism points out that there are three levels of consciousness. The gross level corresponds to the functioning of the brain and its interaction with the body and the external world. The subtle level is next and it is where the mind performs introspection to examine the mind's essential nature. Our belief structure lies at this level, including all of our habitual tendencies. The third level is the very subtle where we gain access to the self-realization of our essence. When we achieve access to this level, we discover that emotions are not a part of the ultimate nature of mind, further underscoring that emotions are not an essential part of who we are. We achieve access to the higher levels of consciousness sequentially by practicing meditation and mindfulness during periods when we are not meditating.

Concluding Thoughts

When we become self-aware, we quickly understand the dominant role that thoughts and emotions play. Everything in our mind relates to emotions and thoughts that are inseparable because of their intertwined nature. If we are to discipline the mind, we need to discipline emotions and thoughts. While meditation and antidotes are highly effective, we typically also need industrial strength skills to manage effectively the constant barrage of emotions and thoughts. The skills of EI and optimists help supplement the basic skills of meditation and antidotes.

The goal is to manage negative thoughts and emotions out of our life. They are barriers to self-realization. Through self-realization, we gain access to ultimate happiness at levels so high that they are unimaginable today for most of us. Ultimate happiness brings us to the threshold of joy. As noted earlier, joy is a level of positive experience beyond happiness. With joy, we experience our soul that is the spark of the Supreme Being residing in all of us. For most of us, our soul lies shrouded in the delusion that we are this mixture of thoughts, emotions, and physical being. In reality, we are so, so much more. We gain access to this reality by gradually disciplining the mind which we accomplish through mastering and controlling our thoughts and emotions.

Chapter Fifteen

The Five Steps for Effective Personal Growth

To become happier we need to change. In earlier

chapters, we learned *what* we can do to become happier,

but unfortunately, most people are unaware of *how* to

achieve the personal growth necessary to become

happier. It takes much more than an interest in changing.

As a result, most people may try to change only to find

their efforts fail and the only tangible result is frustration.

The experience convinces many people that their brain is

"hard wired," making significant change impossible.

This is unfortunate because humans have the potential for

great growth, a degree of growth classified as

revolutionary by most standards. Western science has

recently concluded that the brain is much more plastic

and moldable than fixed. Dr. Richard Davidson of the

University of Wisconsin who conducted experiments on

meditation's brain effects concluded, "The idea that our

brains are the result of the unfolding of a fixed genetic

program is just shattered by the data on neuroplasticity."[clx] Translated this means that the brain is capable of significant changes that directly influence our life.

The challenge is how to realize this potential. Again, the barrier to realizing our potential is ignorance, in this instance it is ignorance of the process of personal growth. This ignorance persists in spite of thousands of personal growth books and seminars. Many of these books and seminars are very helpful when we use them at the right time in the personal growth process. That right time happens to be the last step of a five-step personal growth process. Regrettably, almost none of these books and seminars on personal growth details the five steps required for personal growth. When we do not follow the five steps sequentially, it greatly increases the chances for failure, which accounts for the high failure rate by people trying to change their life. For example, studies report that the vast majority of people fail to stop smoking after they try to stop and weight loss efforts often lead to regaining all or more of the weight loss. These are high profile attempts to change that are supported with large dedicated service industries. If dieting and stopping smoking have these high failure rates, then other less supported personal growth and change topics probably also experience high failure rates.

My sense is that ignorance of how to effectively change and grow causes much of this high failure rate. This chapter outlines the five steps for effective personal growth. Buddhist psychology (with almost 2,500 years of experience) describes these five steps, as do Westerners who study effective personal growth.

The steps follow a sequence that we should not skip. In fact, there are increased risks of failure if we try to skip. The five-step process also frequently stops or pauses, permanently or temporarily. In the early steps, we may have limited perception that we are engaged in a personal growth process. As we become more aware of the actual process, we can more easily gauge where we are and the required next steps for effective change. The development of self-awareness detailed in earlier chapters is critical to personal growth, especially self-awareness of what step we are at in the five-step personal growth process.

Step One: Longing

Longing starts with some level of dissatisfaction with our life. The object of this dissatisfaction varies by person. As mentioned earlier it can be dissatisfaction with our weight or our smoking habit. It can also be dissatisfaction with:

- Behavior that contributes to relationship conflict—personal and/or business, for example

- An inability to achieve desired objectives (athletic, business, and personal, for example)

- Relationship(s) and job(s)

- With global concerns—politics, government, environment, for example.

- The state of our spiritual life.

- How unhappy we are.

It is not unusual for a crisis to trigger our dissatisfaction, although dissatisfaction can also gradually grow in our awareness. When we are dissatisfied, we can strike out in two basic directions in search of a solution.

The first broad direction is to strike out at the external world. For example, we can blame others, like our boss or significant other, or innate items, like laws and policies for our dissatisfaction. Blaming something external to us for our dissatisfaction is the most common direction for our actions and, unfortunately, it seldom produces a satisfactory solution. We discover that the external world seldom acts to resolve our dissatisfaction.

The second broad focus for our dissatisfaction is to focus on our internal world. For example, we may look at the causes of our dissatisfaction. We may examine our beliefs that led to actions and consequences. In other words, we take personal responsibility for our dissatisfaction. This focus has much greater chances for eventually resolving our dissatisfaction, although resolution is seldom fast or easy.

When we are dissatisfied, we may focus our attention on either our external or internal world, but in both instances, our dissatisfaction is an internal, personal experience. Our sense of dissatisfaction ranges between a vague sense that something is not right to a very clear sense of what is not right. Vague senses often result from blocked or unresolved issues or problems. The vagueness may be a protective mechanism if the issues or problems are painful. The issues may remain unresolved until there is enough critical mass of experience to get us to stop, reflect, and address our dissatisfaction.

When dissatisfaction becomes more global and less single incident focused, it can be a signal that we are getting ready for evolution to the next personal growth step. This occurs when current beliefs do not answer all the questions we have about our dissatisfaction. At this point, we may wonder if there is a better way or better answers. It is this sense of wondering that leads to a desire for a better way that produces the longing. If the longing for change requires our external world to change, as when we blame others, the longing is likely to smolder. When we direct our longing internally, we have greater control over eventual next steps, which increases the likelihood that we effectively progress to subsequent steps in the personal growth process.

Ken Wilber, a great American philosopher, describes the power of dissatisfaction.

> The moment of...discovery begins at the moment you consciously become dissatisfied with life...For concealed within this basic unhappiness with life and existence is the embryo of a growing intelligence, a special intelligence usually buried under the immense weight of social shams. A

person who is beginning to sense the suffering of life is, at the same time, beginning to awake into deeper realities, truer realities…In a special sense, suffering is almost a time of rejoicing, for it marks the birth of creative insight.[clxi]

Whatever the object of our dissatisfaction, we want something to resolve the dissatisfaction. Longing can exist at a range of levels. On the low end, it can be a minimal curiosity level and on the high end, it can be deep hunger for something better. With longing, we want something better but have little idea about how to satisfy our longing.

In the personal growth process, longing plays the critical role of self-defining a personal need. This personal ownership and understanding have the potential power to drive more of the process. When the longing becomes strong enough, we are ready to be inspired.

My Story

The story I relate here is a long-term process of personal growth.

Before longing for change developed, I was a hard working, competitive, and somewhat Type A personality. Determining what was real was easy. Either science said it was true or it did not. In determining personal truths, I relied on a logical mind that tested thinking and facts to determine what was real.

My very gradually awakening started when I heard my wife was gong to see a psychic. After losing the debate that it was a waste of money, I invited myself along as an observer. What I experienced shocked me. The psychic related very specific details (names, dates, descriptions) about our lives that no one in the city knew or could know. Clearly, the psychic tapped into some source that I had no knowledge of and related very accurate information. Since we taped the session, I was able to replay it several times, which I needed to do to believe what I had just experienced.

For the first time, there was a crack of dissatisfaction with my understanding of life. This led to an increasing number of efforts to satisfy my curiosity. I read a series of channeling books by psychics and mediums. Many of these were fascinating. Edgar Casey, Shirley Maclaine, and people channeling the entity Michael were noteworthy. Two cities later, when I lived in the Bay Area of California, I met with additional channels with a variety of results.

By this time, I knew that there was clearly something very powerful that I did not understand. I longed for answers. I read more books and only became more intrigued by the phenomenon the authors shared about abilities and powers beyond anything I knew about or could deduce from of my traditional scientific resources.

While channeling was intriguing, two major unanswered questions prevented it from being an inspirational experience. First, while channelers had accurate perceptions and insights about the past, their predictions and suggestions about future events were spectacularly and consistently inaccurate. Second, I could not determine the source of this channeled information. Was it from God? Not likely, because God would certainly be far more accurate about the future. Was it the figment of the channel's imagination? No, because they had insights that no amount of personal research could have accurately determined. (Later in my journey, I learned the answers to both questions.) These questions and concerns did not stop me from longing to know more about parts of life that were both real (I had personally experienced the events multiple times) and a mystery at the same time. This period of longing lasted for almost five years.

Step Two: Inspiration

When the longing reaches a high enough level, we are open to possible answers and solutions that we may previously have ignored because we had no need.

Unlike longing, which comes from our internal experience, inspiration comes from our external world. Longing produces a desire for answers and our external world provides them if we are alert and open to answers coming from both expected and unexpected sources. Potential sources include but are not limited to:

- Books, especially ones we feel strongly drawn to or are suggested by others
- Seminars that we find intriguing and our curiosity is aroused
- Events where we see what others have done that relate to our longing.
- People ranging from loved ones to strangers. It can come from respected authority figures to people with unknown credentials at the time you first encounter them.

While longing we can be very focused on our self, inspiration lifts us out of self-preoccupation. Inspiration can be sudden recognition or something that we only recognize years later as the event that inspired us to move forward in a new direction. Inspiration provides a sense of potential answers to our longing. In a way, longing is the negative perspective and inspiration provides a potential positive attractive force. (In the personal growth process, longing is clearly a very positive and necessary element.)

Inspirations often have a dream like quality where we feel little need to be realistic. That comes later. The power of inspiration is its ability to introduce new possibilities. Inspirations often provide sharp and exceptionally positive contrast with our current reality. When we feel inspired, we feel a deep sense of wanting to move forward from our current realty. We sense answers to our questions and we start developing a desire to live the dream.

There can be various degrees of inspiration. On the low end, we have a momentary high from an uplifting encounter with one of the inspirational sources mentioned earlier. Its power is often limited because we discover it is not as good as we initially thought. On the other hand, inspiration can come from a powerful, life-changing event. Mark Albion in his book *Making a Living, Making a Life* presents the case studies of talented people who were inspired to change from very successful jobs (as measured by career and financial success) to jobs that they were personally passionate about. Many of them had inspiring influences that were powerful enough to drive the subsequent personal growth steps. A third option is a series of inspirational moments that accumulate power over time. It is not unusual for there to be several cycles of longing and inspiration before we are ready to move onto the next step. Of note, many people stop at this step because the longing and inspiration are not powerful enough to motivate them to move to the next step. About the time we are ready to move to the next step, we may do a realty check on our inspiration. In many cases, we need it to represent a real possibility before we are willing to move forward.

My Story

My gradually building longing led to exploration of a number of areas, which included the mind and body connection with healing and meditation. These interests drew me to a workshop at Esalen taught by someone I had never heard of and a name that was unlike any I had ever seen—Sogyal Rinpoche. I talked about my experiences with him in chapter five. I attended his meditation and healing weekend workshop for four consecutive years. Each time was an inspiring experience. I was in the presence of a human who was dramatically more happy and wise than any I had ever known or heard about. After my fourth year at his workshop, I finally started to "get" his message. The meditation practice and study I did in between workshops contributed to my ability to awaken gradually my inner knowing.

Fours years of experiencing him inspired me to bring more happiness and wisdom into my life. His example created grand possibilities that excited and motivated me. I spoke to others about him with great enthusiasm only to discover the inadequacies of words to describe such a wonderful human being. So, I internalized his example into an inspiring image of new possibilities.

Step Three: Aspiration

When the cycle of longing and inspiration builds sufficient intensity and momentum, we develop aspiration for a vision or goal. The time required to build this varies but it seldom is fast. A month and even years may be required to complete the cycles of longing and inspiration before we are ready to move onto the aspiration step.

At this point, the inspiration takes on a more concrete form. We may develop tentative plans and thoughts about how we would manifest the vision. This is the step where the grand inspirational dream goes through a reality check. We consider the challenges we face, including basics like time, money, and energy. We consider the resources needed and where we can get needed help. If it passes these checks, then we seriously consider acting on our aspirations.

With aspirations, we can see a direction for our growth and path to getting there. This is an important next step, although it is no guarantee that we will actually decide to embark on a journey along the path. The process can stop or pause at any step. This often occurs when practical barriers emerge that overwhelm the inspiration and longing of the two previous steps. Barriers frequently emerge and we develop the ways around them or they become too imposing of a hurdle to overcome. Barriers are usually unexpected surprises that can bring the aspiration crashing to earth. In other cases, overcoming a barrier can be reinvigorating experience that propels us further along the aspiration step.

As the aspiration step advances, we increasingly want to move forward and our plan becomes increasingly motivating. At the end of this step, we are very interested in moving forward but we do not begin acting on the plan. Aspiration plays a critical role in personal growth. It takes the dream of the previous step and makes it seemingly realistic and achievable. If we try to skip this step, we run a high risk of disillusionment and struggle. The effect can be to kill potentially very beneficial personal growth and, maybe more importantly, convince us that personal growth is not possible.

My Story

Following my inspiring experiences with Sogyal Rinpoche, I set out to learn how I could progress towards the inspiring possibility of being ultimately happy that he presented. I wanted to be more like him and less like I was at the time.

I began new studies into spiritual topics. There was some study of Buddhism, which was a natural result of my experience with Sogyal Rinpoche, a revered Tibetan Buddhist. I experimented with Christianity through Unity and I studied other world religions, primarily through the great works of Huston Smith.

While this study provided some help and hope, there was not the clear path forward I sought. This study did teach me a very important point—the core esoteric message of all the world's great religions and teachers (Jesus, Krishna, De Chardin Pier Teilhard, Patanjali, Lao Tzu, and others) was the same. They used different words and presented some different dimensions of key points but the essence was the same.

It was at about this time that I learned about another great teacher, Paramahansa Yogananda. I read his famous *Autobiography of a Yogi* and it impressed me immediately with his integral thinking that was a powerful blend of East (Krishna and his enlightened teachers in India) and West (Jesus). His recommended scientific spiritual understandings and practices were another powerful integration.

When I learned that the Self Realization Fellowship, which he founded, offered almost three years of weekly, step-by-step lessons written by him, I saw a path forward that I aspired to follow.

Step Four: Vow

After the thinking and planning of the aspiration step, we may be ready to commit to achieving the vision and associated goals for our personal growth. This is a big step but it can be doomed to failure if the level of commitment is not strong enough to sustain the time, effort, and resources necessary to achieve our goals. When we attempt to achieve a goal, there are at least four levels of commitment people typically have and three of them have high risks of failure.

"I could grow."

This is about the lowest level of commitment and if this is honestly our level of commitment, we are almost certain to fail unless achievement of growth is very easy and fast. This is seldom the case.

This level expresses a theoretical ability to accomplish the goal. It is one level above "I cannot grow." At this level, we feel we might possibly achieve the goal, but it is clear that our intention and commitment are low. The expression of our theoretical ability to accomplish the goal is seldom well thought out, a pro and con analysis, for example.

If we decide to act with this level of commitment, we may stop our effort at the first sign of trouble or barriers. There is little personal investment in the goal's achievement and we are seldom disappointed when we fail to achieve the goal.

"I should grow."

While this is a higher level of commitment than the previous one, it also runs a high risk of eventual failure to achieve our goals. The motivation to act usually comes from outside sources, like parents, friends, and significant others. They can put strong pressure on us to change and grow. They may feel a strong need for us to change or grow but at this level of commitment, we do not share the same level of need. Our primary motivation is to release or diminish the external pressure on us. The motivation is to act for others more than ourselves. Whenever this condition exists, we are unlikely to persist in our efforts when challenges emerge. There is often effort followed by frustration and discouragement.

It is important to recognize that the desire to grow can come from for both ourselves and others, but at this level most of the perceived benefit is for others. To increase our chances for success there needs to be much higher perceived personal benefit.

"I must grow."

This level of commitment has higher chances of success than the two previous levels but still has significant chances of failure. Again, the preponderance of motivation comes from external sources. At this level, those external sources can have greater meaning and importance in our life. In one instance, our boss insists we grow or we risk losing our job. In another case, our doctor strongly recommends lifestyle changes or we run a high risk of premature death. Both of these can be powerful motivations but since we did not create the need and we may not own it, it is less effective than the next level of commitment.

This can be a strong enough level of commitment to produce success even when there are serious challenges. In some cases, we can start at this level of commitment and through additional efforts graduate up to the next level of commitment. That seldom happens with either the "could" or "should" levels of commitment.

The Vow: "I will grow."

This level of commitment is a vow we make to ourselves. A vow has elements of swearing a solemn oath, making a promise, giving our word, and guaranteeing an outcome. Commitment does not get much higher than this for most of us.

We can make a vow even when we do not know all the steps required for success. The vision and goal are so important that we know we will expend every effort to achieve the desired outcome. When unexpected events occur, we take it on as a challenge to overcome. We have almost absolute confidence in our ability overcome virtually every challenge.

A vow creates single-minded focus and purpose. When the previous personal growth steps have been strong and when they build in intensity on each other, they frequently lead to this level of commitment. Energy and momentum build and finally crystallize into a decision to act.

Unlike the previous two levels of commitment, internal reasons propel this level forward. External forces can play a role but more of a supporting role than a lead role. This level of commitment is very heartfelt. When we take this vow, it defines major allocations of time, energy, and resources often over a long period. While chances for success are not 100%, they are very high. Typically, only learning along the way that the vision and goal are not right for us ends our pursuit of the goal.

My Story

After starting the Fellowship lessons and readings, I encountered a choice. The teachings of Yogananda and other respected teachers suggested focusing on the message of one teacher when we are ready to do so. Since I had previously determined that the core messages were the same, I was open to this.

Yogananda suggests that there comes a point for people to consider accepting a teacher as their guru for life. This was a big thought for me. Had I explored enough to know that he was the right guru for me? My answer was

a resounding "yes". His teachings and love of God clearly
demonstrated to me that he knew God. The passion and
beauty of his expressions of love for God were uplifting
and awe-inspiring. h
I then reached a point that I very easily and totally made a
vow that Yogananda was my guru for life. As he indicates,
it is important to note we can have only one guru or
supreme teacher to whom we are committed but we can
have many teachers. Taking this vow cemented my
connection to him and his teachings. Inherent in this vow
was a firm decision to become happier and use that
happiness to help others.

Step Five: Purposeful Action

This is the step where many people start their personal
growth efforts. The vast majority of personal growth
books and seminars provide resources for just this step.
Skipping the previous steps or partially completing them is
the primary cause of high personal growth failure rates.
Having completed the previous steps, we are now ready
to move beyond the limits we have created for ourselves.
In the aspiration step, we identified elements of a potential

plan of action. We then committed to the objective and plan, and in this step, we act on the plan.

It is critical at this step to trust our plan and all of the steps that brought us to acting on the plan. If we do not trust it, we will remain stuck where we are. Distrust is a powerful barrier to progress. Conversely, when we trust our plan we are create the freedom to grow.

There is an exceptional array of resources for personal growth. We need to be careful because there are many resources that do not make us happier when we realize our goals. For example, there are many personal growth resources to help us make more money. When we exclude those resources, we still have an abundance of programs to help us. Some of them are more proven and successful than others. A very few utilize what leading western and eastern thinkers know contribute to helping us become happier more consistently.

Concluding Thoughts

We can change and become happier. That is a proven fact. Failure to focus on improving the life areas that contribute to greater happiness is a major cause of today's very low levels of happiness.

There are steps we need to follow to become happier. This also is a proven fact. Failure to follow the necessary steps to become happier is a key reason why people are stuck at their current level of happiness. The feeling of being stuck can easily grow into feeling trapped.

The combination of not focusing on the life elements contributing to greater happiness and not following the proven personal growth steps explains why self reported levels of happiness are low and declining.

The good news is that we can become much happier by focusing on the life elements known to increase happiness and developing these by following proven steps. This is profoundly good news!

Chapter Sixteen

The Ultimate Happiness Fast Start Program

If you want to become happier faster, you can do so. From the earlier chapters, you already know what ultimate happiness is and the practices that can help you progress towards this destination. This chapter pulls those elements together into a fast start plan. Like with any plan, it is powerless to achieve its goal until you harness willpower and energy to it.

Regardless of your starting point today, for the vast majority of us achieving ultimate happiness is at least a lifelong endeavor. The good news is that while the destination of ultimate happiness is far out on the horizon, becoming happier than you are today is achievable starting now. It is very realistic for most people to become twice as happy as they are today. Throughout the course of this plan, you will validate your progress both subjectively (personal sense of progress) and objectively (validated assessments).

Fast Start Plan for Personal Growth Steps One-Four

We determine our starting point today by assessing where we are in the personal growth process, recalling the steps outlined in the previous chapter. If you want to be happier, it is important to understand and respect the process of personal growth and honestly and objectively evaluate you current status. The inclination for many is to dive in and start with step five, but if you are not ready for this step, you greatly increase chances for failure.

Starting Point: Longing.

If you are dissatisfied with how happy you are today, you want to be happier, and you are not yet inspired by any particular way of satisfying that need, then you probably are at the longing step. Your fast start program includes efforts to translate a subtle inner dissatisfaction into something more specific and clearer. If you do not address your longing, it can simmer for years before you give up. Sometimes we do not focus on our longings because of fear and uncertainty. The vague unknown, which is what longing can feel like, can create these two feelings that stymie efforts to understand and resolve longings.

Journal writing is an effective means to understand better your longings. Before attempting to write, it is often helpful to ask yourself the question "What am I experiencing and feeling?" Attempt to capture whatever response you feel. Do not force the process. Let answers naturally emerge. It is important to maintain the integrity of your inner sense and resist urges to fast forward to something very specific and clear, but partly artificial and incomplete. The longing process can be encouraged but not forced.

If you determine that what you are experiencing and feeling is a vague sense that you want to be, can be, or must be happier, the next step is determining a general sense of what "happier" looks like and feels like. Again, a journal can be a helpful tool for crafting a clearer picture. For example, it may be that your greater happiness picture focuses primarily on a personal relationship or your work. These are important distinctions because you can focus the method's tools on a very specific to the objective.

Beyond journal writing, it can also be helpful to discuss your longing with a trusted friend. In the beginning, the conversation may be rambling and imprecise, but it is often very helpful to hear ourselves attempt to bring a vague inner sense into a form that is more concrete. You may or may not get insights from the other person, but invariably just the attempt to verbalize your longing makes it clearer and more specific.

After multiple attempts at writing and talking about your sense of a personal need, you eventually reach a point where it crystallizes into something you can articulate. When you see it or hear it in words, your inner sense is "Yes, that is what I am looking for."

You are now ready to be inspired about potential ways to satisfy that need.

Starting Point: Inspiration

Most people think of inspiration as something that just happens and, as such, is something we have little control over. The truth is we can nurture and create opportunities for inspiration.

When we have a sense of what we want ("I want my work and home life to be happier."), we can start the process of inspiration by asking a simple question, "How do I do that?" If we repeatedly confirm our interest and desire for an answer, it triggers an openness enabling us to see answers that we might previously have ignored.

The answer or parts of an answer often come from unexpected sources. The source can be a newspaper article we would not normally read, a piece of junk mail, or an unexpected visitor. Often parts of an answer unfold in a sequence we could never predict. Once we ask the question, we need to let go of expectations about how the answer will come and what it will be.

Inspiration often builds slowly. It is not unusual for inspiration to recycle back to longing. When we revisit our longing, the result can be confirmation, change, or elimination. When there is either confirmation or change, we typically return to seeking inspiration.

At some point in the process, the inspiration crystallizes and we move forward to the next step or the longing and search for inspiration cease to be important and we stop. When inspiration crystallizes, we feel uplifted, motivated, and energized. We have a general direction and hope that our longing can be satisfied.

Starting Point: Aspiration.

As we begin the aspiration step, committing our aspiration to writing via journal writing or other comfortable means is a good place to start. It is important to gain maximum clarity about what we aspire to. This is so important that we need to rigorously write and rewrite before we get it right. Our goal is to crisply define what success looks like. Fully developing our aspirations often requires research and learning. For example, we could consult with people who are already really good at being happy. As official or unofficial mentors, they represent a wonderful opportunity to learn. We can also consult people who we trust and objective authority figures, which can be someone like a clergy member or coach trained in positive psychology. Other potential sources include consulting with people that have known us for a long time and visiting with the wisest person you know.

The purpose of this work is to further clarify *what* we want and define *how* we think we can accomplish it. After connecting with external resources, you always need to return to your own personal thoughts and insights. You know that your search for aspiration is complete when you smile inwardly with a deep sense that you have the aspiration you need. This aspiration includes a clear understanding of what you want and a confident understanding about how to achieve it.

Starting Point: Vow

Before fully committing to achieving what you aspire for, you need to deeply search inside for how committed you are to its achievement. As mentioned in the previous chapter, commitment that includes the words "could", "should", and "must" have lower chances for success than a commitment that says, "I will." It is critical that you be honest with yourself about your level of commitment or you seriously risk investing considerable effort and not succeeding. If you are not ready to vow "I will", then you need to re-examine the depth of your longing, the power of your inspiration, and the clarity of your aspirations. Doing this will either reveal opportunities to strengthen them or discover reasons for discontinuing your efforts, at least for now.

Often you can raise your level of commitment by examining how much dynamic tension exists for the achievement of your aspirations. This examination includes contrasting the consequences of doing nothing and accomplishing your aspirations. When there is a sharp, powerful contrast between the two, it creates the energy to become deeply committed or take a vow to accomplish your aspirations. When you vow that you will accomplish your goals, you do not need a specific step-by-step plan, you just need to know where you are going to start. While there can be some sense of a potential step-by-step plan, you increase our chances for success by remaining open to possibilities. You do not want to be constrained by a detailed plan that may or may not be the best path forward. It is important to understand this because some people refuse to commit unless they know exactly and precisely all the necessary details. I suggest for your consideration that this depth of planning may actually reduce your chances for success. Often when you commit to a very specific plan, you tend to reject new learnings and unexpected events, both of which may be critical to achieving your aspirations.

Starting Point: Purposeful Action

Now is the time to energize willpower and take purposeful action to become happier. As an overview, there are three basic parts of purposeful action. First, begin the benchmarking process by completing assessments that determine your starting level of happiness from different perspectives. Second, start the foundational greater happiness practices of meditation, love and compassion, and self-awareness. Third, choose the secondary practice that best fits your immediate needs.

Benchmarking Current Happiness

As you take actions to become happier than you are today, it is important to determine the effectiveness of those actions. If they are working, you want to continue them, but if they are not, you need to take new actions. There are two methods for determining progress. First, you can subjectively assess your well-being. In answering the question "How am I doing?" it is often difficult to determine progress with this method because of your feeling or a mood at the time you make the assessment and the relatively slow pace of most change. Second, you can supplement subjective evaluation with validated objective assessments. The good news is that these assessments are free and developed by leaders in the positive psychology field.

Go to www.ultimate-happiness.com and complete the free registration for the two online assessments. The first assessment evaluates the level of your skills necessary to become happier over the long-term. The second assessment enables you to evaluate ten levels of happiness to determine where you are today.

Also go to www.authentichappiness.org, complete the free registration, and then log on to your account. Complete two questionnaires—the Fordyce Emotions Questionnaire and General Happiness Questionnaire. It is very important that you complete these questionnaires honestly and carefully. As a part of your fast start program, retake these questionnaires each month. The web site retains all your records so you can track your progress.

When you combine your subjective evaluation with these objective assessments, you will have a clear idea of how well you are progressing toward your goal of becoming happier. When you take the vow to become happier, you commit yourself to long-term hard work. This evaluation process is critical to calibrating progress and making adjustments to optimize your personal progress.

Foundation Practice: Meditation

Achieving ultimate happiness, which necessitates disciplining the mind, requires a regular, deep meditation practice. While you can progress towards the goal of ultimate happiness without meditation, it will be slower and ultimately incomplete.

Chapter nine discussed various meditation methods. When you begin your meditation practice, the mantra or following the breath method is often easiest and most effective. It is important to note that you can use these same methods for a lifetime and they will be highly effective. My fast start recommendation is to start meditating with one of these two methods and then later in the first year try focusing on the spiritual eye (the point between your eyebrows). Some people find this method more effective, but this is a decision you need to make for yourself.

The Ultimate Happiness Fast Start Program provides recommendations for four three-month periods. After a week or two of following the recommended process, you may feel that you are ready to move on to the recommendation for the next three-month period. Please resist the urge to do this. Each of the practices recommended in this program are probably first-time experiences for most readers. You have embarked on a long-term journey with an exceptionally important goal— living ultimate happiness. To achieve this important but very challenging goal, you need to develop your skills carefully and deeply. Three months is the minimum time necessary to develop the recommended skills. When I first started using this program, it was not unusual for me to extend the minimum three-month recommendation for a practice to as many as eight months. You move on when it is very clear that you have developed a high level of skill, which almost never happens faster than three months.

The following outlines the recommended type of meditation, frequency per week, and number of minutes per day. While these elements are important, the most important meditation element is the intensity and duration of concentration. Stay focused on the purpose and goal of meditation--disciplining the mind to achieve a calm mind.

- Months 1-3: 10-15 minutes/day of mantra/breath meditation, 7 days/week

- Months 4-6: 15-20 minutes/day of mantra/breath meditation, 7 days/week

- Months 7-9: 20 minutes/day of mantra/breath meditation, 7 days/week plus one 45 minute meditation per week

- Months 10-12: 20 minutes/day of spiritual eye meditation, 7 days/week plus one 60-minute meditation per week. Participate in group meditation 1-4/times per month.

Complete the recommended number of minutes of meditation each day in a single session. After completing the first twelve months, you can add to your meditation practice in several ways. First, you can meditate more than once per day, typically early morning and later evening. Second, you can extend the time for each meditation session to 45-60 minutes each. Again, remember that quality of time is far more important than quantity of time. Third, you can learn more advanced meditation practices. Your major options include transcendental meditation, various Buddhist schools of meditation, and Self-Realization Fellowship lessons.

Foundation Practice: Self-Awareness

Since happiness is an inner experience requiring the discipline of our mind, self-awareness or mindfulness is the crucial practice for disciplining the mind outside of meditation. Before any disciplining can occur, you need to be aware of your mind's workings.

The self-awareness fast start program helps you shift today's predominately external focus to an increasingly internal one. Being self-aware in the moment is a challenging, advanced skill. As a result, the recommended program starts with developing retrospective self-awareness. You start by looking back at high profile, memorable events in the current day. After an intensive first three months of this effort, you gradually expand self-awareness into the present moment. The easiest present moment times are friendly, relaxed experiences. The most difficult present moment times are high-pressure, negative experiences where actual defensive mechanisms often take charge and blind our self-awareness.

The following fast start recommendation may be the most aggressive timing of all the recommended practices. As a result, be ready to extend the first three months of activity until you feel that you have a strong and deep awareness of recent past events.

- Months 1-3: evening daily journal writing—at least one page, review the day's most important event, detail your thoughts and emotions, learnings, and how you might do it differently.

- Months 4-6: continued journal writing about the day's most important event, develop live awareness each day during a known, easy, and friendly event with a focus on feelings and thoughts, and making mid-conversation adjustments to achieve a happier outcome.

- Months 7-9: continued journal writing about the day's most important events, prepare for live awareness each day during a known challenging event with a focus on feelings and thoughts and making mid conversation adjustments to achieve a happier outcome.

- Months 10-12: continued journal writing about the day's most important events, develop the ability to be aware during unexpected events--monitor, learn, and make adjustments to achieve a happier outcome.

Longer term you can extend the focus of months 10-12 for the balance of your life. Achieving self-awareness in unexpected, challenging life events is very difficult because strong thoughts and emotions want to dominate the situation. The more you create calm inner conditions, the better your self-awareness becomes. Self-awareness is critical to interrupting habitual reactions that typically have unhappy consequences. Developing and using self-awareness to create happier consequences may be the single most difficult task you have ever undertaken in your life. Be patient, persistent, and courageous.

Foundation Practices: Love and Compassion

Actively searching for opportunities to love and to demonstrate compassion are two of the most powerful proactive actions available to us to become increasingly happier. If you have not been actively meditating and attempting to become more self-aware, then investing energy in these areas may not have obvious rewards. On the other hand, if you have experience expressing and feeling love then you know how rewarding it is. While you may have less experience with compassion, most likely you can recall the satisfaction of helping someone who was struggling and needed your help.

All of these foundation practices require significant reallocation of energy in your life. You need to slow down and focus. As easy as this sounds, it can be one of the most difficult tasks you have ever undertaken.

The recommended fast start program for bringing more love into your life includes the elements first outlined in Chapter Twelve.

- Months 1-3: discover the beauty around you. Consider photographing expansive landscape scenes, sunrises or sunsets, and close-ups of natural phenomena. Minimize the physical and technical process of photography and maximize the heartfelt appreciation of beauty. With people that you already love, each week identify one person and send them a note or have a conversation telling them what you love about them.

- Months 4-6: continue your beauty quest. Make it a daily objective to express heartfelt love to another person. Be careful not to make this mechanical or routine. Also deepen the feelings of love by writing about those feelings in your personal journal.

- Months 7-9: continue both your beauty quest and daily expressions of love. Expand your expressions of love to new people. At first, you can share thoughts and feelings limited to specific actions or aspects associated with the person. For example, you love how they help another person or how they stay focused on what is really important in life.

- Months 10-12: continue both your beauty quest and daily expressions of love. Expand your circle of people who you share your feelings of love with and the frequency with which you share your feelings. Gradually expand your sharing of loving thoughts and feelings to multiple times per day.

Focusing on one special loving and caring relationship can also provide significantly greater happiness. Fortunately, there are many resources to help you create more loving and caring relationships in your life. It is important that you identify a resource that you are comfortable with and in couples work that both of you are comfortable with. The focus of the fast start recommendations is more on the process than the tools that you utilize. It is important to establish specific objectives, and you need the ability to track progress even if the best method is entirely subjective. Setting objectives needs to be a collaborative process that you give the careful attention it deserves. Once you achieve the initial objectives, it is often appropriate to set new objectives. Most people will be amazed at how loving and caring relationships can really be and this is true for people who already believe they have a good relationship.

- Months 1-3: Discussion and agreement to objectives, identify resources—therapy, couple's groups, books, friends, clergy; begin your work, measure progress, celebrate success.
- Months 4-6: Continued assistance, evaluating and revising objectives with an emphasis on daily practices, measure progress, celebrate success.
- Months 7-9: Continued assistance as needed, evaluating and revising objectives with an emphasis

on daily practices; extend focus to another close relationship (son/daughter, sibling, parents, etc) and establish objectives and the resources needed to accomplish them, measure progress, celebrate success.

- Months 10-12: Continued assistance as needed, evaluating and revising objectives with an emphasis on daily practices; continue focus to another close relationship (son/daughter, sibling, parents, etc) and establish objectives, the resources needed to accomplish them, measure progress, and celebrate success.

Some of the secondary practices can be very helpful in creating more loving and caring relationships. The obvious ones are forgiveness and gratitude, which can play a strong role in strengthening relationships. From a personal standpoint, applying antidotes to habitual negative thoughts and emotions often prevents relationship damage. For people who either have been in a relationship for a long time or have fixed views on relationship potential, one of the major changes that needs to occur is expanding understanding about how positive, loving, and caring a relationship can be. Typically, this understanding does not develop without proof, and the strongest proof is firsthand learning from people who are in a loving and caring relationship.

The fast start recommendations for expressing compassion involve increasing involvement in organizations dedicated to helping the needy. Each of us will have a point of connection with people with particular needs, like the homeless, disabled, hungry, culturally challenged, and disaster victims. This list can obviously be much longer. Consider using your expanding self-awareness to determine your strongest personal connection with a particular type of need. If nothing clearly emerges from this effort, consider volunteering with two or three organizations over the course of the first year to determine a personal best fit.

In both your personal and career life consider frequently asking others, "How can I help you today?" This will open up unexpected opportunities to provide help by sharing kindness with another person. Remember that compassion is action we take to relieve the suffering or struggling of others. Even without making an explicit offer to help, we can often help people just by performing unexpected acts of kindness. Consider making this a daily objective.

Secondary Practice Overview

In addition to the foundation practices of meditation, self-awareness, love, and compassion, I recommend that you choose only one secondary practice to begin your fast start program. Meditation, self-awareness and love and compassion are major new activities in your life. Your top priority to become happier is establishing these practices as new regular life routines. Achieving this requires considerable time and energy.

Choose the *one* secondary practice that is most appealing to you and fits a clear perceived personal need. For example, if repairing injured relationships would create immediate happiness improvements for you, then consider the gratitude and forgiveness practices. If your greatest source of unhappiness is your work, then consider the passionate and meaningful activity practices.

There is an alternative for those who are not quite sure if they want to dedicate themselves to the serious work of meditation, self-awareness and love and compassion. You can experiment with one or two of the secondary practices to determine if you want to become more deeply committed.

When you undertake the three foundation practices plus one secondary practice, it is unlikely you will complete the progress you want to make in all four areas within the first year. Please remember throughout this process that depth of skill building and understanding are far, far more important than speeding through the various practices. Frankly, you could focus only on the three foundation practices for the next five years and make major progress toward your goal of living ultimate happiness. Achieving ultimate happiness requires high-level skill and proficiency in the foundation skills and the appropriate secondary practices.

Secondary Practice: Releasing Negative Thoughts and Emotions

Using any of the three methods for releasing negative thoughts and emotions requires a moderate to high level of self-awareness. As such, it probably is not an initial secondary practice for most people, unless there is already a substantial level of self-awareness present. The following is the suggested fast start program for using antidotes to release negative thoughts and emotions. The basic process is the same for the other two methods--the Sedona Method and visualization.

Applying an antidote requires five steps. First, you need awareness of the specific negative thoughts and emotions. Second, you need to interrupt their momentum and put them on pause. Third, identify an appropriate positive thought and emotion as an antidote. In the beginning, some powerful all-purpose antidotes are love, beauty, empathy, and compassion. Fourth, shift your total focus onto your antidote. For example, look for beauty somewhere around you. It can be as simple as a flower, picture, or the sunlight. Fifth, maintain your focus until the negative thoughts and emotions are no longer present. If you find yourself slipping back to the negative thoughts and emotions, focus on your positive antidote and keep applying it until there is no reoccurrence of the negative thoughts and emotions. This is analogous to taking medicine until the illness is gone.

The following is the recommended fast start antidote program that slowly and solidly builds your ability to apply an antidote. The program starts with applying an antidote in private, reflective moments where you are aware of a lingering negative thought and emotion. It gradually builds your abilities to eventually applying them first in friendly interpersonal situations and then more challenging and even adversarial ones.

- Months 1-3: apply an antidote in a private moment once/day, consider a journal entry about your experience.

- Months 4-6: apply an antidote in private moments several times/day; consider a journal entry about each experience.

- Months 7-9: apply an antidote in low-moderate degree of difficulty interpersonal situations 1-2/day; consider a journal entry about each experience.

- Months 10-12: apply an antidote in low-moderate degree of difficulty interpersonal situations 1-2/day, apply an antidote in very difficulty interpersonal situations 1-2/day, and consider a journal entry about each experience.

Longer term, you can use your developing self-awareness to apply antidotes earlier in the development of negative thoughts and feelings. The earlier you can apply an antidote, the easier it becomes and the faster you experience its effectiveness.

Secondary Practice: Gratitude and Forgiveness

Expressing gratitude and forgiveness do not require the degree of self-awareness required for applying antidotes. It is important to remember that both practices are a means (to becoming happier), not an end in themselves. Becoming very good at both practices results in constantly reinforcing happy events and letting go of the grasp of unhappy events in your life. As you will discover, at its best the expression of gratitude and forgiveness is heartfelt. Typically, this requires delving deeply into the experience that is the target of your gratitude or forgiveness. Unlike most forgiveness opportunities, many expressions of gratitude can be for others' relatively small kind acts or your positive inner experiences.

The fast start program for gratitude and forgiveness quickly makes both a part of life. As you become happier, you discover there are fewer opportunities for forgiveness and more opportunities for gratitude. The recommended program starts with gratitude only because the benefits are greater and quicker by reinforcing positive, happy life events. The program recommends beginning forgiveness after the first six months, but if there are significant opportunities to benefit from forgiveness, feel free to start earlier.

- Months 1-3: make a gratitude journal entry every 3-5 days, at least one-page per entry and openly and personally share your gratitude with another person at least once a week.

- Months 4-6: make a gratitude journal entry every 1-3 days, at least one-page per entry, a gratitude letter once/month, and openly and personally share your gratitude with another person at least twice a week.

- Months 7-9: make a gratitude journal entry every 1-3 days, at least one-page per entry, deliver a gratitude letter once/month, openly and personally share your gratitude with another person at least twice a week, and a forgiveness journal entry 1-3/month

- Months 10-12: make a daily gratitude journal entry (at least one-page per entry) coupled with doing unexpected acts of kindness once/day, deliver a gratitude letter once/month, openly and personally share your gratitude with another person at least twice a week, forgiveness 2-4/month.

At the end of your first year with this program, gratitude and forgiveness will make strong contributions to your personal happiness and the happiness of others. Gratitude and forgiveness can make strong contributions to developing loving and caring relationships. When you share your gratitude and express your forgiveness to others, it strengthens the bonds with them and can convert acquaintances into close friends.

Secondary Practice: Passionate and Meaningful Activity

While the primary focus of this practice is work, it is not limited to work. While the ideal might be having a life filled with passionate and meaningful activities, you may build to that goal. For example, you may want to start by filling your community contributor life role with passionate and meaningful activities. For example, this might lead you to volunteering at your local Red Cross chapter and become a member of their disaster services team. After satisfying this need for passionate and meaningful activities, you may move on to develop these activities in other roles like your role as a husband/wife, family member, recreational activities, and work.

The definition of passionate and meaningful activities differs for all of us. As a first step, it is important to understand clearly our needs. You do this best with a combination of objective and subjective evaluations. Objective evaluations range from ones that help us in all of our life roles, like the Signature Strengths and Myers-Briggs assessments, to ones that focus on only one life role, like work where the Strong Interest Inventory (http://www.cpp.com/products/strong/index.asp) is helpful in determining the best career fit for us. Other resources include some good books including *I Could Do Anything If I Only Knew What It Was* and *Making a Living, Making a Life.* Lastly, many talented life and career coaches regularly help people discover the best career fit for people and then help them to make the dream a reality. A good resource is the International Coach Federation web site where you can search for a coach that meets your specific needs. Quality subjective evaluations include identifying your past dreams and actual experiences with and about meaningful and passionate activities. Sometimes your childhood dreams, hobbies, and one specific project at work provide quality clues about the activities that you have been most passionate about in the past and found to be most meaningful for you.

The ultimate happiness fast start recommendations focus on doing the quality assessment work up front followed by real world exploration and learning. Activities that sound positive on paper may be in reality very disappointing.

- Months 1-3: complete the appropriate assessments, explore real world possibilities, and begin one new activity that enables you to utilize your signature strengths

- Months 4-6: develop a long-term vision, learn about specifics of your vision by studying people and activities that already are closest to your vision, establish a network of people and resources capable of helping you achieve your vision.

- Months 7-9: begin efforts to become a part of passionate and meaningful activities by, for example, applying for specific jobs or community roles, consider hiring a life or career coach.

- Months 10-12: begin actual experience with passionate and meaningful activities, continue to learn and create opportunities for even greater fulfillment of your vision.

At the end of this first year, you will be living some important aspects of your vision of passionate and meaningful activities. In software terms, please understand that this is version 1. As you continue to learn about yourself and opportunities, you may discover several subsequent versions. View this as a dynamic learning, experiential process and never lose sight of that exciting inner sense that defines your dream.

Version 1 may be a hobby or part-time activity that can gradually grow into full-time activity. Many successful entrepreneurs started this way. This is one process that you want to "make haste slowly." If you set the expectation that this should happen easily and quickly, you may be frustrated and give up. If today's reality is not close to your dream of meaningful and passionate activities, manifesting your vision will require a combination of intelligent diligence and inspired courage.

Secondary Practice: Spiritual and Religious Practice

I am not recommending any one religious practice over another in this program. As mentioned earlier, the core esoteric teachings of all the world's great religions are remarkably similar. What is important is that if you connect with a religion; choose one that feels like a good fit to you. If possible, avoid connecting with a religion that suggests it is better than any other alternative religion and if you believe in one of those alternative religions, you are not a good person for whatever reason.

This fast start program supplements your religious and spiritual practices with recommendations to learn from the teachings and writings of the many enlightened teachers from the last 3,000 years. In an appendix, I list some books I have found very helpful, but you need to make your own discriminating choices. It is often helpful to visit a quality bookstore and review books in the spiritual, religious, philosophy, and personal growth sections to determine if there is a book that you feel especially attracted to reading. Respect this inner sense of attraction when it occurs.

The focus of the following fast start program is not on quantity of books read, but on the quality of the reading experience. I am suggesting a process of purposeful reading where you regularly read a small portion of the book, a section or chapter at most, and reflect on its meaning and relevance to you.

- Months 1-3: Purposeful reading 1 book/month, journal entries for especially relevant and helpful learnings.

- Months 4-6: Purposeful reading 1 book/month, journal entries for especially relevant and helpful learnings; attend one group book discussion session/month

- Months 7-9: Purposeful reading 2-3 books/month—books by enlightened teachers; journal entries for especially relevant and helpful learnings, and attend one group book discussion session/month

- Months 10-12: Book discussion group for books by enlightened teachers, purposeful reading 2-3

books/month, journal entries for especially relevant
and helpful learnings

At some point, you may discover the best book to read is
one you have previously read. This can be a wonderful
experience, almost like reading it for the first time,
especially when it has been a year or more since you read
it. It is amazing sometimes how much more you learn
from even your favorite books when you reread them.

Secondary Practice: Becoming More Positive and
Optimistic.

Optimists are much happier and more successful by
almost any measure you choose. Optimists do not
experience fewer challenges and unexpected life events
than the pessimist does. Optimists make different choices
in response to these challenges and events that
consistently produce happier consequences. These
choices have a much stronger logical foundation than the
choices made by the pessimist who finds their logical mind
almost paralyzed by challenges and unexpected events.
The fast start program recommendation focuses on
extensive learning in the beginning followed by increasingly
more challenging use of learned skills. The learning phase

includes work by Dr. Norman Vincent Peale on the power of positive thinking, which is more than 30 years old, to current studies, many pioneered by Dr. Martin Seligman. A key book for everyone to consider is Dr. Seligman's book *Learned Optimism*. A suggested reading list is in an appendices.

- Months 1-3: Study books and materials on optimism; develop ideas on how to best use the skills; use daily affirmations that specify your new beliefs and desired actions, take the Optimism Test at www.authentichappiness.org each month to track progress

- Months 4-6: 2-4 times/week, resolve a negative event after the event via journal writing; take the Optimism Test at www.authentichappiness.org each month to track progress

- Months 7-9: 3-5 times/week, resolve a negative event while it is going on using the disputing and learning skills, take the Optimism Test at www.authentichappiness.org each month to track progress

- Months 10-12: 4-6 times/week, resolve a negative event while it is going on using the disputing and learning skills, help others experience the benefits of disputing and optimism skills, take the Optimism Test at www.authentichappiness.org each month to track progress

As you become a skilled optimist, you respond faster and faster to the initial wave of negative thoughts and emotions. Ultimately, you detect the early warning signs of events with the potential to have unhappy consequences and you use your optimism skills before negative thoughts and emotions trigger unhappy consequences. For example, someone tells you that they have bad news and before they get into the details, you immediately engage the optimism skills necessary to properly understand the news.

Secondary Practice: Emotional Intelligence

The core skill of emotional intelligence is self-awareness. In the emotional intelligence system, self-awareness focuses on very specific subjects. For example, a goal of self-assessment is a clear and accurate understanding of our strengths and weaknesses. Creating this picture requires a combination of objective and subjective evaluations. There are many objective evaluations like Myers-Briggs and the FIRO-B assessments. Also, strongly consider taking the online emotional intelligence assessment (Go to www.hayresourcesdirect.haygroup.com and click on "Competency" on the left side of the page.).

Subjective evaluations include feedback from friends and work supervisors. Self-assessment goes beyond just the collection of inputs. It also includes learning from the subjective and objective inputs to improve our interpersonal effectiveness and happiness. People who are skilled at self-assessment see it as a continuous process of learning and improvement.

Emotional intelligence also uses self-awareness and self-assessment to create a strong, reality based self-confidence. It is a self-confidence based on personal understanding and validation and is not subject to the whims of other people's opinions about you.

Developing emotional intelligence requires a combination of both general and specific training and learning programs. Learning about the general subject of emotional intelligence can be done effectively through reading key books like *Emotional Intelligence* and *Working with Emotional Intelligence* plus participating in one of many emotional intelligence training seminars.

On the specific subjects of self-assessment, self-control, developing empathetic skills, becoming a better listener, and more effective at influencing others, there are also many specific training resources--books, group training programs, and coaching.

The recommended fast start process includes five steps. First, identify the skill and ability capable of making the greatest contribution to your success and happiness. Second, learn about both the general and very specific resources that can assist your development of these skills and abilities. Third, actually use more than one resource during your initial efforts. Fourth, develop an ongoing program to refresh and build your skills, recognizing that it may take you several years to become highly proficient. Fifth, repeat the process for the next most important skill.

Concluding Thoughts.

The purpose of this book is to deliver a message of great hope. Each of us can be much happier than we are today.

We have personal control over how happy we can become. We very clearly know what does not and what does contribute to greater happiness. We know how to use these practices to become happier. We have the ability to live Ultimate Happiness, which is a level of happiness almost unimaginable to most people today because of our very low expectations about how happy we can be.

The suggested methods and practices in this book are proven and practical. Used correctly, you can rely on them to help you become happier. For most of us, becoming much happier is the most challenging and rewarding task of our lives. Achieving and living ultimate happiness requires courage, deep commitment, moment-to-moment persistence, assistance, and an inspiring vision. To get updates on our latest understandings about how to live ultimate happiness, visit our web site at www.ultimate-happiness.com. Thank you very much for your patience.

Appendix: Suggested Further Study & Reading

- Visit www.ultimate-happiness.com for:
  - Free services: 1) Ten Point Ultimate Happiness Assessment, 2) Happiness Skills Assessment, 3) Information brochure.
  - Order the Mediation Program: An audio file that enables to you try the major forms of meditation.
  - Order the Releasing Program: An audio file that enables to experience the major forms of releasing negative thoughts and emotions.
  - Order the book, *Ultimate Happiness:* order individual chapters, groups of chapters, and the entire book as a downloadable audio file, downloadable printable/readable file, or deliverable printed copy.
  - Register for Ultimate Happiness seminars and events.
- *Autobiography of a Yogi,* Paramahansa Yogananda: Great insight into the founder of the Self Realization Fellowship.

- *The Art of Happiness*, His Holiness the Dalai Lama and Dr. Howard Cutler: A landmark book detailing the Tibetan Buddhist view of the path to happiness. Also *The Art of Happiness at Work* by the same authors adds some helpful perspective.

- Ken Wilber, A Theory of Everything: A wonderful introduction to the biggest Western thinker of our time.

- *The Sedona Method*, Hale Dwoskin: A powerful method that everyone should become familiar with because you can learn to quickly release negative thoughts and emotions.

- *Spiral Dynamics*, Don Beck and Christopher Cowan: THE book of the evolution of values and beliefs.

- *Emotional Intelligence* and *Working with Emotional Intelligence*, Daniel Goleman: I like the second better but both are must reads for effectively managing emotions which are one of the biggest barriers to achieving Ultimate Happiness.

- *Authentic Happiness,* Dr. Martin E. P. Seligman: The state of the art from a western science perspective about what contributes to lasting increases in personal happiness. His book *Learned Optimism* is also the best book on this important topic.

- *Love & Survival,* Dean Ornish: The power of love is confirmed by Western science.

- *The Seven Spiritual Laws of Success* and *The Book of Secrets,* Deepak Chopra: He brings an extraordinary Eastern and Western perspective to all of his powerful works.

- *The Tibetan Book of Living and Dying,* Sogyal Rinpoche: An extraordinary book that reveals some of the most helpful insights from Tibetan Buddhism's most powerful teachings.

[i] Goleman, Destructive Emotions, Page 138.
[ii] Goleman, Destructive Emotions, Page 85.
[iii] Swinyard, Kau, and Phua, Happiness, Materialism, and Religious Experience in the United States and Singapore, Journal of Happiness Studies, 2: 13-32, 2001
[iv] *The Progress Paradox*, p. 170
[v] Karasu, Serenity, p. 51
[vi] Authentic Happiness, p. 52
[vii] Seligman, Dr. Martin E. P. , Authentic Happiness, p. 49
[viii] Howard, Dr. Howard C. and His Holiness the Dali Lama, The Art of Happiness at Work, p. 48
[ix] Myers, Dr. David, The Pursuit of Happiness, p. 42
[x] Ouwneel, Piet, Social Security and Well Being of the Unemployed in 42 Nations, Journal of Happiness Studies, 3: 167-192, 2002
[xi] Brickman, P. ; Coates, D. ; & Janoff-Bulman, R. ; (1978), Lottery winners and accident victims: Is happiness relative? Journal of Personality and Social Psychology, 36, 917-927
[xii] Barry Schwartz, *The Paradox of Choice*, pp.108-109
[xiii] Yogananda, The Second Coming of Christ, vol. 1, p. 518
[xiv] Gregg Easterbrook, *The Progress Paradox*, p. 9
[xv] Ibid, page 18
[xvi] Ibid, p. 19
[xvii] Ibid, p. 21
[xviii] Ibid, p. 28
[xix] Ibid, Pages 35 -- 36
[xx] Ibid, pp. 38, 39
[xxi] Ibid, pages 41, 42
[xxii] Ibid, p. 49
[xxiii] Baker, Dr. Dan, What Happy People Know, p. 50
[xxiv] Easterbrook, The Progress Paradox, p. 27
[xxv] Howard, Dr. Howard C. and His Holiness the Dali Lama, The Art of Happiness at Work, p. 30
[xxvi] Roper Starch, p. 50
[xxvii] Trends Affecting the Market for Alcoholic Beverages in the 1990s, Roper Starch, February 1996, p. 27
[xxviii] Howard, Dr. Howard C. and His Holiness the Dali Lama, The Art of Happiness at Work, p. 17
[xxix] Barry Schwartz, *The Paradox of Choice*, Pages 172 -- 173

[xxx] Piquart, Martin, Age Differences in Perceived Positive Affect, Negative Affect, and Affect in Middle and Old Age, Journal of Happiness Studies, 2: 375-405

[xxxi] Influential Americans: Trendsetters for the New Millennium, Roper Starch Worldwide Report, 4th edition, p. 31

[xxxii] Seligman, Dr. Martin E. P. , What You Can Change and What You Can't, pp. 106-107

[xxxiii] Yogananda, The Second Coming of Christ, vol. 1, p. 526

[xxxiv] Roper Starch, p. 33

[xxxv] Seligman, Martin, Authentic Happiness, p. 6

[xxxvi] Seligman, Authentic Happiness, p. 55

[xxxvii] The Science of Hope and Optimism, edited by Jane Gillham, article Hope and Happiness, p.330

[xxxviii] Seligman, p. 260

[xxxix] Seligman, pp. 140-145

[xl] Mitroff, Ian I. , A Spiritual Audit of America, p. 36

[xli] Myers, Dr. David G. , The Pursuit of Happiness, p. 89

[xlii] Seligman, p. 75

[xliii] Dalai Lama and Cutler, Dr. Howard, The Art of Happiness, p. 17

[xliv] Karasu, Serenity, p. x

[xlv] Dalai Lama, Cutler, Howard C. , The Art of Happiness, p. 13

[xlvi] Dalai Lama, Cutler, Howard C. , The Art of Happiness,, p. 52

[xlvii] Rinpoche, Sogyal, Finding Peace, Compassion, and Wisdom in a Complex World, CD of a talk in Adelaide, 2/2//2004

[xlviii] Soul Happy, compiled by Kobi Yamada, (no page numbers)

[xlix] The Art of Happiness, p. 58

[l] Dalai Lama, Cutler, Dr. Howard, The Art of Happiness at Work, pp. 195-196

[li] The Art of Happiness, p. 15

[lii] The Art of Happiness, p. 26

[liii] Ken Wilber, No Boundary, page 27.

[liv] The Art of Happiness, pp. 54-55

[lv] Yogananda, The Second Coming of Christ, page 1069

[lvi] Where There Is Light, p. 105

[lvii] Yogananda, The Second Coming of Christ, volume 2, page 1186

[lviii] Time, October 25, 2004, Jeffrey Kluger, "Is God in Our Genes?", pp 64-65

[lix] Where There Is Light, p. 107

[lx] Where There Is Light, pp. 107-108

[lxi] Where There Is Light, p. 93

[lxii] Inner Peace, p. 5

[lxiii] Spiritual Diary, October 7

[lxiv] Where There Is Light, p. 47

[lxv] Inner Peace, p. 51

[lxvi] Where There Is Light, p. 47

[lxvii] Where There Is Light, p. 52

[lxviii] http://www.wisdomquotes.com/001357.html

[lxix] The Law of Success, p. 29

[lxx] The Law of Success, p. 31

[lxxi] The Law of Success, p. 21

[lxxii] The Law of Success, p. 21

[lxxiii] Inner Peace, p. 26-27

[lxxiv] Inner Peace, p. 3

[lxxv] Inner Peace, p. 84

[lxxvi] Lesson 53, p. 2

[lxxvii] Where There Is Light, p. 108

[lxxviii] Where There Is Light, p. 119

[lxxix] Where There Is Light, p. 122

[lxxx] Lesson 12, p. 4

[lxxxi] The Law of Success, p. 19

[lxxxii] Yogananda, The Second Coming of Christ, volume 2, page 1084

[lxxxiii] ibid., page 1085

[lxxxiv] ibid. page 1086

[lxxxv] Abraham Lincoln, quoted in Happiness is a Choice, Barry Neil Kaufman, p. 65

[lxxxvi] Visions of Compassion, edited by Richard J. Davidson and Anne Harrington, page 42.

[lxxxvii] Ibid, p. 68

[lxxxviii] Ibid, Page 69.

[lxxxix] Ibid, p. 90.

[xc] Live & Survival, p. 1

[xci] Ibid, p. 2

[xcii] Yogananda, *The Second Coming of Christ*, volume 2, page 1186

[xciii] Seligman, What you can change and what you can't, p. 243

[xciv] Ibid, p. 251

[xcv] Ibid, p. 245

[xcvi] John Marks Templeton, Worldwide Laws of Life, 200 Eternal Spiritual Principles, p. 7

[xcvii] The Second Coming of Christ, volume 1, p. 677

[xcviii] Tolle, The Power of Now, p. 14

[xcix] Yogananda, Spiritual Diary, August 24

[c] Tolle, The Power of Now, p. 28

[ci] Mihaly Csikszentmihalyi, *Flow, the Psychology of Optimal Experience,* pp. 48-67

[cii] Authentic Happiness Coaching lecture, Master Class 10, slide 9 Karen Reivich.
[ciii] Seligman, Learned Optimism, p. 219
[civ] Integral Psychology, Ken Wilber, p. 47
[cv] Dictionary.com
[cvi] Karasu, The Art of Serenity, p. 197
[cvii] Ibid, p. 203
[cviii] Easterbrook, *The Progress Paradox*, p. 249
[cix] Ibid, p. 249
[cx] Karasu, The Art of Serenity, p. 222
[cxi] http://www.brainyquote.com/quotes/authors/p/pierre_teilhard_de_chardi.html
[cxii] 11/1 Yogananda Spiritual Diary
[cxiii] http://www.brainyquote.com/quotes/authors/b/buddha.html
[cxiv] Spiritual Audit of America, p. 39
[cxv] http://www.brainyquote.com/quotes/authors/b/buddha.html
[cxvi] http://www.brainyquote.com/quotes/authors/b/buddha.html
[cxvii] Karasu, Serenity, p. 202
[cxviii] Visions of Compassion, edited by Richard J. Davidson and Anne Harrington, Page 69.
[cxix] http://www.wisdomquotes.com/cat_love.html
[cxx] http://www.brainyquote.com/quotes/authors/p/pierre_teilhard_de_chardi.html
[cxxi] Wayne Dyer, Intention, p. 26
[cxxii] http://www.wisdomquotes.com/cat_love.html
[cxxiii] Ornish, Love and Survival, p. 28
[cxxiv] Esoteric Healing, p. 262
[cxxv] Ibid, p. 20
[cxxvi] 7 Laws, p. 3
[cxxvii] Chopra, 7 Laws, p. 40
[cxxviii] HTTP://WWW.WISDOMQUOTES.COM/001798.HTML
[cxxix] http://www.wisdomquotes.com/cat_compassion.html
[cxxx] Templeton, Worldwide Laws of Life, p. 49
[cxxxi] Matthew 7:12, Luke 6:31
[cxxxii] The Seven Spiritual Laws of Success, p. 25
[cxxxiii] Templeton, p. 2
[cxxxiv] Ibid, p. 1
[cxxxv] Ibid, p. 236
[cxxxvi] Ibid p. 344
[cxxxvii] Ibid, p. 436
[cxxxviii] Dali Lama and Cutler, The Art of Happiness, p. 239

[cxxxix] Spiritual Diary, Yogananda, March 22

[cxl] Ibid, March 24

[cxli] Dali Lama and Cutler, The Art of Happiness, p. 239

[cxlii] Ibid, p. 255

[cxliii] Easterbrook, *The Progress Paradox*, p. 229

[cxliv] Ibid, p. 232

[cxlv] Mathew 6:14-15

[cxlvi] Easterbrook, *The Progress Paradox*, Pages 238 -- 239

[cxlvii] Seligman, Authentic Happiness, pp. 132-3

[cxlviii] Yogananda, The Second Coming of Christ, volume two, p. 944

[cxlix] Easterbrook, *The Progress Paradox*, Page 232.

[cl] Seligman, Learned Optimism, p. 218

[cli] Compact Oxford Dictionary, www.askoxford.com

[clii] Goleman, EI, p. 289

[cliii] Ibid

[cliv] Goleman, Destructive Emotions, p. 134

[clv] Ibid, p. 159

[clvi] Ibid, p. 133

[clvii] Goleman, Destructive Emotions, Page 158

[clviii] Ibid, Page 143.

[clix] Ibid, p. 84

[clx] Yogananda, The Second Coming of Christ, vol 1, p.414

[clxi] Ken Wilber, No Boundary, page 85.